# GRAMMAR AND BEYOND ESSENTIALS

# 4

John D. Bunting
Luciana Diniz
with Randi Reppen

CAMBRIDGE
UNIVERSITY PRESS

CAMBRIDGE
UNIVERSITY PRESS & ASSESSMENT

Shaftesbury Road, Cambridge CB2 8EA, United Kingdom

One Liberty Plaza, 20th Floor, New York, NY 10006, USA

477 Williamstown Road, Port Melbourne, VIC 3207, Australia

314–321, 3rd Floor, Plot 3, Splendor Forum, Jasola District Centre, New Delhi – 110025, India

103 Penang Road, #05-06/07, Visioncrest Commercial, Singapore 238467

Cambridge University Press & Assessment is a department of the University of Cambridge.

We share the University's mission to contribute to society through the pursuit of education, learning and research at the highest international levels of excellence.

www.cambridge.org
Information on this title: www.cambridge.org/9781009212915



First published 2019
Update published 2022

20 19 18 17 16 15 14 13 12 11 10 9 8 7 6 5 4 3

Printed in Malaysia by Vivar Printing

*A catalogue record for this publication is available from the British Library*

ISBN 978-1-009-21291-5 Student's Book with Digital Pack

Additional resources for this publication at www.cambridge.org/essentials

# Scope and Sequence

| Unit | Theme | Grammar | Topics | Avoid Common Mistakes |
|---|---|---|---|---|
| **PART 1** | **Social Responsibility** | **Cause and Effect** | | |
| UNIT 1 page 2 | Cause and Effect 1: The Environment and You | Sentence Structure; Common Patterns with Nouns That Show Cause | Sentence Structure: Simple and Compound Sentences (p. 4)<br>Complex Sentences (p. 8)<br>Common Patterns with Nouns That Show Cause (p. 11) | Avoiding fragments; avoiding *cuz* and *coz* in written academic English; avoiding beginning sentences with *and* in written academic English |
| UNIT 2 page 16 | Cause and Effect 2: Consumer Behavior | Subordinators and Prepositions That Show Cause; Transition Words and Common Patterns with Nouns That Show Effect | Subordinators and Prepositions That Show Cause, Reason, or Purpose (p. 18)<br>Transition Words and Phrases That Show Effect (p. 21)<br>Common Patterns with Nouns That Show Effect (p. 24) | Remembering the correct preposition in expressions with *cause*, *result*, and *effect*; remembering *of* in *because of* |
| UNIT 3 page 28 | Cause and Effect 3: Social Responsibility | Real and Unreal Conditionals; Common Phrases with *If* and *Unless* | Present and Future Real Conditionals (p. 30)<br>Present and Future Unreal Conditionals (p. 34)<br>Common Phrases with *Unless* and *If* (p. 37) | Remembering the base form of the verb following a modal; remembering the correct form of the modal in real and unreal conditionals |
| UNIT 4 page 40 | Cause and Effect 4: Alternative Energy Sources | *-ing* Participle Phrases and Verbs That Show Cause and Effect | *-ing* Participle Phrases That Show Effect (p. 42)<br>*-ing* Participle Phrases That Show Cause (p. 44)<br>Verbs That Show Cause and Effect (p. 46) | Remembering to use *result in* and *result from* correctly; remembering subject-verb agreement with *contribute to* |

| Unit | Theme | Grammar | Topics | Avoid Common Mistakes |
|---|---|---|---|---|
| PART 2 | Human Behavior | Comparison and Contrast | | |
| UNIT 5 page 50 | Comparison and Contrast 1: Family Size and Personality | Identifying Relative Clauses; Comparatives with *As . . . As*; Common Patterns That Show Contrast | Identifying Relative Clauses (p. 52)<br>Comparatives with *As . . . As* (p. 56)<br>Common Patterns That Show Contrast (p. 59) | Avoiding omitting the relative pronoun in subject relative clauses; avoiding *the same than* |
| UNIT 6 page 62 | Comparison and Contrast 2: Men, Women, and Equality | Complex Noun Phrases; Parallel Structure; Common Quantifiers | Complex Noun Phrases (p. 64)<br>Parallel Structure (p. 67)<br>Common Quantifiers (p. 70) | Remembering parallel structure |
| UNIT 7 page 74 | Comparison and Contrast 3: Family Values in Different Cultures | Comparative and Superlative Adjectives and Adverbs; Articles; Common Expressions That Show Similarity | Comparative and Superlative Adjectives and Adverbs (p. 76)<br>Articles (p. 81)<br>Common Expressions That Show Similarity (p. 85) | Avoiding using both *more* and *-er* in comparisons; avoiding using *most* before nouns; remembering *the* in *the same as* |
| UNIT 8 page 88 | Comparison and Contrast 4: Intercultural Communication | Adverb Clauses of Contrast and Concession; Transition Words and Phrases That Show Contrast and Concession | Adverb Clauses of Contrast and Concession (p. 90)<br>Transition Words and Phrases That Show Contrast and Concession (p. 93) | Avoiding *another* in *on the other hand*; avoiding *but* in sentences with adverb clauses of concession |
| PART 3 | Society and Culture | Narrative | | |
| UNIT 9 page 98 | Narrative 1: The American Dream | Past Perfect; Past Modals; Common Time Clauses | Past Perfect and Past Perfect Progressive (p. 100)<br>Past Modals and Modal-like Expressions (p. 103)<br>Common Time Clauses (p. 107) | Remembering to use the past participle with the past perfect |
| UNIT 10 page 112 | Narrative 2: Immigration | Demonstratives; Common Time Signals | Demonstratives (p. 114)<br>Common Time Signals (p. 117) | Remembering to use *this/that* with singular nouns and *these/those* with plural nouns |

| Unit | Theme | Grammar | Topics | Avoid Common Mistakes |
|---|---|---|---|---|
| **PART 4** | **Business** | **Classification and Definition** | | |
| UNIT 11<br>page 122 | Classification and Definition 1: Job Interviews | The Passive; Common Words and Phrases Used to Classify | The Passive (p. 124)<br>Common Words and Phrases Used in Classification Writing (p. 128) | Remembering to put the adverb after the modal in passive sentences |
| UNIT 12<br>page 134 | Classification and Definition 2: Your Ideal Job | The Language of Definition; Appositives | The Language of Definition (p. 136)<br>Appositives (p. 139) | Remembering to use the correct form in definitions; remembering to use *who* only with animate nouns |
| **PART 5** | **Nutrition and Health** | **Problem–Solution** | | |
| UNIT 13<br>page 144 | Problem–Solution 1: Food and Technology | Present Perfect and Present Perfect Progressive; Noun Phrase Structures | Present Perfect and Present Perfect Progressive (p. 146)<br>Common Noun Phrase Structures (p. 150) | Avoiding the plural with noncount nouns; avoiding *this* in *the fact that* |
| UNIT 14<br>page 156 | Problem–Solution 2: Children and Health | Reporting Verbs; Adverb Clauses and Phrases with *As*; Vocabulary for Describing Information in Graphics | Reporting Verbs (p. 158)<br>Adverb Clauses and Phrases with *As* (p. 161)<br>Common Vocabulary for Describing Information in Graphics (p. 164) | Remembering to use the base form of *be* after modals in the passive |
| UNIT 15<br>page 168 | Problem–Solution 3: Health and Technology | Adverb Clauses and Infinitives of Purpose; Reduced Adverb Clauses; Vocabulary to Describe Problems and Solutions | Adverb Clauses of Purpose and Infinitives of Purpose (p. 170)<br>Reducing Adverb Clauses to Phrases (p. 174)<br>Common Vocabulary to Describe Problems and Solutions (p. 177) | Avoiding the plural with *for example*; avoiding a comma before *so that* |
| UNIT 16<br>page 182 | Problem–Solution 4: Leading a Healthy Life | *It* Constructions; Transition Words to Indicate Steps of a Solution | *It* Constructions (p. 184)<br>Common Transition Words to Indicate Steps of a Solution (p. 189) | Remembering *to* or *for* after *impossible*; avoiding *than* to introduce next steps |

| Unit | Theme | Grammar | Topics | Avoid Common Mistakes |
|---|---|---|---|---|
| PART 6 | Social Issues and Technology | Summary–Response and Persuasion | | |
| UNIT 17<br>page 194 | Summary–Response: Privacy in the Digital Age | Past Unreal Conditionals; Phrases Used in Summary–Response Writing | Past Unreal Conditionals (p. 196)<br>Common Phrases Used in Summary–Response Writing (p. 200) | Remembering to use the past participle after modals in past unreal conditionals |
| UNIT 18<br>page 204 | Persuasion 1: Violence in the Media | Nonidentifying Relative Clauses; Phrases That Limit Overgeneralization | Nonidentifying Relative Clauses (p. 206)<br>Phrases That Limit Overgeneralization (p. 210) | Remembering the relative pronoun in nonidentifying relative clauses; avoiding *that* in nonidentifying relative clauses |
| UNIT 19<br>page 214 | Persuasion 2: Living in an Age of Information Overload | Noun Clauses with *Wh-* Words and *If / Whether*; Phrases for Argumentation | Noun Clauses with *Wh-* Words and *If / Whether* (p. 216)<br>Phrases for Argumentation (p. 219) | Avoiding *whether* to express a condition; remembering to spell *whether* correctly |
| UNIT 20<br>page 224 | Persuasion 3: Social Media | Expressing Future Actions; Common Words and Phrases in Persuasive Writing | Expressing Future Actions (p. 226)<br>Common Words and Phrases in Persuasive Writing (p. 230) | Remembering when to use the noun or verb forms of *claim* and *argue*; avoiding *according for* and *according with* |

# Introduction to Grammar and Beyond *Essentials*

*Grammar and Beyond Essentials* is a research-based and content-rich grammar series for beginning to advanced-level students. The series focuses on the most commonly used English grammar structures and practices all four skills in a variety of authentic and communicative contexts. It is designed for use both in the classroom and as a self-study learning tool.

## *Grammar and Beyond Essentials* is Research-Based

The grammar presented in this series is informed by years of research on the grammar of written and spoken English as it is used in college lectures, textbooks, academic essays, high school classrooms, and conversations between instructors and students. This research, and the analysis of over one billion words of authentic written and spoken language data known as the *Cambridge International Corpus*, has enabled the authors to:

- Present grammar rules that accurately represent how English is actually spoken and written
- Identify and teach differences between the grammar of written and spoken English
- Focus more attention on the structures that are commonly used, and less on those that are rarely used, in writing and speaking
- Help students avoid the most common mistakes that English language learners make
- Choose reading topics that will naturally elicit examples of the target grammar structure
- Introduce important vocabulary from the Academic Word List

# Special Features of *Grammar and Beyond Essentials*

## Realistic Grammar Presentations

Grammar is presented in clear and simple charts. The grammar points presented in these charts have been tested against real-world data from the *Cambridge International Corpus* to ensure that they are authentic representations of actual use of English.

## Data from the Real World

Many of the grammar presentations and application sections include a feature called Data from the Real World. Concrete and useful points discovered through analysis of corpus data are presented and practiced in exercises that follow.

## Avoid Common Mistakes

Each unit features an Avoid Common Mistakes section that develops students' awareness of the most common mistakes made by English language learners and gives them an opportunity to practice detecting and correcting these errors. This section helps students avoid these mistakes in their own work. The mistakes highlighted in this section are drawn from a body of authentic data on learner English known as the *Cambridge Learner Corpus*, a database of over 35 million words from student essays written by non-native speakers of English and information from experienced classroom teachers.

## Academic Vocabulary

Every unit in *Grammar and Beyond Essentials* includes words from the Academic Word List (AWL), a research-based list of words and word families that appear with high frequency in English-language academic texts. These words are introduced in the opening text of the unit, recycled in the charts and exercises, and used to support the theme throughout the unit. By the time students finish each level, they will have been exposed several times to a carefully selected set of level-appropriate AWL words, as well as content words from a variety of academic disciplines.

# Series Levels

The following table provides a general idea of the difficulty of the material at each level of *Grammar and Beyond Essentials*. These are not meant to be interpreted as precise correlations.

| | **Description** | **TOEFL IBT** | **CEFR Levels** |
|---|---|---|---|
| Level 1 | Beginning | 20 – 34 | A1 – A2 |
| Level 2 | Low Intermediate to Intermediate | 35 – 54 | A2 – B1 |
| Level 3 | High Intermediate | 55 – 74 | B1 – B2 |
| Level 4 | Advanced | 75 – 95 | B2 – C1 |

# Student Components

## Student's Book with Digital Pack

Levels 1 through 3 teach all of the grammar points appropriate at each level in short, manageable cycles of presentation and practice organized around a high-interest unit theme. Level 4 focuses on the structure of the academic essay in addition to the grammar rules, conventions, and structures that students need to master in order to be successful college writers. Please see the Tour of a Unit on pages xvi–xix for a more detailed view of the contents and structure of the units.

## Digital Workbook

The Digital Workbook provides extra practice to help students master each grammar point. Automatically-graded exercises give immediate feedback. Each unit offers practice correcting the errors highlighted in the Avoid Common Mistakes section in the Student's Book. Self-Assessment sections at the end of each unit allow students to test their mastery of what they learned. Look for in the Student's Book to see where additional practice in the Digital Workbook is available.

## Kahoot!

Kahoot! is a game-based learning platform that makes it easy to create, share, and play learning games and quizzes in minutes. Kahoot! can be played on any mobile device or laptop with an Internet connection.

Kahoots can be used for review, formative assessment, or homework.

Cambridge has developed a number of Kahoot! quizzes for *Grammar and Beyond Essentials* - see cambridge.org/kahoot/grammarandbeyond. You can play these Kahoot quizzes before starting a unit as a diagnostic, during a unit as formative assessment, or at the end of a unit to test student knowledge.

# Teacher Resources

A variety of downloadable resources are available on Cambridge One (cambridgeone.org) to assist instructors, including the following:

## Teacher's Manual

- Suggestions for applying the target grammar to all four major skill areas, helping instructors facilitate dynamic and comprehensive grammar classes
- An answer key and audio script for the Student's Book
- Teaching tips, to help instructors plan their lessons

## Assessment

- Placement Test
- Ready-made, easy-to-score Unit Tests, Midterms, and Final in .pdf and .doc formats
- Answer Key

## Presentation Plus

Presentation Plus allows teachers to digitally project the contents of the Student's Books in front of the class for a livelier, interactive classroom. It is a complete solution for teachers because it includes the answer keys and audio.

## Communicative Activity Worksheets

Downloadable, photocopiable worksheets organized by grammar topic provide communicative activities to facilitate more in-class speaking practice. Each worksheet has an instructor's page and a student's page.

## Lesson Mapping Guides

*Grammar and Beyond Essentials* is designed to be used easily alongside academic English titles from Cambridge University Press. These include: *Academic Encounters, Final Draft, Making Connections, Prism,* and *Prism Reading*.

# About the Authors

John D. Bunting is a Senior Lecturer in the Intensive English Program in the Department of Applied Linguistics & ESL at Georgia State University. Prior to this, John taught EFL in Venezuela. He wrote *College Vocabulary 4* (Cengage, 2006) and worked on a revision of *Vocabulary in Use High Intermediate* (Cambridge, 2010). His research interests are corpus linguistics, vocabulary, academic writing, technology in language learning, and teacher education.

Luciana Diniz is the ESOL Department Chair at Portland Community College and an instructor. She has an MA and a PhD in Applied Linguistics from Georgia State University, and she has been teaching EFL/ESL for nearly 15 years. Luciana's research interests focus on the use of corpus linguistics in vocabulary and grammar teaching/learning. She has presented a number of papers at national and international conferences.

Randi Reppen is Professor of Applied Linguistics and TESL at Northern Arizona University (NAU) in Flagstaff, Arizona. She has over 20 years' experience teaching ESL students and training ESL teachers, including 11 years as the Director of NAU's Program in Intensive English. Randi's research interests focus on the use of corpora for language teaching and materials development. In addition to numerous academic articles and books, she is the author of *Using Corpora in the Language Classroom* and a co-author of *Basic Vocabulary in Use*, 2nd edition, both published by Cambridge University Press.

# Advisory Panel

The ESL advisory panel has helped to guide the development of this series and provided invaluable information about the needs of ESL students and teachers in high schools, colleges, universities, and private language schools throughout North America.

Neta Simpkins Cahill, Skagit Valley College, Mount Vernon, WA

Shelly Hedstrom, Palm Beach State College, Lake Worth, FL

Richard Morasci, Foothill College, Los Altos Hills, CA

Stacey Russo, East Hampton High School, East Hampton, NY

Alice Savage, North Harris College, Houston, TX

# Acknowledgements

The publisher and authors would like to thank these reviewers and consultants for their insights and participation:

Marty Attiyeh, The College of DuPage, Glen Ellyn, IL
Shannon Bailey, Austin Community College, Austin, TX
Jamila Barton, North Seattle Community College, Seattle, WA
Kim Bayer, Hunter College IELI, New York, NY
Linda Berendsen, Oakton Community College, Skokie, IL
Anita Biber, Tarrant County College Northwest, Fort Worth, TX
Jane Breaux, Community College of Aurora, Aurora, CO
Anna Budzinski, San Antonio College, San Antonio, TX
Britta Burton, Mission College, Santa Clara, CA
Jean Carroll, Fresno City College, Fresno, CA
Chris Cashman, Oak Park High School and Elmwood Park High School, Chicago, IL
Annette M. Charron, Bakersfield College, Bakersfield, CA
Patrick Colabucci, ALI at San Diego State University, San Diego, CA
Lin Cui, Harper College, Palatine, IL
Jennifer Duclos, Boston University CELOP, Boston, MA
Joy Durighello, San Francisco City College, San Francisco, CA
Kathleen Flynn, Glendale Community College, Glendale, CA
Raquel Fundora, Miami Dade College, Miami, FL
Patricia Gillie, New Trier Township High School District, Winnetka, IL
Laurie Gluck, LaGuardia Community College, Long Island City, NY
Kathleen Golata, Galileo Academy of Science & Technology, San Francisco, CA
Ellen Goldman, Mission College, Santa Clara, CA
Ekaterina Goussakova, Seminole Community College, Sanford, FL
Marianne Grayston, Prince George's Community College, Largo, MD
Mary Greiss Shipley, Georgia Gwinnett College, Lawrenceville, GA
Sudeepa Gulati, Long Beach City College, Long Beach, CA
Nicole Hammond Carrasquel, University of Central Florida, Orlando, FL
Vicki Hendricks, Broward College, Fort Lauderdale, FL
Kelly Hernandez, Miami Dade College, Miami, FL
Ann Johnston, Tidewater Community College, Virginia Beach, VA
Julia Karet, Chaffey College, Claremont, CA
Jeanne Lachowski, English Language Institute, University of Utah, Salt Lake City, UT
Noga Laor, Rennert, New York, NY
Min Lu, Central Florida Community College, Ocala, FL
Michael Luchuk, Kaplan International Centers, New York, NY
Craig Machado, Norwalk Community College, Norwalk, CT
Denise Maduli-Williams, City College of San Francisco, San Francisco, CA
Diane Mahin, University of Miami, Coral Gables, FL
Melanie Majeski, Naugatuck Valley Community College, Waterbury, CT
Jeanne Malcolm, University of North Carolina at Charlotte, Charlotte, NC
Lourdes Marx, Palm Beach State College, Boca Raton, FL
Susan G. McFalls, Maryville College, Maryville, TN
Nancy McKay, Cuyahoga Community College, Cleveland, OH
Dominika McPartland, Long Island Business Institute, Flushing, NY

Amy Metcalf, UNR/Intensive English Language Center, University of Nevada, Reno, NV
Robert Miller, EF International Language School San Francisco – Mills, San Francisco, CA
Marcie Pachino, Jordan High School, Durham, NC
Myshie Pagel, El Paso Community College, El Paso, TX
Bernadette Pedagno, University of San Francisco, San Francisco, CA
Tam Q Pham, Dallas Theological Seminary, Fort Smith, AR
Mary Beth Pickett, Global LT, Rochester, MI
Maria Reamore, Baltimore City Public Schools, Baltimore, MD
Alison M. Rice, Hunter College IELI, New York, NY
Sydney Rice, Imperial Valley College, Imperial, CA
Kathleen Romstedt, Ohio State University, Columbus, OH
Alexandra Rowe, University of South Carolina, Columbia, SC
Irma Sanders, Baldwin Park Adult and Community Education, Baldwin Park, CA
Caren Shoup, Lone Star College – CyFair, Cypress, TX
Karen Sid, Mission College, Foothill College, De Anza College, Santa Clara, CA
Michelle Thomas, Miami Dade College, Miami, FL
Sharon Van Houte, Lorain County Community College, Elyria, OH
Margi Wald, UC Berkeley, Berkeley, CA
Walli Weitz, Riverside County Office of Ed., Indio, CA
Bart Weyand, University of Southern Maine, Portland, ME
Donna Weyrich, Columbus State Community College, Columbus, OH
Marilyn Whitehorse, Santa Barbara City College, Ojai, CA
Jessica Wilson, Rutgers University – Newark, Newark, NJ
Sue Wilson, San Jose City College, San Jose, CA
Margaret Wilster, Mid-Florida Tech, Orlando, FL
Anne York-Herjeczki, Santa Monica College, Santa Monica, CA
Hoda Zaki, Camden County College, Camden, NJ

We would also like to thank these teachers and programs for allowing us to visit:

Richard Appelbaum, Broward College, Fort Lauderdale, FL
Carmela Arnoldt, Glendale Community College, Glendale, AZ
JaNae Barrow, Desert Vista High School, Phoenix, AZ
Ted Christensen, Mesa Community College, Mesa, AZ
Richard Ciriello, Lower East Side Preparatory High School, New York, NY
Virginia Edwards, Chandler-Gilbert Community College, Chandler, AZ
Nusia Frankel, Miami Dade College, Miami, FL
Raquel Fundora, Miami Dade College, Miami, FL
Vicki Hendricks, Broward College, Fort Lauderdale, FL
Kelly Hernandez, Miami Dade College, Miami, FL
Stephen Johnson, Miami Dade College, Miami, FL
Barbara Jordan, Mesa Community College, Mesa, AZ
Nancy Kersten, GateWay Community College, Phoenix, AZ
Lewis Levine, Hostos Community College, Bronx, NY
John Liffiton, Scottsdale Community College, Scottsdale, AZ
Cheryl Lira-Layne, Gilbert Public School District, Gilbert, AZ
Mary Livingston, Arizona State University, Tempe, AZ
Elizabeth Macdonald, Thunderbird School of Global Management, Glendale, AZ
Terri Martinez, Mesa Community College, Mesa, AZ
Lourdes Marx, Palm Beach State College, Boca Raton, FL
Paul Kei Matsuda, Arizona State University, Tempe, AZ
David Miller, Glendale Community College, Glendale, AZ
Martha Polin, Lower East Side Preparatory High School, New York, NY
Patricia Pullenza, Mesa Community College, Mesa, AZ
Victoria Rasinskaya, Lower East Side Preparatory High School, New York, NY
Vanda Salls, Tempe Union High School District, Tempe, AZ
Kim Sanabria, Hostos Community College, Bronx, NY
Cynthia Schuemann, Miami Dade College, Miami, FL
Michelle Thomas, Miami Dade College, Miami, FL
Dongmei Zeng, Borough of Manhattan Community College, New York, NY

# Tour of a Unit

## GRAMMAR IN THE REAL WORLD

presents the unit's grammar in a realistic context using **contemporary** texts.

UNIT 5

# Comparison and Contrast 1: Identifying Relative Clauses; Comparatives with *As . . . As*; Common Patterns That Show Contrast

**Family Size and Personality**

## 1 Grammar in the Real World

You will read an essay that discusses how a child's birth order in the family – being the oldest child, middle child, youngest child, or an only child – may affect his or her personality as an adult. The essay is an example of a type of comparison and contrast writing in which the ideas are organized using the block method.

**A** Before You Read **How many siblings (brothers and sisters) do you have? Do you think that some of their personality traits come from the order of their birth? Read the essay. How strong are the effects of birth order, according to the information in the essay?**

**B** Comprehension Check **Answer the questions.**

1 How are former presidents Jimmy Carter, George W. Bush, and Barack Obama connected to the main idea of the text?

2 According to the writer, why are firstborn children usually more ambitious than their siblings?

3 Which of the different birth order types – firstborn, middle born, youngest, and only child – do you think has the fewest advantages in life? Explain.

**C** Notice **Follow the instructions below to help you notice and understand comparison and contrast sentences from the essay that use *as . . . as*.**

1 Read the *as . . . as* sentence in the third paragraph. Are middle children likely to be equally determined, more determined, or less determined than firstborn children? Explain.

2 Read the *as . . . as* sentence in the fourth paragraph. Are youngest children likely to be equally creative, more creative, or less creative than middle children? Explain.

3 Read the *as . . . as* sentence in the fifth paragraph. Are only children likely to be equally intelligent, more intelligent, or less intelligent than children with siblings? Explain.

50

Comparison and Contrast 1

# Birth Order and Adult Sibling Relationships

What do U.S. Presidents Jimmy Carter, George W. Bush, and Barack Obama all have in common? In addition to being elected president of the United States, these men all share the same birth order. Each one is the oldest child in his family. In fact, many very successful people in government and business have been "firstborn" children. While there is always some variation, some experts agree that birth order can have an influence on a person's personality in childhood and in adulthood.

Firstborn children often share several traits. First, in contrast to their siblings, they are more likely to be responsible, ambitious, and authoritarian. This is probably because they are born into an environment of high expectations, and they usually receive a great deal of attention. They are used to being leaders, taking responsibility for others, and sometimes taking on an almost parental role.

Middle children, on the other hand, exhibit different characteristics from firstborns. They are often not as determined as firstborns. They tend to be more passive and solitary. Having to share family attention with older and younger siblings, middle children have a tendency to be more realistic, creative, and insightful.

Youngest children are often more protected than their older siblings. As a result, they are more likely to be dependent and controlling. They are often as creative as middle children, but usually more easygoing and social.

A child with no siblings, or an "only child," also exhibits some unique characteristics. While some parents worry that an only child will have difficulties socializing and making friends, studies show that an only child is just as intelligent, accomplished, and sociable as a child with siblings. In fact, some research indicates that being an only child has some benefits. These children tend to have better vocabulary, perform better at school, and maintain closer relationships with their parents than children with siblings.

Even though it is assumed that birth order dictates some personality traits, individuals can free themselves from the roles they played when they were young, but it can be difficult. According to Vikki Stark, family therapist and author of *My Sister, My Self*, change requires letting go of familiar ways of being and patiently asserting new behaviors that express one's true self.

Family Size and Personality **51**

## NOTICE ACTIVITIES

draw students' attention to the structure, guiding their own analysis of form, meaning, and use.

## GRAMMAR PRESENTATION

begins with an overview that describes the grammar in an **easy-to-understand** summary.

# 2 Identifying Relative Clauses

## Grammar Presentation

| | |
|---|---|
| A relative clause modifies a noun and follows the noun it modifies. Identifying relative clauses provide necessary information about the noun. They are used in all kinds of academic writing, but they are especially useful in comparison and contrast writing to describe characteristics of elements that are being compared. | *Children who/that have no siblings are often very close to their parents. People gradually behave in ways which/that are more consistent with their preferred self-image.* |

### 2.1 Identifying Relative Clauses

| | |
|---|---|
| **A** An identifying relative clause modifies a noun. It begins with a relative pronoun: *that, which, who, whom,* or *whose*. (It is often called a *restrictive relative clause*.)<br>An identifying relative clause answers the question, "Which one?" It gives necessary information about the noun or noun phrase in the main clause. Without that information, the sentence would be incomplete. | IDENTIFYING RELATIVE CLAUSE<br>*People who do not have children may not be aware of differences in birth order.*<br>IDENTIFYING RELATIVE CLAUSE<br>*Creativity is a trait that all middle children share.* |
| **B** *Who, that,* and *whom* refer to people. Use *whom* for object relative clauses. In informal speaking and writing, the use of *who* for *whom* is common. | PEOPLE<br>*Researchers who/that study families have different views.*<br>*My siblings are the people in my life whom I will always trust.* |
| **C** *Whose* shows possession. It is followed by an animate or inanimate noun in academic writing. | POSSESSION<br>*Researchers whose work focuses on families disagree about the importance of birth order.*<br>*She cited a study whose results supported previous research.* |
| *Which* and *that* refer to things. In academic writing, *that* is often preferred to *which* in identifying relative clauses. | THINGS<br>*The study examines characteristics that/which are common in firstborn children.* |



**Data from the Real World**

In academic writing, the relative pronoun ***who*** is more commonly used than ***that*** to refer to people.

In speaking, the relative pronoun ***that*** is more commonly used than ***who*** to refer to people.

## Grammar Application

**Exercise 2.1** Identifying Relative Clauses

**A** Read the paragraph about birth order. Complete each sentence with *that, who, whom,* or *whose*. Sometimes more than one answer is possible.

Birth order researchers have discovered some interesting information ___that___ (1) can help us understand our colleagues better. Do you have a difficult boss ________ (2) authoritarian personality makes your life difficult? If so, your boss might be a firstborn child. Children ________ (3) are born first are often more authoritarian than their younger siblings. Do you have a co-worker ________ (4) is passive, but particularly creative and insightful? This person may be a middle child. People ________ (5) have both older and younger siblings are often passive because their older siblings were responsible for their well-being when they were young. The creativity ________ (6) they exhibit might be the effect of their having spent a lot of time on their own due to having to share parental attention with their older and younger siblings. People ________ (7) you work with ________ (8) are controlling may be youngest children. These people are also likely to be more social than co-workers ________ (9) are middle children. Of course, these are only generalizations. There are countless factors ________ (10) help form people's personalities, but birth order research may shed some helpful light on people's behavior in the workplace.



## CHARTS

provide clear guidance on the form, meaning, and use of the target grammar for ease of **instruction and reference.**

## GRAMMAR APPLICATION

keeps students engaged with a wide variety of exercises that introduce new and stimulating content.

## DATA FROM THE REAL WORLD

takes students beyond traditional information and teaches them how the unit's grammar is used in authentic situations, including differences between spoken and written use.

## QR CODES

give easy access to audio at point of use.

**Data from the Real World**

In academic writing, 75 percent of relative clauses with *whose* modify inanimate nouns.

*The report included the results of a study funded by an organization* ***whose*** *mission is to help children reach their potential.*

**Exercise 3.2** Comparatives with *As . . . As*

**A** Listen to the story of two famous sisters – Venus and Serena Williams. Complete the chart.

| | Venus Williams | Serena Williams |
|---|---|---|
| 1 Birth date | *June 17, 1980* | |
| 2 Height | *6'1"* | |
| 3 Year turned professional | | |
| 4 Wimbledon singles victories (individual years) | | |
| 5 U.S. Open singles victories (individual years) | | |

**B** On a separate sheet of paper, use the information from A and the cues below to write sentences with the following *as . . . as* phrases: *almost as . . . as; just as . . . as; not nearly as . . . as* and *not quite as . . . as*. Sometimes more than one answer is possible.

1 Serena / is / tall / Venus.
*Serena is not quite as tall as Venus.*
2 Serena / has / played / long / Venus.
3 Serena / is / old / Venus.
4 Serena / has / experience / Venus.
5 Serena / is / important to U.S. sports / Venus.
6 Serena / has / won / Wimbledon singles / Venus.
7 Venus / is / famous / Serena.

Serena and Venus Williams

8 Serena / has had / Wimbledon singles victories / Venus has had.
9 Venus / has had / success in business / Serena. They are both successful businesswomen.

**C** Pair Work **Tell a partner about two people you know well. Compare them using *as . . . as* structures. Next, write five sentences about them using *as . . . as*. Use adjectives, adverbs, and noun phrases as well as phrases such as *almost, not nearly,* and *not quite* in your sentences where possible.**

*Younsil does not have as many children as Victoria.*
*Younsil is not quite as shy as Victoria.*

## HOW TO USE A QR CODE

1. Open the camera on your smartphone.
2. Point it at the QR code.
3. The camera will automatically scan the code. If not, press the button to take a picture.

* Not all cameras automatically scan QR codes. You may need to download a QR code reader. Search "QR free" and download an app.

## CONTEXTUALIZED PRACTICE

moves from controlled to open-ended, teaching meaningful language for real communicative purposes.

## AVOID COMMON MISTAKES

is based on a database of over 135,000 essays. Students learn to avoid the most common mistakes English language learners make and develop self-editing skills to improve their speaking and writing..

### Vocabulary Application

**Exercise 4.1** Vocabulary That Shows Contrast

**A** Complete the following sentences about children in the United States using the words and phrases in the box.

| | | |
|---|---|---|
| differ from | ~~major difference between~~ | unlike |
| in contrast | significantly different from | |

1 One *major difference between* children in the United States in 1900 and now is that children in the past didn't get a lot of individual attention from their parents, while children today get a lot of individual attention.

2 Another way that today's children are ______ children in the past is that in the past, children often worked to help their families, but children now often work for their own extra spending money.

3 Today's children also ______ children in 1900 in that they are required to attend school.

4 Children in the past often had large families with several siblings. ______, many children today have one or two siblings or are only children.

5 In 1900, children were very independent. ______ them, children today depend on their parents a lot.

**B** Pair Work With a partner, draw a chart like the one below. Write five contrasting pieces of information about children in the 1900s and now in a culture that you are familiar with. Then present your information to the class, using vocabulary from A.

| Children in the 1900s | Children Now |
|---|---|
| | |

*One major difference between young children in my native country today and in the 1900s is that in the 1900s, they used to work in factories. Today that's illegal.*

60 Unit 5 Comparison and Contrast 1

Comparison and Contrast 1

### 5 Avoid Common Mistakes

**1 Do not use *who* with inanimate nouns.**

*A study ~~who~~ that showed the benefits of being an only child was published last year.*

**2 Do not omit the relative pronoun in subject relative clauses.**

*Children who have older siblings tend to be somewhat dependent.*

**3 Remember that the subject and the verb must agree in relative clauses.**

*Children who ~~has~~ have siblings often become secure and confident adults.*

**4 Use *the same as*, not *the same than*.**

*Middle children often have the same level of creativity ~~than~~ as youngest children.*

### Editing Task

Find and correct eight more mistakes in this body paragraph from an essay comparing trends in families in the past and today.

Families Past and Present

A major way that families have changed is the number of families that have only one child. The number of families had only one child was low in the United States in the 1950s and 1960s. However, one-child families began increasing in the 1970s and are very common today. This is especially true in households who have only one parent. One reason families are smaller is the cost of living. It is not the same than it was 40 years ago. For example, it costs about 10 times more to send a child to college than it did 40 years ago. As a result, many parents choose to have only one child because they do not have enough money for more children. In addition, attitudes about only children are also not the same than attitudes about them in the past. In the 1950s and 1960s, people avoided having only one child. At that time, many people thought that children did not have siblings had many disadvantages. For example, people thought that they did not learn good social skills. However, recent studies who focus on only children show a different picture. These studies show that only children tend to have the same social skills than children who has siblings.v

Family Size and Personality 61

## THEME-RELATED EXERCISES

boost fluency by providing grammar practice in a variety of different contexts.

## EDITING TASK

gives learners an opportunity to identify and correct commonly made errors and develop self-editing skills needed in their university studies.

UNIT 1

# Cause and Effect 1: Sentence Structure; Common Patterns with Nouns That Show Cause

## The Environment and You

## 1 Grammar in the Real World

You will read an essay about ecological footprints, a measurement of the impact each person has on the world's natural resources. The essay is an example of one kind of cause and effect writing in which one cause leads to several effects.

**A** Before You Read **What are three common things that people do in their everyday lives that have an impact on the environment? Read the essay. According to the writer, what might be one effect of mining for natural resources such as coal and oil?**

**B** Comprehension Check **Answer the questions.**

1 In your own words, what is an ecological footprint? Provide examples of activities that could cause a large and a small ecological footprint.

2 According to the essay, what are three major consequences of large ecological footprints?

3 "We do not inherit the Earth from our ancestors; we borrow it from our children" is a Native American proverb. How is this proverb related to the essay?

**C** Notice **Follow the instructions below to help you notice sentence structures that state causes and describe effects.**

1 In the first paragraph, find the sentence about easily accessible resources and large ecological footprints on lines 10–14. Write *C* above the clause that gives a reason or cause and *E* above the clause that states the effect. Circle the word that introduces the cause.

2 In the third paragraph, find the sentence that states the effect of releasing dangerous gases in the air. Circle the phrase that introduces the effect.

3 In the fourth paragraph, underline the first sentence. Does the sentence describe a cause or an effect? What phrase does the writer use to introduce it?

# Ecological Footprints

Environmentalists are increasingly concerned about the impact that individuals have on our planet, and many people now want to help protect the environment. A good place to start is reducing one's ecological footprint. An ecological footprint is an estimate of how much land, water, and other natural resources are being used by a person or a group. Because resources are easily accessible in developed countries like the United States, people in these countries tend to have large ecological footprints. For example, they may take long showers, leave their computers on for the whole day, buy new things they do not need, and fly frequently between cities. The consequences of large ecological footprints can be disastrous.[1]

One of the worst effects of large ecological footprints is the loss of natural resources, such as oil, water, and wood. These resources are being consumed so fast that the Earth does not have time to renew them. Approximately 99 million barrels of oil are produced daily in the world. People use oil to run their cars, heat their homes, and create products such as clothes, paint, and plastic.

Plastic is now one of the biggest threats to our environment, and in fact to each of us. The naturalist David Attenborough shocked the world by showing images of sea birds attempting to feed their young on plastic shopping bags. It is estimated that eight million tonnes of plastic end up in our oceans every year. Unless this stops, there will be more plastic than fish in the ocean by 2050. Already, billions of people around the world are drinking water that is contaminated by plastic. The United States is the country worst affected, with 94% plastic contamination in its tap water.

Large ecological footprints also lead to higher greenhouse gas emissions. The mining of oil, natural gas, and coal, as well as the use of these resources in electrical power plants and automobiles, releases dangerous gases into the air, where they trap[2] heat. As a result, the Earth gets warmer.

It is our responsibility to find ways to decrease our impact on our planet. Even small changes can make a difference and help to protect the environment. If we do not start reducing our ecological footprints right away, it may be too late for future generations to contain[3] the damage.

[1]**disastrous:** causing a lot of damage

[2]**trap:** prevent from leaving

[3]**contain:** limit

# 2 Sentence Structure: Simple and Compound Sentences

## Grammar Presentation

| | |
|---|---|
| In cause and effect writing and in academic writing in general, it is effective to use a variety of sentence types. Writers use simple sentences to express facts or opinions strongly. They use compound sentences to link related ideas such as causes and effects. | Simple sentence:<br>*Lack of natural resources is one of the results of large ecological footprints.*<br>Compound sentence:<br>*Large ecological footprints cause many problems, and it is our social responsibility to solve them.* |

### 2.1 Simple Sentences

| | |
|---|---|
| **A** A simple sentence has only one clause, called a *main clause* or an *independent clause*. Like all sentences, a simple sentence must have a subject and a verb. | SUBJECT: *Millions of barrels of oil* VERB: *are produced*<br>*Millions of barrels of oil are produced daily.* |
| Many different elements may come after the verb, including: | |
| object | SUBJECT VERB OBJECT<br>*Plastic pollution has devastated **our oceans**.* |
| prepositional phrase | SUBJECT VERB PREP. PHRASE<br>*Ozone and other greenhouse gases are often **in the news**.* |
| adjective | SUBJECT VERB ADJECTIVE<br>*The Earth is becoming **warmer**.* |
| adverb | SUBJECT VERB PREP. PHRASE<br>*Natural resources that provide energy will run out **eventually**.* |
| **B** The subject of a sentence must be a noun phrase. There are many different kinds of noun phrases, including: | |
| adjective + noun | ***Small changes** can make a difference.* |
| pronoun | ***This** has devastated many oceans.* |
| noun and noun | ***Ozone and other greenhouse gases** are often in the news.* |
| noun + prepositional phrase | ***The health of our oceans** remains critical.* |
| noun + relative clause | ***Natural resources that provide energy** will run out eventually.* |
| gerund | ***Reducing our ecological footprints** is crucial.* |

## 2.1 Simple Sentences *(continued)*

| | |
|---|---|
| **C** The verb of a sentence can consist of a single main verb or a main verb with an auxiliary verb such as *be*, *do*, and *have*, or a modal such as *can* and *will*.<br><br>A verb phrase can consist of more than one verb. | MAIN VERB<br>*The health of our oceans* ***remains*** *critical.*<br><br>AUXILIARY VERB<br>*This* ***has*** *devastated many oceans.*<br><br>MODAL<br>*People* ***may*** *take long showers.*<br><br>*The average temperature* ***rises and falls****.* |

## 2.2 Using Simple Sentences

| | |
|---|---|
| **A** Use short simple sentences to emphasize an important point within the larger discourse. | *The consequences of these footprints can be disastrous.* |
| **B** If the subject or a verb is missing, the sentence is incomplete. It is called a *fragment*.<br><br>Avoid fragments by making sure all sentences have a subject and a verb. | FRAGMENT (MISSING SUBJECT): *In the future, will probably be much warmer on Earth.*<br><br>CORRECTION: *In the future,* ***the temperature*** *will probably be much warmer on Earth.*<br><br>FRAGMENT (MISSING VERB): *The worst effect of large ecological footprints the loss of natural resources.*<br><br>CORRECTION: *The worst effect of large ecological footprints* ***is*** *the loss of natural resources.* |
| **C** Academic writers connect independent clauses with transition words to make the relationship between two ideas very clear.<br><br>Some examples of transition words are: *as a result, consequently, furthermore, however*<br><br>You can use a period or a semicolon before a transition word to connect the independent clauses. Use a comma after a transition word. | *These gases trap heat in the air.* ***As a result****, the Earth gets warmer.*<br><br>*These gases trap heat in the air;* ***as a result****, the Earth gets warmer.* |
| **D** You can connect two independent clauses with a semicolon. This is a good choice if the ideas in the two clauses are closely related. | INDEPENDENT CLAUSE 1 / INDEPENDENT CLAUSE 2<br>*People should buy less; they should replace items only when absolutely necessary.* |

## 2.3 Compound Sentences

**A** Use compound sentences to connect two ideas. A compound sentence includes at least two independent clauses that are connected by a coordinating conjunction (*and*, *but*, *or*, *so*, *yet*). Use a comma before the coordinating conjunction.

INDEPENDENT CLAUSE 1
*Some people are concerned about the environment,*
INDEPENDENT CLAUSE 2
***so** they recycle as much as they can.*

**B** Avoid run-on sentences and comma splices. A run-on sentence is two independent clauses without a coordinating conjunction.

Use a comma and coordinating conjunction when connecting two independent clauses.

RUN-ON: *These gases trap heat in the air the Earth gets warmer.*

CORRECTION: *These gases trap heat in the air, **so** the Earth gets warmer.*

A comma splice is two independent clauses combined with a comma.

Use a period between the two independent clauses.

COMMA SPLICE: *Humans are the cause of many environmental problems, it is our responsibility to resolve them.*

CORRECTION: *Humans are the cause of many environmental problems**.** It is our responsibility to resolve them.*

**C** The use of *and* and *but* to introduce a sentence is common in some types of writing, such as in newspapers and magazines. However, it is not usually appropriate in academic writing.

*Natural resources are being consumed so fast that the Earth does not have time to renew them. **And** as a result, these resources are becoming scarce.*

*There are efforts to clean up the oceans. **But** the health of our oceans remains critical.*

# Grammar Application

## Exercise 2.1 Subjects and Verbs

**Read about energy resources in Iceland. Underline the subject, and circle the verb in each independent clause.**

1 Iceland has huge frozen glaciers, but it also has more than 100 volcanoes.

2 In 1998, Iceland decided to become independent from fossil fuels.

3 It began to increase its use of renewable energy sources.

4 Electricity in Iceland's homes is generated by geothermal springs, or it comes from the energy of the rivers and glaciers.

5 The water in geothermal springs is already hot, so Icelanders use it instead of fossil fuels to heat their homes.

6 Basic services such as transportation in Iceland are switching to electric vehicles, and all ships in the large fishing industry may eventually operate on hydrogen fuel.

7 Iceland satisfies its country's need for energy without relying heavily on fossil fuels.

## **Exercise 2.2** Fragments, Run-on Sentences, and Comma Splices

**A** Read the following sentences about the environment. Check (✓) each complete sentence. Write *F* for each fragment, *R-O* for each run-on, and *CS* for each comma splice.

1 (a) ___✓___ Over time, people have destroyed the natural habitats of many plants and animals in order to build more homes and grow more food. (b) ___*F*___ For this reason, many of our forests now gone. (c) ___*R-O*___ Plants and animals are losing their homes they may become extinct.

2 (a) ________ Water pollution a serious problem. (b) ________ For many years, people got rid of waste by dumping it into the water. (c) ________ As a result, the quality of the water in many of our oceans, rivers, and lakes unacceptable. (d) ________ In fact, nearly about two billion people in the world do not have safe drinking water, and over two million people die each year from diseases related to water.

3 (a) ________ Environmentalists are constantly trying to come up with ideas to protect the environment nobody knows what the environment will be like in the future. (b) ________ However, researchers believe that much has already improved. (c) ________ Individuals are becoming more aware of the environment around them.

4 (a) ________ Trying to protect nature in various ways. (b) ________ Some people are helping to clean up the environment by driving electric cars, others are working to preserve endangered plants and animals. (c) ________ These efforts will allow future generations to have clean air and water and to enjoy the world's natural beauty.

5 (a) ________ The forests of the Earth are being cut down. (b) ________ The destruction of the forests is the result of human and natural disasters. (c) ________ Has negative consequences on the environment.

**B** Rewrite the fragments, run-ons, and comma splices in A. Use coordinating conjunctions, transition words, and punctuation to correct run-ons and comma splices. Check your answers with a partner.

1 *For this reason, many of our forests are now gone. Plants and animals are losing their homes. As a result, they may become extinct.*

2 ________________________________________

3 ________________________________________

4 ________________________________________

5 ________________________________________

# 3 Complex Sentences

## Grammar Presentation

| | |
|---|---|
| Another way to link cause and effect ideas is with complex sentences. Complex sentences have one independent clause and at least one dependent clause. | *Because resources are readily accessible in developed countries like the United States, people in these countries tend to have large ecological footprints.* |

### 3.1 Complex Sentences

| | |
|---|---|
| A complex sentence has an independent clause and a dependent clause introduced by a subordinator. Subordinators show the relationship between the two ideas.<br>Some examples of subordinators are: *although, after, as if, because, before, if, since, whereas, whether, while*<br>When the dependent clause comes first, use a comma to separate it from the independent clause. | INDEPENDENT CLAUSE<br>*Future generations will suffer*<br>DEPENDENT CLAUSE<br>***if** pollution is not reduced.*<br><br>DEPENDENT CLAUSE<br>***Although** people try to save energy,*<br>INDEPENDENT CLAUSE<br>*global demand for energy increases every year.* |

### 3.2 Using Complex Sentences

| | |
|---|---|
| **A** In academic writing, use complex sentences with the subordinators *because, if, since,* and *when* to express cause and effect relationships. | CAUSE EFFECT<br>***If** pollution is reduced, global health will improve.* |
| **B** A dependent clause that is not connected to an independent clause is a fragment.<br>Avoid dependent clause fragments in the following ways:<br>Connect the dependent clause to an independent clause. (Remember to use a comma after a dependent clause if it comes before an independent clause.)<br>*OR*<br>Change the subordinator to a transition word that can introduce an independent clause. | FRAGMENT: ***Because** energy use is high in the developed world. People there use a lot of resources.*<br><br>DEPENDENT CLAUSE<br>CORRECTION: ***Because** energy use is high in the*<br>INDEPENDENT CLAUSE<br>*developed world, people there use a lot of resources.*<br><br>CORRECTION: *Energy use is high in the developed world. **As a result**, people there use a lot of resources.* |

# Grammar Application

## Exercise 3.1 Complex Sentences

**A** For each pair of sentences about bald eagles, write *C* next to the sentence that shows the cause and *E* next to the sentence that shows the effect. Next, combine the sentences using *because*, *if*, *since*, or *when*. Sometimes more than one answer is possible.

1 __E__ The United States government declared bald eagles an endangered species.

__C__ Bald eagles were almost extinct in the 1960s.

*Because bald eagles were almost extinct in the 1960s, the United States government declared them an endangered species.*

2 ____ The bald eagle showed the qualities of impressive strength and courage.

____ The bald eagle was chosen in 1782 to be the symbol for the United States.

3 ____ The government enacted laws that included banning the use of the pesticide DDT.

____ The bald eagle population began to recover.

4 ____ In 2007, the bald eagle was taken off the Endangered Species Act's "threatened" list.

____ The bald eagles' numbers had greatly increased since the 1960s.

5 ____ The bald eagle population may decrease once more.

____ The habitats of the bald eagles are not protected in the future.

6 ____ Some biologists are urging wind energy companies to develop safer turbines.

____ The birds are sometimes killed by the blades of wind turbines.

7 ____ People can help protect the bald eagle.

____ People volunteer to clean up the habitats where eagles nest.

**B** Pair Work With a partner, think of two endangered animals. Discuss why the animals are endangered (habitat loss, pesticides, overfishing, etc.) and what is being done to protect the animals. Next, do the role play below. Use *because*, *if*, *since*, and *when* where possible.

A You are a reporter. Interview Partner B about one of the animals you talked about. Ask why the animal is endangered and what the impact of environmental policies has been.

B You are an environmentalist. Answer Partner A's questions.

Partner A *Tell me about an endangered animal that people should know about.*

Partner B *Sea turtles are an endangered animal.*

Partner A *Why are they endangered?*

Partner B *One reason is the fishing industry. Many turtles die when they bite the hooks and get caught in the fishing lines.*

Partner A *How are they today?*

Partner B *Since there are now programs that protect the turtles, their numbers have improved in recent years.*

Switch roles and do the role play again using information about the second animal.

## Exercise 3.2 More Complex Sentences

Read the questions below. Then listen to the radio interview about bikeshare programs in large cities. As you listen, take notes. Finally, answer the questions. Use *because*, *if*, *since*, and *when*.

1 Why are bikeshares becoming so popular in large cities?

*Bikeshares are becoming popular because they are a great way to reduce pollution.*

2 Why do people use a bikeshare?

3 What do people have to do if they want to use the bikes?

4 What happens when riders get a flat tire?

5 If a city wants a bikeshare program to be successful, what two things are required?

6 What can bikeshare riders do in some cities when they want to find a bike or an empty space at a station?

7 Why do some people feel uncomfortable riding the bikes?

# 4 Common Patterns with Nouns That Show Cause

## Vocabulary Presentation

Cause and effect relationships can be shown in many different ways. One important way is through the use of the nouns *cause*, *reason*, and *factor*.

*One important cause of overpopulation is lack of education.*
*Low cost is the primary reason why many communities use coal for energy.*
*Emissions from cars are a major factor in the increase in air pollution.*

### 4.1 Nouns That Show Cause: *Cause, Reason, Factor*

| | |
|---|---|
| **A** The following expressions and patterns are commonly used with the noun *cause* and a form of the verb *be*:<br>NOUN PHRASE ______ *is a/one cause of* ______ NOUN PHRASE.<br>*Another cause of* ______ NOUN PHRASE *is* ______ NOUN PHRASE. | *A higher birth rate is one major cause of overpopulation.*<br>*Another leading cause of overpopulation is the decline in death rates.* |
| **B** Expressions with cause generally describe a negative effect. *Cause* does not usually occur with words that are related to success or positive results. | *Some researchers believe that the primary cause of global warming is large ecological footprints.* |

## 4.1 Nouns That Show Cause: *Cause, Reason, Factor* (continued)

| | |
|---|---|
| **C** These expressions and patterns are commonly used with the noun *reason* a form of the verb *be*:<br><br>CLAUSE CLAUSE<br>*One reason (why)* _______ *is* _______ .<br><br>CLAUSE NOUN PHRASE<br>*One reason (why)* _______ *is* _______ .<br><br>NOUN PHRASE CLAUSE<br>*The reason for* _______ *is* _______ .<br><br>NOUN PHRASE NOUN PHRASE<br>*The reason for* _______ *is* _______ .<br><br>SENTENCE<br>_______ . *For this reason / these*<br>CLAUSE<br>*reasons,* _______ . | ***One reason (why)*** *the population* ***is*** *growing so fast* ***is*** *that death rates have fallen dramatically.*<br><br>***One reason (why)*** *the population is growing so fast* ***is*** *the decline in the death rate.*<br><br>***The*** *real* ***reason for*** *our concern about overpopulation* ***is*** *that our resources are limited.*<br><br>***The*** *primary* ***reason for*** *our concern about overpopulation* ***is*** *limited resources.*<br><br>*People are living longer, healthier lives.* ***For this reason,*** *the population has been increasing.* |
| **D** These expressions and patterns are commonly used with the noun *factor* and a form of the verb *be*:<br><br>NOUN PHRASE NOUN PHRASE<br>_______ *is a / one factor in* _______ .<br><br>NOUN PHRASE NOUN PHRASE<br>*Another factor in* _______ *is* _______ . | *Mortality* ***is one*** *key* ***factor in*** *the current growth in population.*<br><br>***Another*** *critical* ***factor in*** *water pollution* ***is*** *the increase in fertilizer use by farmers.* |

### Data from the Real World

Adjectives that most frequently occur with *cause* are:
*leading, probable, common, root, underlying, exact, major, likely, main, important, primary*
*Scholars are not sure whether poverty is an* ***underlying cause*** *of overpopulation.*

Adjectives that most frequently occur with *reason* are:
*good, major, real, main, primary, biggest*
*One* ***good reason*** *to recycle is to save money.*

Adjectives that most frequently occur with *factor* are:
*important, another, major, key, significant, critical*
*Decreasing the number of cars on the road is a* ***critical factor*** *in the effort to reduce air pollution.*

# Vocabulary Application

## Exercise 4.1 Nouns That Show Cause

**A** Complete the online article about ways to get around. Use *cause*, *reason*, or *factor* and appropriate adjectives from the Data from the Real World box above.

### Changing with the Times

Some experts say that one *leading cause* (1) of air pollution is the carbon emissions from cars. To reduce these emissions, many people have changed how they get around. James Kendall of Cincinnati, Ohio, sold his gas-guzzling car and purchased a hybrid vehicle. Kendall says, "One ________ ________ (2) I bought a hybrid is that it's better for the environment. However, another ________ ________ (3) in my decision was money. I spend a lot less on gas now."

Linda Wong of Los Angeles, California, takes public transportation as often as she can. "Carbon emissions from cars is the ________ ________ (4) of smog and air pollution in L.A.," she explains. "I don't want to add to that. That's the ________ (5) why I don't like to drive. Another ________ ________ (6) in my decision is that driving in L.A. is very stressful."

Pedro Sandoval of Missoula, Montana, started using a carpool to get to and from work two years ago because of his concern for the environment, but he says that the ________ (7) ________ that he has stuck with it has to do with other incentives. "I've met a lot of really nice people and saved a lot of money." He'll take public transportation, but, as he says, buses are a ________ ________ (8) of pollution, too.

**B** Pair Work With a partner, choose three environmentally related issues. Below are some ideas. Explain possible causes and effects for each one using expressions with *factor*, *reason*, and *cause*.

| | | | |
|---|---|---|---|
| noise pollution | nuclear safety | overpopulation | water pollution |

*The use of medicines is a factor in water pollution. The medicines we use end up in our water. For this reason, some communities have started to collect unused medicines so that they don't end up in our water.*

## **Exercise 4.2** More Nouns That Show Cause

**A** Answer the questions about ways that people and cities are lessening their impact on the environment. Use expressions and patterns with *cause*, *reason*, or *factor*, and adjectives from Data from the Real World.

1 What is one reason why some people prefer not to eat meat?

*One primary reason why some people prefer not to eat meat is that they don't want animals to be killed for food.*

2 What do you think is one reason for the rising interest in locally grown food?

______________________________________________

3 What are two causes of pollution in cities?

______________________________________________

4 What is one important factor in a city's decision to start a bikeshare program?

______________________________________________

5 Some cities have decided to ban the use of plastic bags in grocery stores. What do you think is the reason for this ban?

______________________________________________

**B** Pair Work With a partner, take turns asking and answering the questions in A. Do you agree or disagree with each other's answers? Tell why.

*I disagree that people don't eat meat because they don't want animals to be killed.*
*I think that some people don't eat meat because they can't afford it.*

# 5 Avoid Common Mistakes

**1 Avoid fragments. Make sure sentences have a subject and a verb.**

*The result of a large ecological footprint* ^*is* *often pollution.*

**2 Use *because*, not *cuz or coz*, in written academic English.**

*Animals are becoming extinct* ~~*cuz*~~ *because* *humans have moved into their habitats.*

**3 Do not confuse *cause* with *because*.**

~~*Cause*~~ *Because* *water pollution is widespread, there is a shortage of clean drinking water in many parts of the world.*

**4 Avoid beginning sentences with *and* in written academic English.**

*Shoppers should bring their own bags to stores because paper bags lead to* ~~*deforestation. And*~~ *deforestation, and* *plastic bags are dangerous for birds and marine life.*

# Editing Task

**Find and correct eight more mistakes in this paragraph from an essay about ocean pollution.**

One significant cause of ocean pollution *is* the accidental spilling of crude oil by large ocean-going ships. The consequences of oil spills can be disastrous to both plant and animal marine life. For example, oil that spills on the surface of the water blocks oxygen from getting to marine plant life. Cause oxygen is necessary for survival, marine plants die. And the fish that eat them can die as well. In addition, oil spills can coat the feathers of marine birds. Oil-coated birds can become weighted down, so cannot fly. Furthermore, oil often removes the natural coating on marine birds' feathers. As a result, the birds can die from overexposure cuz the coating protects them from the elements. Oil spills also affect the human food chain. This occurs coz shellfish such as mussels and clams filter water through their bodies. If the water is polluted with oil, the flesh of the shellfish becomes polluted as well. And this makes them harmful for human consumption. Cause oil spills affect human, animal, and plant life, many people agree that these spills one of the most serious environmental problems in the world today.

UNIT 2

# Cause and Effect 2: Subordinators and Prepositions That Show Cause; Transition Words and Common Patterns with Nouns That Show Effect

## Consumer Behavior

## 1 Grammar in the Real World

You will read an essay about the factors that influence consumers' buying behavior. The essay is an example of one type of cause and effect writing in which several causes lead to one effect.

**A** Before You Read **What is the biggest purchase you made in the past six months? What influenced you in making your decision? Read the essay. What does the writer state are the key factors that affect consumer buying behavior?**

**B** Comprehension Check **Answer the questions.**

1 According to the text, what is the definition of consumer behavior? Use your own words.

2 Name one factor from the essay that might influence someone to buy more and one factor from the essay that might influence someone to buy less.

3 Why does the writer believe it is important to understand consumer behavior?

**C** Notice **Follow the instructions below to help you notice the words the writer uses to state causes and describe effects.**

1 Find the word *effect* in the first paragraph and circle it. Underline the verb, adjective, and preposition that combine with the word *effect.* Notice how the author uses the word *effect* twice in the fifth paragraph with different adjectives. Underline the phrases with *effect* and circle the adjectives.

2 Find the sentence in the second paragraph that describes a possible effect of being hungry when one shops. Circle the words that introduce the result in the sentence that follows it.

# Understanding Consumer Behavior

Consumer behavior is the process consumers go through in making purchasing decisions. This process includes the steps they take from the moment they become aware of a particular need through the final decision to purchase or not purchase a product. According to marketing experts, this process includes the time spent planning where to shop and comparison shopping. Along the way, consumers are influenced by many factors, including psychological and physical ones. Many experts agree on four factors that have a significant effect on consumer behavior.

One set of factors that influence consumer behavior is physical factors – how a person physically feels when shopping. For example, being hungry when grocery shopping affects how people shop. The result is that people often buy more food than they would if they were not hungry. In contrast, feeling tired leads people to buy less.

Cultural and social factors also have an effect on consumer behavior. Some people make choices because of what their friends do. One example is the importance attached to owning a particular item, such as an expensive pair of jeans, in a person's social network. Another social factor is whether the culture encourages or discourages a behavior, such as bargaining for a lower price.

A third factor that impacts consumer behavior is a person's self-image. People often try to match their purchases, from paper towels to cars, to their idea of self. For example, some people care very much about the environment and health of the planet. Therefore, they might choose to drive an electric car due to its low impact on the environment. Other people might see themselves as economical shoppers. As a result, they might buy only simple, inexpensive clothing in order to maintain that aspect of their self-image.

Finally, a person's own experience is a factor. Memories about a certain product or place can have a direct effect on later decisions. For instance, people will tend to go back to a restaurant because they had a good eating experience there. On the other hand, if a person becomes ill eating seafood, it might have a negative effect on his or her future desire for that kind of food.

Every day, people make choices about what to buy. However, they are often unaware of the process behind their decision making. As a result, they can become vulnerable to[1] advertising and other marketing techniques that target the factors that convince people to buy more. Consumers may want to make changes in their purchasing patterns, but they might not know how to make these changes. One important step is for them to become more aware of why they make choices. Becoming educated about their behavior as consumers is an important way for people to make better buying decisions.

[1] **vulnerable to:** able to be easily hurt or influenced

# 2 Subordinators and Prepositions That Show Cause, Reason, or Purpose

## Grammar Presentation

| | |
|---|---|
| Some subordinators and prepositions show cause, reason, or purpose in academic writing. They answer the question *why*. Both subordinators and prepositions may be a word or a phrase. | *Some people buy products they do not need only* ***because*** *they are on sale.*<br>*We often choose what products to buy* ***as a result of*** *past experience.* |

### 2.1 Using Subordinators That Show Cause, Reason, or Purpose

| | |
|---|---|
| **A** Subordinators connect dependent clauses to independent clauses. These dependent clauses are adverb clauses. | INDEPENDENT CLAUSE<br>*Some consumers purchase certain products*<br>DEPENDENT CLAUSE<br>***because*** *they want to maintain their self-image.* |
| **B** As taught in Unit 1, use the subordinators *because* and *since* to indicate the cause or reason. | EFFECT / CAUSE / REASON<br>*Some consumers buy products* ***because*** *they want to be like their friends.* |
| **C** Use the following subordinators to indicate purpose:<br>*so / so that* | PURPOSE<br>*Some consumers buy "green" products* ***so (that)*** *they can appear environmentally aware.* |

### 2.2 Using Prepositions That Show Cause or Reason

| | |
|---|---|
| Use the following prepositions to indicate cause or reason. Unlike subordinators, they are followed by noun phrases:<br>*because of, as a result of, due to* | EFFECT / CAUSE / REASON<br>*Some people choose products* ***because of*** *their past experiences.*<br>EFFECT / CAUSE / REASON<br>*Shoppers will buy more food* ***as a result of*** *being hungry when they shop.*<br>EFFECT / CAUSE / REASON<br>*Some consumers choose an electric car* ***due to*** *its low impact on the environment.* |

# Grammar Application

## **Exercise 2.1** Subordinators That Show Cause, Reason, or Purpose

**A** In each pair of clauses about consumer behavior, write *C* above the clause that states a cause and *E* above the clause that states an effect. Next, combine the clauses using the words in parentheses. Sometimes more than one answer is possible.

C E

1 our decisions affect our financial future / it is important for us to make responsible buying decisions (*because*) *It is important for us to make responsible buying decisions because they affect our financial future.*

2 it is not easy to ignore advertising / consumers need to learn how to shop wisely (*since*)

____________________

3 make a list before you leave home / you do not buy something you do not need (*so that*)

____________________

4 people can get into debt easily / it is easy to buy things using a credit card (*because*)

____________________

5 children see the snack foods and ask their parents for them / stores put snack foods on low shelves (*so that*)

____________________

6 people will impulsively buy products that they don't need / stores put fun items like candy and toys by the checkout counters (*so*)

____________________

**B** Group Work **Complete the sentences with your own ideas on a separate sheet of paper. Then share your sentences with your group and explain them. Ask your classmates if they agree or disagree with your ideas and tell why.**

1 Sometimes people buy things they don't need because . . .
2 Sometimes people spend more money than they make because . . .
3 Manufacturers of cereals often include cartoon characters in their commercials so . . .
4 Fast-food restaurants often air commercials during late-night TV so that . . .
5 Stores sometimes advertise a few items at very low prices because . . .
6 Some people prefer to buy products online since . . .

A *My sentence is* People buy things they don't need because they want to feel better. *For example, when I have a bad day, sometimes I go out and buy something – even something small like a book – to make myself feel better.*

B *I agree with you because I do that, too, but I think more often people buy things they don't need because they are bored.*

## Exercise 2.2 Subordinators and Prepositions That Show Cause, Reason, or Purpose

**Complete the sentences about consumer buying habits. The subordinators and prepositions are missing one word each. Write the missing word.**

Consumers buy things for a lot of different reasons. Most frequently, people buy products ___*because*___ (1) of their individual tastes. For example, they might buy the same snacks or cereals every time they go shopping __________ (2) to their family's likes and dislikes. They don't even think about whether or not they want those items. People also make purchases as a __________ (3) of need. They buy an air conditioner __________ (4) of severe hot weather, or they purchase fire alarms in their house __________ (5) that their family stays safe. Finally, sometimes people make impulse purchases. They buy things they haven't planned to buy and may not necessarily need or even want. Sometimes they make these purchases __________ (6) a result of effective advertising or in the case of food, because __________ (7) hunger while they are shopping. They also make impulse purchases due __________ (8) their own personalities. Some people are more prone to impulse buying than others are.

## Exercise 2.3 More Subordinators and Prepositions That Show Cause, Reason, or Purpose

**A** You will listen to an interview about a person's buying habits. First read the questions. Then listen and take notes on the answers. Finally, write answers to the questions using sentences with the words in parentheses.

1 Why does Roger sometimes go shopping when he doesn't need anything?

(because) *He goes shopping when he doesn't need anything because he's happy when he is shopping.*

2 How does he control his spending?

(*so that*) __________

3 Does he use a credit card or debit card for his purchases? Why or why not?

(*because of*) __________

4 Why does he do a lot of research when he has to buy an expensive product?

(*as a result of*) __________

5 Does he eat out a lot?

(*due to*) ______________________________________________

______________________________________________

**B Pair Work** Rewrite questions 2–5 in A to interview your partner. On a separate sheet of paper, write sentences with his or her answers. Try to use the same prepositions and subordinating conjunctions. Share your sentences with another pair. How similar are your habits and experiences?

# 3 Transition Words and Phrases That Show Effect

## Grammar Presentation

Another important way to link cause and effect in academic writing is with transition words and phrases. Transition words often signal a cause, a reason, or an effect.

*Sometimes people buy products that show that they are part of a social network.* ***Therefore,*** *they might choose an expensive pair of jeans because the jeans are popular with their friends.*

### 3.1 Using Transition Words and Phrases That Show Effect

| | |
|---|---|
| **A** Transition words and phrases connect two independent clauses. | |
| Separate the clauses with a semicolon or use two separate sentences. | *Environmental values might affect some purchases****;*** ***consequently,*** *many merchants offer green products.* |
| Use a comma after the transition word or phrase. | *Environmental values might affect some purchases****.*** ***Consequently,*** *many merchants offer green products.* |
| **B** The following transition words and phrases are used to show effect or result:<br>*as a consequence, as a result, consequently, therefore, thus*<br>*Note: Thus* is rarely used in informal speech or informal writing. | *Many consumers are concerned about the environment.* ***As a result****, they buy products that are environmentally safe.*<br>*Some consumers feel the need to be part of a certain group;* ***therefore****, they buy products that are expensive and fashionable.* |

## Grammar Application

### Exercise 3.1 Transition Words and Phrases

**A** Unscramble the sentences about the effects of advertisements on consumers, using the prompts in parentheses. Remember to use a comma after the transition words and phrases.

1 People see and hear over 2,500 advertisements per day.

*As a result, people need to be aware of the effects of advertising.*
(of advertising / be / people / need to / aware of / the effects / as a result)

2 Candy and sugary cereals are advertised during children's television shows.

______________________________
(for them / a desire / children / develop / as a consequence)

3 Public television does not show advertisements for sugary foods.

______________________________
(exposed to / not / children / are / them / as a result)

4 The effects of smoking are serious and possibly deadly.

______________________________
(it / not / on TV / them / legal / to advertise / is / therefore)

5 Happy people are often shown eating snack foods.

______________________________
(think / them / viewers / too / snack foods / happy / will make / eating / consequently)

**B** Pair Work With a partner, choose two different products. How is each product advertised? What effects do you think the advertisements have on consumers? On a separate sheet of paper, write five sentences about each product using the cause and effect words in A. Then share your ideas with another pair of students.

*The first product we discussed was an exercise shoe. Every ad shows young, thin women who are very pretty wearing the shoes. They have handsome boyfriends, and they seem very happy. Consequently, when I see the advertisements, I always think I should buy the shoes.*

### Exercise 3.2 More Transition Words and Phrases

**A** Match the causes and effects of advertising techniques and their influence on consumers' buying decisions.

| Causes | Effects |
|---|---|
| 1 Advertisements equate high prices with effectiveness. | *1* a Consumers end up buying expensive brands. |
| 2 Some advertisements target children. | ___ b Consumers buy more than they need. |
| 3 Prices for large quantities of food are discounted. | ___ c Consumers sometimes buy products that might not be good for them. |
| 4 Advertisements often show beautiful people. | ___ d Children start to become consumers early. |
| 5 Sometimes ads do not focus on the ill effects of the products. | ___ e Consumers believe the products will make them beautiful, too. |

**B** Combine each pair of causes and effects in A. Write sentences using *as a consequence*, *as a result*, *consequently*, and *therefore*. Use each transition word or phrase once.

1 *Advertisements equate high prices with effectiveness. As a result, consumers end up buying more expensive brands.*

2 ______________________________

3 ______________________________

4 ______________________________

5 ______________________________

**C** Group Work Discuss recent purchases that your group has made. What factors influenced you in your buying decision? Write five sentences based on the answers from your group using transition words and phrases such as *as a consequence*, *as a result*, *for this reason*, and *therefore*. Share the information with another group of students.

*A friend of Amy's daughter had her ears pierced recently. For this reason, Amy's daughter wanted to get her ears pierced, too.*

*Julia Rozzio watched a very funny commercial about electric cars. As a result, when it was time to buy a new car, she decided to buy an electric one.*

# 4 Common Patterns with Nouns That Show Effect

## Vocabulary Presentation

| | |
|---|---|
| There are several common expressions with the nouns *effect* and *result* that are used to show effect in cause and effect writing. | *Advertising* ***can have a big effect on*** *children and teens.*<br>*The increase in sales* ***is a direct result of*** *our ad campaign.* |

### 4.1 Expressions with *Effect* and *Result*

| | |
|---|---|
| **A** Some common expressions and patterns with the noun *effect* are:<br>*The/One effect of* ________ (NOUN PHRASE) *on* ________ (NOUN PHRASE) *is* ________ (NOUN PHRASE) . | ***One effect of*** *advertising* ***on*** *the public* ***is*** *overconsumption.* |
| ________ (NOUN PHRASE) *have an effect on* ________ (NOUN PHRASE) . | *Advertising* ***can have a*** *significant* ***effect on*** *children and teens.* |
| **B** Some common expressions and patterns with the noun *result* are:<br>________ (NOUN PHRASE) *is a result of* ________ (NOUN PHRASE) . | *Overconsumption* ***is a*** *predictable* ***result of*** *consumers' unawareness of sophisticated advertising techniques.* |
| *When/If* ________ (CLAUSE) *, the result is* ________ (NOUN PHRASE) . | ***When/If*** *consumers are unaware of their behavior,* ***the*** *primary* ***result may be*** *overconsumption.* |
| ________ (NOUN PHRASE) *have a result.* | *Consumer awareness of advertising techniques often* ***has a*** *positive* ***result.*** |

### Data from the Real World

| | |
|---|---|
| Adjectives that most frequently occur with *effect* are:<br>*no, little, significant, some* | *Research suggests that advertising has* ***little effect*** *on a family's food budget.* |
| Adjectives that most frequently occur with *result* are:<br>*direct, positive, predictable, primary* | *Women's desire to be thin is a* ***direct result*** *of advertising.* |

# Vocabulary Application

## Exercise 4.1 Common Patterns with Nouns That Show Effect

**A** Complete the following paragraph about the consumer behavior of working parents using the phrases in the box. Add appropriate punctuation as needed.

| | | |
|---|---|---|
| a direct result can be | one effect of | effect on |
| a positive effect on | effect of | ~~have a significant effect on~~ |

These days, both parents work full-time in many families. This fact can *have a significant effect on* (1) their consumer behavior. In general, too, the behavioral change will have ______ (2) the economy. Parents with full-time jobs may not have time to cook dinner when they get home from work. As a result, they may spend more money in restaurants than families with non-working parents do. Dual-income families may eat out a lot or bring prepared food home. Some parents who work full-time may want to spend a lot of time with their children when they are not working. ______ (3) that they do special activities with their children that cost money. For example, they might take their children to amusement parks or go to the movies with them on the weekends. Some parents may also have to wear business attire for their jobs, which has an ______ (4) their clothing expenses. Another ______ (5) a dual-income lifestyle may be higher commuting expenses. The working parents may have two cars or pay twice the amount in public transportation costs. In sum, ______ (6) a dual-income lifestyle is that it will benefit the economy.

**B** Pair Work **Write answers to the questions about the consumer behavior of parents below. Then share your answers with a partner. Use the common patterns with nouns to show effect with an appropriate adjective in each sentence.**

1 How does having two working parents in a family affect the family's consumer behavior?

*One positive effect of working parents on children is that the children need to become more responsible.*

2 How does the fact that working parents may not have time to cook dinner affect their lives?

______________________________

3 What effect can having a dual income have on entertainment expenses?

______________________________

4 How might working parents' jobs affect a family's clothing expenses?

______________________________

5 How does a dual-income lifestyle affect a family's commuting expenses?

______________________________

## Exercise 4.2 More Common Patterns with Nouns That Show Effect

**A** **Answer the questions about consumer behavior. Use the expressions with *effect* and *result* and adjectives from Data from the Real World where appropriate in your answers.**

1 Some stores, especially clothing stores, play loud music. If a store plays loud music, does the store have a positive or negative effect on you? Why? Would you walk into the store or not?

*Music always has a positive effect on me. If I like the music, then I'll go into the store.*

2 Do brand names have a significant effect on your decision to buy clothes? Why or why not?

______________________________

3 Why do some people prefer to buy expensive brands? What is it a direct result of? Explain your opinion.

______________________________

4 What do you think the primary result of advertising is on young children?

______________________________

5 What kind of effect do consumer reviews on websites have on you as a consumer?

______________________________

6 Why are some people thrifty? What could it be the result of?

______________________________

**B** Group Work **Share your answers in a group. Decide on answers to each question that you all agree on. Share them with the class.**

# 5 Avoid Common Mistakes

**1** **Do not confuse *affect* and *effect*. *Affect* is almost always a verb; *effect* is almost always a noun.**

*Product placement in movies usually has a strong ~~affect~~ effect on sales.*

**2** **Remember to use the correct preposition in expressions with *cause*, *result*, and *effect*.**

*Cartoon characters in ads have a significant effect ~~in~~ on children.*

*As a result ~~on~~ of advertising on Saturday mornings, the company reached their target market – children.*

**3** **Do not confuse *because* with *because of*. Follow *because* with a subject and verb; follow *because of* with a noun.**

*Advertisers are coming up with new ways to market products because ~~of~~ young consumers are paying less attention to ads.*

*Advertisers are coming up with new ways to market products because of young people's disinterest in ads.*

## Editing Task

Find and correct six more mistakes in this body paragraph from an essay about effective advertising campaigns.

Overexposure to advertising has gradually resulted ~~on~~ *in* consumer inattention. In fact, studies have shown that most advertisements have little affect in consumers. One way in which manufacturers are responding to this problem is by a technique known as product placement. Rather than spending money on advertisements that consumers ignore, companies place their products in TV shows or films. For example, characters drink a particular brand of soda, drive a particular type of car, or use a certain computer. An example of successful product placement is the use of Apple products in various TV shows and films. In 2010, Apple's products were present in 30 percent of that year's top 33 films. This resulted on increased sales for Apple because product placement. Product placement has a second beneficial affect. Placing products in movies and TV shows, allows film companies to lower production costs because of they can use products for free. For example, the TV show *My Fair Wedding* features several jewelry and makeup brands in each episode. Without product placement, producers might have to purchase the jewelry and makeup. As a result on using product placement, the show's producers use the jewelry and makeup for free.

UNIT 3

# Cause and Effect 3: Real and Unreal Conditionals; Common Phrases with *If* and *Unless*

## Social Responsibility

## 1 Grammar in the Real World

You will read an essay that describes what might happen if corporations were to make socially responsible decisions. The essay is another example of cause and effect writing in which one cause leads to several effects.

**A** Before You Read **What do you think it means for a company to act in a socially responsible manner? What can companies do to help local communities? Read the essay. According to the writer, what are the benefits of companies being socially responsible?**

**B** Comprehension Check **Answer the questions.**

1 According to the writer, how can corporate social responsibility benefit the community?

2 Why does the writer argue that it is important that companies implement green policies?

3 Explain this sentence in the last paragraph: "Supporters say that it is not just that a company makes money, but *how* it makes money."

**C** Notice **Follow the instructions below to help you notice sentence structures that state causes and describe effects.**

1 Find a sentence in the first paragraph that contains an *if* clause. This sentence contains ideas that express cause and effect. Does the *if* clause or the main clause state the effect (result)? How certain is the writer of this effect? What word in the main clause gives the certainty?

2 Underline the sentence in the fifth paragraph that contains an *if* clause. Compare the meaning of this sentence with the sentence in 1. Which effect seems more likely to happen? Why?

3 Look at lines 36–41. Compare the sentence containing the *when* clause with the one containing the *if* clause that immediately follows it. Which sentence contains an effect that is more likely to happen? Which words tell you?

# CORPORATE SOCIAL RESPONSIBILITY: The Wave of the Future

Most managers would be in agreement that the main goal of a modern company is to make a profit. If a company does not make money, it will go out of business. In addition, while pursuing profit, companies should be ethical in their business practices. However, more and more people believe that the ethical pursuit of profit is no longer enough for modern companies. They argue that companies should also incorporate a strong sense of corporate social responsibility. This means managing a business while attempting to have a positive impact on the community. There are many reasons why companies may choose to embrace social responsibility.

According to proponents of corporate social responsibility, if companies make socially responsible decisions, they can improve life in the community. For example, companies can make an impact on a local community when they sponsor local cultural events or science fairs for high school students. To make a broader impact, companies can give money to charitable organizations that are connected to the core beliefs of the company. An example of this is People Water, which helps develop and support clean water programs around the world. Companies can also try to improve public policy. For instance, they may stop doing business with companies that use child labor, even if that means higher manufacturing costs and lower profits.

Corporate social responsibility can also benefit the environment. For example, companies can implement green policies, such as restricting printing to important documents, buying locally grown products, or conducting an electronics recycling fair. When companies conduct their business with an awareness of the environment, they set an example for the community. If these policies are part of the culture of the company, employees are likely to follow them outside the workplace.

Finally, if a company makes social responsibility part of its corporate mission, it can potentially have a better public image. A socially responsible company will be seen as an ally[1] of the community. This positive public image may set the company apart from its competitors. It will also attract investors, which will improve the company's finances. Companies like Patagonia, Inc. are very aware of this benefit. They hire executives to focus on corporate social responsibility throughout the business.

Many companies see the value of corporate social responsibility for the community as well as for their own organization. However, corporate social responsibility could play a role in every company. Supporters say that it is not just that a company makes money, but how it makes money. They argue that if more companies embraced corporate social responsibility, there would be more instances of positive social change in the world.

[1]**ally:** a person, country, or organization that provides help and support

# 2 Present and Future Real Conditionals

## Grammar Presentation

| | |
|---|---|
| Present and future real conditionals describe possible situations or conditions in the present and future and their likely results. They are often used to express cause and effect relationships in academic writing. | *Companies* ***improve*** *life in the community* ***if*** *they* ***are*** *socially responsible.*<br>***If*** *companies* ***follow*** *green policies, they* ***will set*** *a good example for their employees.* |

### 2.1 Present Real Conditionals

| | |
|---|---|
| The present real conditional is formed as follows:<br>*If* clause (present), + main clause (present) | IF CLAUSE (PRESENT)<br>***If*** *companies* ***donate*** *to charity programs,*<br>MAIN CLAUSE (PRESENT)<br>*they* ***set*** *good examples for other companies.* |
| The *if* clause can come first or last in the sentence. When the *if* clause comes first, use a comma to separate the clauses. If it comes last, do not use a comma.<br>*Note:* You can use *then* to start the main clause. The meaning does not change. | *Companies* ***set*** *a good example for other companies* ***if*** *they* ***donate*** *to charity programs.*<br>*If companies donate to charity programs,* ***then*** *they set a good example for other companies.* |

### 2.2 Using Present Real Conditionals

| | |
|---|---|
| **A** You can use present real conditionals to describe general truths, habits, routines, and scientific facts. | ***If*** *companies* ***recycle,*** *employees generally* ***recycle****, too.* |
| **B** In real conditional sentences, the *if* clause describes what action or event is necessary (the condition) for the action or event in the main clause to happen (the result). | IF CLAUSE: CONDITION<br>***If*** *companies* ***contribute*** *to charity,*<br>MAIN CLAUSE: RESULT<br>*many programs* ***benefit****.* |
| **C** You can use *when* or *whenever* to replace *if* when something is a general fact or a routine. | *Companies help the community* ***if/when/whenever*** *they are socially responsible.* |

## 2.3 Future Real Conditionals

| | |
|---|---|
| **A** The future real conditional is formed as follows:<br>*If* clause (present) + main clause (*be going to/modal* + base form of verb)<br>The *if* clause can come first or last. Use a comma only when the *if* clause comes first. | IF CLAUSE (PRESENT)<br>*If we* ***get*** *a tax refund this year,*<br>MAIN CLAUSE (*BE GOING TO* + BASE FORM)<br>*(then) we* ***are going to buy*** *an electric car.*<br>MAIN CLAUSE (MODAL + BASE FORM)<br>*We* ***will/might buy*** *a hybrid car*<br>IF CLAUSE (PRESENT)<br>*if we* ***get*** *a tax refund this year.* |
| **B** The *if* clause states a possible future situation or condition, and the main clause states the likely result. | CONDITION RESULT<br>***If I get a raise****, we will be able to buy a new car.* |

## 2.4 Using Future Real Conditionals

| | |
|---|---|
| **A** You can use future real conditionals to offer predictions. They describe possible future situations and their likely result. | ***If*** *a company* ***does not make*** *a profit, it* ***will go*** *bankrupt.* |
| **B** You can use different modals in the main clause. The modal indicates how likely the result is. | |
| *will* = It is certain. | *If a company has a good public image, it* ***will*** *attract investors.* |
| *can/could* = It is possible. | *If a company addresses social responsibility, it* ***can*** *result in a better public image.* |
| *should* = It is a strong possibility. | *If the company installs solar panels at its factories, this* ***should*** *cut energy costs in half within two years.* |
| *may/might* = It is not certain. | *Employees* ***might*** *consider ways to make their companies greener if they receive rewards for their ideas.* |

## Grammar Application

### **Exercise 2.1** Present Real Conditionals

**A** Each pair of sentences below describes a way (condition) for companies to be socially responsible and the effect that the condition can have. Write *C* next to each condition and *E* next to each effect.

1 ___C___ Car companies produce electric cars.

___E___ The companies help decrease the amount of pollution in the atmosphere.

2 ______ Workers are happier and more productive.

______ Companies offer generous salaries.

3 ______ The government gives tax breaks to companies that donate to organizations.

______ Company donations to schools increase.

4 ______ Employees feel good about themselves, and the community benefits.

______ Companies encourage their employees to volunteer.

5 ______ The countries that allow child labor feel more pressure to change their laws.

______ Companies refuse to do business in countries that allow child labor.

6 ______ The companies help the environment and save money.

______ Companies use environmentally friendly (green) technology.

**B** Combine the pairs of sentences in A. Write sentences using an *if* clause in the way indicated in parentheses. Remember to use commas where necessary.

1 (*if* clause first) *If car companies produce electric cars, they help decrease the amount of pollution in the atmosphere.*

2 (main clause first) ______

3 (*if* clause first) ______

4 (main clause first) ______

5 (*if* clause first) ______

6 (main clause first) ______

**C** Pair Work Take turns reading the sentences in B aloud with a partner. Replace *if* in the sentences with *when* or *whenever*. Talk with a partner. Does the meaning of each sentence change? Why or why not?

## Exercise 2.2 Future Real Conditionals

**A** Johnny's Chicken Restaurant has poor sales. Below are some suggested actions and results to improve sales. Match the actions and results.

| Suggested Actions | Results |
| --- | --- |
| *f* 1 Offer inexpensive lunch specials. | a Save money on gas. |
| ____ 2 Donate the profit of a sandwich to a nonprofit organization. | b Attract customers who don't eat meat. |
| ____ 3 Have some vegetarian choices. | c Lower its electricity bills. |
| ____ 4 Create a website. | d Show people that it supports local farmers. |
| ____ 5 Install energy-efficient ovens. | e Improve its public image. |
| ____ 6 Use bikes – not cars – to deliver food. | ~~f~~ See an increase in its lunch business. |
| ____ 7 Buy local produce. | g Get more online orders. |

**B** Combine the actions and results in A and write suggestions for improving the restaurant. Use future real conditionals and modals that best express the meanings of the words in parentheses.

1 (strong possibility) *If the company offers inexpensive lunch specials, it should see an increase in its lunch business.*

2 (possible) ____________________

3 (strong possibility) ____________________

4 (not certain) ____________________

5 (possible) ____________________

6 (certain) ____________________

7 (certain) ____________________

**C** Pair Work Work with a partner. Think of a company you know that is not doing well. On a separate sheet of paper, list three reasons why the company is having problems. Next to each reason, write a suggestion to the manager to fix the problem. Use a future real conditional and the appropriate modal to show how confident you are that your suggestion would work. Next, trade papers with another pair. Read their reasons and suggestions. Do you agree that the suggestions would work? Explain your opinions.

*For the problem of rude waiters, your suggestion is* If you train your waiters to be kind and helpful, your business will improve. *We agree that training is helpful, but we think* could *is more accurate because we don't think training is enough to change people's behavior. We believe that employees will change if they also feel respected by management.*

# 3 Present and Future Unreal Conditionals

## Grammar Presentation

| | |
|---|---|
| Present and future unreal conditional sentences describe situations that are not true. They describe imaginary situations, and then give the results of those situations as if they were true. In cause and effect writing, unreal conditional sentences are used to propose changes and predict the results of those changes. | *If employees became involved in the community, they would feel good about themselves.*<br><br>*If the restaurant donated money to a community organization, its public image would improve.* |

### 3.1 Present and Future Unreal Conditionals

| | |
|---|---|
| **A** The unreal conditional is formed as follows:<br><br>*If* clause (past) + main clause (modal + base form of the verb). The modal *would* is the most commonly used.<br><br>The *if* clause can come first or last. Use a comma only when the clause comes first. | IF CLAUSE (PAST)<br>*If we **were** socially responsible,*<br>MAIN CLAUSE (MODAL + BASE FORM)<br>*we **would** attract more customers.*<br><br>*Charitable programs **would** help more people if more companies **contributed** to their programs.* |
| **B** Use *were*, not *was*, for singular subjects, including *I*, in formal writing. *Was* is more common in speaking and informal writing. | FORMAL: *If I **were** socially responsible, I would recycle.*<br><br>MORE COMMON: *If I **was** socially responsible, I would recycle.* |
| **C** The modals *would*, *might*, and *could* are used in the main clause:<br>*Would* expresses a more certain or desired effect or result. It is often used in unreal conditionals.<br>*Might* and *could* express less certain results.<br>*Could not* expresses impossibility. | *Communities **would** benefit if more companies donated time and money to local charities.*<br><br>*If your company advertised more, you **might** get more business.*<br><br>*If the organization did not receive donations, it **could not** exist.* |

### 3.2 Using Present and Future Unreal Conditionals

| | |
|---|---|
| **A** In unreal conditional sentences, use the *if clause* to describe a situation that is not real or true. However, the situation may be possible in the present or future. The main clause describes the result of the situation. | IF CLAUSE: CONDITION<br>*If the company **used** more resources on social issues,*<br>MAIN CLAUSE: RESULT<br>*it **would** attract more investors.*<br><br>(It does **not** currently use many resources on social issues, but it might in the future.) |

## 3.2 Using Present and Future Unreal Conditionals *(continued)*

**B** Present unreal conditionals are often used in cause and effect writing to propose changes and predict the results of those changes.

*Less energy **would** be consumed in the world **if** more companies **used** green technology.*

(Not enough companies use green technology in the present. The situation is not real or true at the present time.)

# Grammar Application

## Exercise 3.1 Present and Future Unreal Conditionals

**A Read the article with tips on how individuals can be more socially responsible. Underline four more sentences containing present unreal conditional clauses.**

It always feels good to help other people and know that you are making a positive difference in someone's life. Here are a few tips to get you started. First, decide who you want to help. If you want to help your community, visit a local school and ask if they need help. The school would probably appreciate your help. If there were more volunteers in classrooms, teachers could spend more time with students who need special help. If there's a park or other public place near you that is full of trash, get a group of friends together and volunteer to clean it up. Your actions would have a huge impact. If these places were cleaned up, more people would visit them. As a result of all these visitors, local shops would get more business and hire more staff.

If you want to help people outside of your community or country, find an organization that sends money, supplies, and clothes to troubled areas. Your contributions are crucial. If these organizations didn't get donations and help, they couldn't be as effective as they are.

You could also spend your time or money helping an organization that works for a special cause like cancer or heart disease. If you spent time volunteering for one of these organizations, you might learn more about the organizations and find ways to help them receive more donations. These donations could be used to fund research and lead to breakthroughs or cures. If you made a donation today, you would know that your money is going toward an important cause.

**B** Pair Work **Explain your choices to a partner. Do you agree or disagree?**

## Exercise 3.2 More Present and Future Unreal Conditionals

**A** You will listen to a radio interview about ways to improve your community. First, read the questions. Then listen and take notes on the answers. Finally, write answers to the questions using unreal conditional sentences and the modals *would*, *might*, or *could*, depending on the certainty of the speaker's comments.

1 Why is it important for more people to safely recycle their old electronics?

*If more people safely recycled their old electronics, it would reduce toxins in the environment.*

2 Why is it important for more people to donate their old clothes to community organizations?

______________________________

______________________________

3 Why should more people volunteer at a school?

______________________________

______________________________

4 Why should teenagers volunteer?

______________________________

______________________________

5 Why should more people donate money to community organizations?

______________________________

______________________________

**B** Group Work With your group, decide how the community can encourage people to become involved in solving issues that affect the quality of living. How could the community get more young and old people involved? What would motivate residents to get involved? Explain why you think people – both young and old – are not involved. Then think of five suggestions explaining how you might motivate them and how you would reward them. Present your ideas to another group or the class.

*We think that teenagers are very busy with school, so they don't have time. But they also want to socialize and feel accepted. Teenagers would become more involved if the volunteering was combined with a social event. The city could . . .*

# 4 Common Phrases with *Unless* and *If*

## Vocabulary Presentation

| | |
|---|---|
| *Unless, if . . . not, only if*, and *even if* can also introduce conditions. | ***Unless*** *cities require solar panels for new construction, builders may continue to use older forms of energy delivery.*<br>*People will recycle* ***only if*** *it is required by law.*<br>***Even if*** *companies do a lot for the community, they still need to make a profit.* |

### 4.1 Negative Conditions: *Unless, If . . . not*

| | |
|---|---|
| *Unless* can be used to describe a possible negative condition in the present or future. It suggests that failing to meet the condition will lead to an undesirable or unpleasant result. | NEGATIVE CONDITION<br>***Unless*** *the organization gets more donations,*<br>UNDESIRABLE RESULT<br>*it will have to cut some programs.* |
| *If* with a negative subject (*no one*) or *if . . . not* has the same meaning as *unless*. | ***Unless*** *someone speaks up, the city will not fix the problems. (=* ***If no one*** *speaks up, the city will not fix the problems.)*<br>***Unless*** *more employees volunteer for the event, it will be canceled. (=* ***If*** *more employees* ***don't*** *volunteer for the event, it will be canceled.)* |

### 4.2 Exclusive Condition: *Only if*

| | |
|---|---|
| *Only if* is used to show that the result/effect will happen when a specific condition becomes true. No other condition will have this result. | *Consumers will change their habits* ***only if*** *prices increase dramatically.* |
| When a sentence begins with *only if*, do not use a comma. The modal in the independent clause comes before the subject. | *ONLY IF* + CONDITION / MODAL + SUBJECT<br>***Only if*** *prices increase dramatically* ***will consumers*** *change their habits.* |

### 4.3 Emphatic Condition: *Even if*

| | |
|---|---|
| *Even if* emphasizes that the condition does not matter. The condition may occur or be fulfilled, but the result will be the same. | *EVEN IF* + CONDITION<br>***Even if*** *many people start driving electric cars,*<br>UNCHANGED RESULT<br>*the country's energy needs will not decrease.* (Despite the fulfillment of the condition, the expected change will not occur.) |
| In contrast, there is an expectation that the change will occur with *if* clauses. | *IF* + CONDITION / EXPECTED RESULT<br>***If*** *many people start driving electric cars, the country's energy needs will be lower.* (We would expect this change.) |

## Vocabulary Application

### Exercise 4.1 *Unless, Only If, Even If*

**A** Complete the sentences about the rules for refunds and exchanges for employees of a retail company that values social responsibility. Use *unless*, *only if*, and *even if*.

1 *Even if* the product is broken, offer to exchange the item for another one.

2 The customer can exchange the product ________________ he or she has bought the item within the last 60 days. If it is more than 60 days, get a manager's approval before you make the exchange.

3 Offer an exchange first ________________ the customer appears upset and asks for the money right away. In that case, give them the money.

4 ________________ the customer has a receipt, can you offer an exchange. Do not offer one otherwise.

5 Do not offer the customer a store credit ________________ the product is in good condition because we need to be able to resell it.

6 Give a cash refund ________________ the customer refuses an exchange and a store credit. In general, try to avoid giving full cash refunds.

7 You cannot give a full cash refund ________________ you have approval from a manager. His or her approval is required.

8 ________________ the customer becomes upset, stay calm and patiently explain that you are doing everything you can to help him or her.

**B** Pair Work **Rewrite the sentences with *unless* using *if . . . not*. You will need to change some words.**

### Exercise 4.2 More *Unless, Only If, Even If*

**Complete the sentences about social responsibility in your city with a condition or a result. Use your own ideas and *unless*, *even if*, and *only if* where necessary.**

1 Unless the city provides free recycling pick-up, ____________________________ .

2 Even if people recycle, ____________________________ .

3 If the city doesn't clean up the parks, ____________________________ .

4 Only if the city adds more buses and subway trains, ____________________________ .

5 ____________________________ will people volunteer in the community.

6 ____________________________ , there will continue to be crime downtown.

7 ____________________________ , children won't have a safe place to play.

8 ____________________________ , people will continue to throw litter on the streets.

# 5 Avoid Common Mistakes ⚠

**1** **Remember that the subject and verb in an *if* clause must agree.**

*The restaurant will have more customers if it ~~buy~~* buys *local produce.*

**2** **Remember that the base form of the verb follows a modal.**

*If a company improves its image, it can ~~makes~~* make *a higher profit.*

**3** **Remember to use the correct form of the modal in real and unreal conditional sentences.**

Real: *If companies use recycled paper, they ~~would~~* will *save money.*

Unreal: *Telecommuting ~~will~~* would *work if employees had laptops.*

**4** **Do not confuse *otherwise* with *unless*.**

*Our dependence on oil will not decrease ~~otherwise~~* unless *we start making more electric cars.*

## Editing Task

Find and correct seven more mistakes in a body paragraph from an essay about how companies can make changes to create a better world.

### Making a Better World

If a company allows telecommuting, it can ~~creates~~ create a better working lifestyle for its employees and a better world. If a business have a telecommuting program, it not only improves the environment, it also improves the quality of life for its employees. Take, for example, an employee who usually drives to the office. If he or she can works from home a few days a week, there is one less car on the road. This reduces the levels of carbon dioxide in the air. If there is less carbon dioxide, there would be less pollution in the future. Telecommuting also improves the communities that employees live in. Often employees are too busy to get involved in their communities. If employees spent fewer hours at the office, they will spend more time in their communities. Employees can gets involved in local programs if they can structure their own working days. For example, many telecommuters cannot volunteer in local schools or other neighborhood activities otherwise they have some free time during the week. If more companies offered telecommuting, both the environment and our communities will benefit.

UNIT

# 4

# Cause and Effect 4: *-ing* Participle Phrases and Verbs That Show Cause and Effect

## Alternative Energy Sources

## 1 Grammar in the Real World

You will read an essay that contains several cause and effect ideas about solar energy. In order to persuade the reader that solar energy is a good energy alternative, the writer uses ideas from experts.

**A** Before You Read **What are the advantages and disadvantages of traditional sources of energy, such as oil, natural gas, and coal? Read the essay. What does the writer believe are the advantages of solar energy?**

**B** Comprehension Check **Answer these questions.**

1 Why does the writer believe that it is important to switch from traditional energy sources to alternative energy sources, such as solar power?

2 What is the difference between renewable and nonrenewable resources? Give examples.

3 Does the writer believe that solar energy is a feasible alternative to traditional energy sources? Explain.

**C** Notice **Follow the instructions to help you notice and understand *-ing* participle phrases that show effects and causes.**

1 Look at the lines 39–42 and lines 46–48. They each have a sentence that talks about an effect. Circle the word in each sentence that signals that the writer is going to state an effect of using solar energy.

2 Notice the *-ing* form of the verbs that follow the words that you found in item 1. Underline the verb and all the words that complete each phrase. Notice how you can use *As a result* to restate each phrase as a sentence.

3 Reread the *-ing* phrase in the first sentence in the last paragraph. Does the phrase state a cause or an effect? How is its position different from the *-ing* phrases in item 1?

# Making the Dream a Reality: NEVER RUNNING OUT OF ENERGY

The demand for energy is always increasing. Currently, electricity is produced mainly with nonrenewable fossil fuels, such as coal, oil, and natural gas. Although this use of fossil fuels can meet the world's current energy needs, it can potentially lead to negative consequences. These may include global warming, scarcity of[1] resources, and high prices. Environmental analysts warn us that the reserves of oil in the world are gradually shrinking. Fortunately, there are other alternatives for energy sources. Many experts note that solar energy is one excellent substitute because it is feasible[2] to use and is a clean source of energy.

Solar energy is feasible for several reasons. There are already solar thermal[3] power stations located in many places in the world, including in the United States, Spain, Australia, South Africa, and India. In these power stations, solar energy is converted into thermal energy, providing hot water and heat for homes and offices. Representatives in the solar energy industry point out that the cost of producing solar energy is decreasing. For example, it costs around $50 to produce a mega-watt hour of electricity through solar power, compared with about $100 to produce a mega-watt hour from coal. This lower cost for solar energy is encouraging because it may signal the start of a change in the way we power not only our buildings, but our vehicles, too. This lower cost for solar energy will make it easier to use in more places in the future.

In addition to its feasibility, solar energy is very clean, unlike fossil fuels. It does not create pollution like coal, gas, and oil. It is true that many other materials can also produce energy, such as recycled automobile tires and aluminum cans. However, these materials are nonrenewable and create pollution. Solar energy consumes far fewer nonrenewable materials, making less of an impact on the environment. For example, solar energy uses long-lasting solar panels to convert energy from sunlight, thereby reducing our dependence on coal, oil, and gas.

Being such a clean energy, solar energy is a sensible alternative to fossil fuels. It reduces our dependence on imported fuels and improves the quality of the air we breathe. The world needs energy sources like solar energy that can save resources, thus preserving the environment. The rise of renewable sources of energy – solar, wind, and water energy in particular – shows that we are gradually finding ways to avoid running out of energy. The United Nations Environment Program stated that in 2017 more energy from solar power was created than any other type of energy. There is therefore reason to hope that renewables will eventually win the battle against nonrenewables.

[1]**scarcity of:** lack of

[2]**feasible:** possible to succeed

[3]**thermal:** related to or caused by heat

# 2 *-ing* Participle Phrases That Show Effect

## Grammar Presentation

| | |
|---|---|
| *-ing* participle phrases begin with the *-ing* form of a verb. They can show effects in academic writing. | *Solar energy is converted into thermal energy,* ***providing hot water and heat for homes****.*<br>*Nuclear plants are expensive to build,* ***limiting their desirability****.* |

### 2.1 *-ing* Participle Phrases That Show Effect

| | |
|---|---|
| **A** *-ing* participle phrases that show effect usually come after the independent clause. | INDEPENDENT CLAUSE<br>*Solar energy is very clean,*<br>*-ING* PARTICIPLE PHRASE<br>***causing less pollution****.* |
| **B** A comma separates the *-ing* participle phrase from the independent clause. | *The government is investing large sums of money in alternative energy projects,* ***creating thousands of new jobs****.* |

### 2.2 Using *-ing* Participle Phrases That Show Effect

| | |
|---|---|
| **A** Use an *-ing* participle phrase to show the effect or result of the situation or action in the independent clause. | CAUSE<br>*Some countries give tax credits for wind energy,*<br>EFFECT / RESULT<br>***lowering costs for consumers****.* |
| **B** You can use *thus* or *thereby* to start *-ing* participle phrases. These words strengthen the cause and effect relationship of the ideas. | *The manufacturing of solar energy systems can create jobs,* ***thus*** *stimulating the economy.*<br>*Most solar panels have no moving parts,* ***thereby*** *lowering maintenance costs.* |

## Grammar Application

### Exercise 2.1 *-ing* Participle Phrases That Show Effect

**A** Listen to the lecture about wind power. Match each cause with its effect.

| Causes | Effects |
|---|---|
| d 1 Wind power costs about the same as coal and oil. | a It provides low cost power to everyone. |
| ____ 2 The technology of wind power is improving. | b It is a steady source of power. |
| ____ 3 Wind power will not involve many costs in the near future. | c It reduces air pollution. |
| ____ 4 Wind power produces zero carbon dioxide emissions. | ~~d~~ This makes it an affordable source of alternative energy. |
| ____ 5 Wind energy is renewable. | e It lowers the costs even further. |

**B** Combine the causes and effects in A and write sentences with *-ing* participle phrases that show effect. Remember to put a comma before the phrases.

1 *Wind power costs about the same as coal or oil, making it an affordable source of alternative energy.*

2 ____

3 ____

4 ____

5 ____

## Exercise 2.2 *-ing* Participle Phrases That Show Effect

**A** In each pair of sentences about alternative energy, label the sentences *C* for cause and *E* for effect.

1 *C* Solar energy technology continues to improve.
*E* Solar energy provides more efficient and cost-effective choices.

2 ____ Solar energy reduces noise pollution.
____ Solar cells are silent when collecting energy.

3 ____ Solar energy helps keep our air clean.
____ Solar energy does not release any harmful gases into the atmosphere.

4 ____ Homeowners can sell excess electricity they create through solar energy.
____ Homeowners can produce extra income with no extra effort.

5 ____ Governments often give tax credits for solar power generation.
____ Tax credits lower the cost of installing a solar energy system.

6 ____ Solar energy provides a long-term source of energy.
____ Solar energy exists in the sunlight we enjoy every day.

7 ____ Wind power is another clean source of energy.
____ Wind power offers another renewable option for our future energy needs.

**B Pair Work** On a separate sheet of paper, combine each pair of sentences in A. Introduce the effect using *thus* or *thereby* and an *-ing* participle phrase. Compare your sentences with a partner.

1 *Solar energy technology continues to improve, thereby providing more efficient and cost-effective choices.*

# 3 *-ing* Participle Phrases That Show Cause

## Grammar Presentation

| | |
|---|---|
| In academic writing, *-ing* participle phrases can show causes or reasons. | ***Producing very little waste**, solar power creates an environmentally friendly source of energy.*<br>***Being such a new technology**, solar energy is still in the development stage in many countries.* |

### 3.1 *-ing* Participle Phrases That Show Cause

| | |
|---|---|
| **A** *-ing* participle phrases that show cause or reason almost always come before the independent clause. | ***Providing an almost unlimited clean source of electricity**, solar energy will certainly grow in importance.* |
| **B** The omitted subject of the *-ing* participle phrase must be the same as the subject of the independent clause. | ***Being widely accessible,** hot rocks deep in the earth could be an unlimited source of energy.* |
| **C** Do not confuse *-ing* participle phrases and gerunds.<br>Gerunds can be the subject or object of a sentence. | -ING PARTICIPLE PHRASE<br>***Investing in alternative sources of energy**, the country will be ready for increases in oil prices.*<br>GERUND PHRASE<br>***Investing in solar energy** was once considered a high risk.* |

## 3.2 Using *-ing* Participle Phrases That Show Cause

| | |
|---|---|
| **A** Use an *-ing* participle phrase to show the cause of or reason for the situation or action in the independent clause. | CAUSE / REASON<br>***Using wind energy,***<br>EFFECT<br>*we can lower the cost of electricity for consumers.* |
| **B** You can start *-ing* participle phrases with the prepositions *by* and *in*. Using these words to begin the phrase can strengthen the cause and effect relationship of the ideas. *By* is more frequent than *in* in these expressions. | CAUSE EFFECT<br>***By** using solar energy, we can reduce our ecological footprint.*<br>***In** cutting tax credits for alternative energy, the government has increased our dependence on fossil fuel.* |

# Grammar Application

### Exercise 3.1 *-ing* Participle Phrases That Show Cause

**A** Read the online article about saving energy in the home. Underline each *-ing* participle phrase that expresses a cause. Circle each *-ing* participle phrase that shows an effect.

## Tips for Saving Energy

Many people want to save energy in their homes, but they're not sure how. The truth is there are several simple ways to begin saving energy and money. First, people can keep their appliances unplugged when they're not in use, decreasing small amounts of energy use with each unplugged appliance. In taking that simple step, some consumers have saved hundreds of dollars in energy costs in a single year. Along the same lines, people should not leave the lights on when they're not in a room. By making this change, people can easily save a few dollars a month on their energy bills. Also, by purchasing and installing energy-efficient appliances, people can reduce their energy use. These appliances may cost more money to buy. However, they save consumers money in the long run, using less electricity than regular appliances. Keeping doors and windows closed, people can reduce their use of air conditioning and heating. By setting thermostats lower while they are away or sleeping, people can reduce their energy costs by up to 10 percent. All consumers should take these simple steps, making a positive difference in energy use and reducing electricity bills.

**B Pair Work** Explain your choices in A to a partner.

*I circled "decreasing" because it describes the effect of unplugging appliances when they are not in use.*

**Exercise 3.2** *-ing* Participle Phrases That Show Cause

**A** Complete the sentences about ways to reduce energy consumption. Use *-ing* participle phrases and the prepositions in parentheses. Use the information from 3.1 or your own ideas. Remember to use commas after the phrases.

1 (*by*) *By using dimmers and timers for all the lighting,* hospitals can bring their energy costs down.

2 (*in*) ______________________________ restaurants can reduce their use of electricity.

3 (*by*) ______________________________ hotels would be able to reduce energy costs.

4 (*by*) ______________________________ offices could reduce waste and energy bills.

5 (*in*) ______________________________ airports might be able to reduce their energy costs.

6 (*by*) ______________________________ schools could probably reduce their energy bills.

**B Pair Work** Discuss with a partner three things that a government can do to reduce people's energy use. Agree on three things and write sentences using *in* or *by* and *-ing* participle phrases. Share your sentences with another pair. Are any of your ideas the same?

*I think that by increasing taxes on energy use, people will want to use energy more efficiently.*

# 4 Verbs That Show Cause and Effect

## Vocabulary Presentation

| | |
|---|---|
| The verbs *cause, lead to, produce, contribute to, result in,* and *result from* are commonly used to show cause and effect in academic writing. | *Curiously, increases in efficiency may have* **led to** *greater demand.*<br>*Higher gas prices have* **contributed to** *more consumer awareness of energy issues.* |

## 4.1 Verbs That Show Cause and Effect

| | |
|---|---|
| **A** *Cause* as a verb can be used in active or passive (*be* + *caused* + *by*) sentences. It is usually used to discuss negative issues (disasters, crises, etc.). | *The accident* ***caused*** *a shutdown of the plant's central operations.*<br>*The slow development of alternative energy* ***is caused by*** *cheap oil.* |
| **B** *Lead to* and *produce* are other ways to link cause and effect. They are more neutral than *cause* and are used to discuss positive or negative issues. | *New laws* ***have led to*** *an increase in wind-generated electricity.*<br>*Overreliance on fossil fuels* ***could produce*** *an uncertain future for all of us.* |
| **C** *Contribute to* is used to show one of a number of causes. | *Pollution* ***contributes to*** *many health problems.*<br>*Increased use of wind power* ***contributes*** *directly* ***to*** *a cleaner environment.* |
| **D** *Result in* and *result from* show a connection between cause and effect. Use *result in* to refer to the effect. Use *result from* to refer to the cause. | CAUSE / EFFECT<br>*Strict standards for cars* ***will result in*** *a reduction in energy use.*<br>EFFECT / CAUSE<br>*A reduction in energy use* ***will result from*** *strict standards for cars.* |

# Vocabulary Application

### **Exercise 4.1** Common Verbs That Show Cause and Effect

**Rewrite the sentences about energy sources with the verb phrases in parentheses.**

1 The sharp increase in oil prices in the 1970s created a surge in state-funded energy research and development. (*result in*)

*The sharp increase in oil prices in the 1970s resulted in a surge in state-funded energy research and development.*

2 Growing concerns about environmental issues were a factor in the government's decision in the 1970s to promote alternative energy sources. (*contribute to*)

3 Increase in oil supplies and falling prices in the 1980s were a result of a reduction in U.S. rules requiring more fuel-efficient cars. (*result from*)

4 An increase in fossil fuel usage and nuclear plants was a result of a lack of consistent solar and wind energy supplies. (*was caused by*)

5 In the future, hydrogen-based energy sources could give us pollution-free cities. (*lead to*)

______________________________________________

6 Continued overreliance on oil could create political conflicts in the future. (*cause*)

______________________________________________

## Exercise 4.2 More Common Verbs That Show Cause and Effect

**A** Read the sentences about international energy issues. Circle the correct verbs to complete the sentences.

1 The Japanese nuclear power plant accident in 2010 **resulted in / was caused by** widespread protests against nuclear plants.

2 Japan's position as the world's leading manufacturer of household solar technology **was a result of / produced** the Japanese government's financial assistance for solar roof panels in 1994.

3 High energy needs and low energy production **were caused by / contributed to** Japan's interest in renewable energy sources.

4 In Denmark, a high tax on electricity **produced / resulted from** an incentive for consumers to use less energy.

5 Denmark's interest in reducing dependence on foreign fossil fuels **resulted from / led to** the country's commitment to using natural sources of energy.

6 In Italy, a lack of natural resources **resulted in / resulted from** a need to import foreign electricity.

7 A desire to reduce use of foreign electricity **has been caused by / has contributed to** Italy's current focus on energy efficiency.

**B** Pair Work Discuss with a partner events that occurred in other countries as a result of energy issues. Use the verbs in A to explain the causes and effects.

*In Ecuador in 2009 and 2010, there was an energy crisis. Severe droughts resulted in very low water levels at hydroelectric plants. This led to many blackouts.*

# 5 Avoid Common Mistakes

**1 Remember to use *result in*, not *result of* for verbs that are followed by an effect.**

*The increased demand for oil has resulted ~~of~~ in higher prices for gas.*

**2 Remember to use *result from*, not *result by* for verbs that are followed by a cause.**

*A decrease in carbon dioxide emissions will result ~~by~~ from an increase in electric cars.*

**3 Remember to use *contribute to*, not *contribute for*.**

*The use of solar energy will contribute ~~for~~ to a healthier environment.*

**4 Remember that the subject and the verb must agree when using *contribute to*.**

*This factor ~~contribute~~ contributes to climate change.*

## Editing Task

Find and correct six more mistakes in these paragraphs about alternative energy sources.

Rising awareness of the dangers of carbon emissions and the limits of our natural resources has contributed ~~for~~ to some creative ideas for alternative energy sources. While most scientists think of ways to use renewable resources in the environment to make energy, others are finding ways to generate electricity from the movements of the human body. Michael McAlpine of Princeton University and some of his colleagues placed a material called PZT into flexible silicone rubber sheets. The PZT-filled sheets generate an electrical current when they are bent. Bending the sheets repeatedly results of a significant amount of energy. Placing these crystals in a pair of shoes or even directly into the body could result of enough electricity to charge devices like cell phones or tablets.

Our body heat can help create energy, too. For example, Belgian nanotechnology engineers built thermoelectric devices that allow a person's body heat to contribute for powering medical devices such as EKG machines and brain monitors. In 2010, engineers in Paris discovered a different way to use body heat to conserve electricity. The engineers developed a system that uses geothermal technology to move heat from a metro, or subway, station to heating pipes in a public-housing project above the station. Their system resulted from a 33 percent cut in carbon dioxide emissions in the housing project's heating system. Innovative approaches like these contributes to solving our ongoing need for alternative energy sources.

UNIT 5

# Comparison and Contrast 1: Identifying Relative Clauses; Comparatives with *As . . . As*; Common Patterns That Show Contrast

## Family Size and Personality

## 1 Grammar in the Real World

You will read an essay that discusses how a child's birth order in the family – being the oldest child, middle child, youngest child, or an only child – may affect his or her personality as an adult. The essay is an example of a type of comparison and contrast writing in which the ideas are organized using the block method.

**A** Before You Read **How many siblings (brothers and sisters) do you have? Do you think that some of their personality traits come from the order of their birth? Read the essay. How strong are the effects of birth order, according to the information in the essay?**

**B** Comprehension Check **Answer the questions.**

1 How are former presidents Jimmy Carter, George W. Bush, and Barack Obama connected to the main idea of the text?

2 According to the writer, why are firstborn children usually more ambitious than their siblings?

3 Which of the different birth order types – firstborn, middle born, youngest, and only child – do you think has the fewest advantages in life? Explain.

**C** Notice **Follow the instructions below to help you notice and understand comparison and contrast sentences from the essay that use *as . . . as*.**

1 Read the *as . . . as* sentence in the third paragraph. Are middle children likely to be equally determined, more determined, or less determined than firstborn children? Explain.

2 Read the *as . . . as* sentence in the fourth paragraph. Are youngest children likely to be equally creative, more creative, or less creative than middle children? Explain.

3 Read the *as . . . as* sentence in the fifth paragraph. Are only children likely to be equally intelligent, more intelligent, or less intelligent than children with siblings? Explain.

# Birth Order

## and Adult Sibling Relationships

What do U.S. Presidents Jimmy Carter, George W. Bush, and Barack Obama all have in common? In addition to being elected president of the United States, these men all share the same birth order. Each one is the oldest child in his family. In fact, many very successful people in government and business have been "firstborn" children. While there is always some variation, some experts agree that birth order can have an influence on a person's personality in childhood and in adulthood.

Firstborn children often share several traits. First, in contrast to their siblings, they are more likely to be responsible, ambitious, and authoritarian. This is probably because they are born into an environment of high expectations, and they usually receive a great deal of attention. They are used to being leaders, taking responsibility for others, and sometimes taking on an almost parental role.

Middle children, on the other hand, exhibit different characteristics from firstborns. They are often not as determined as firstborns. They tend to be more passive and solitary. Having to share family attention with older and younger siblings, middle children have a tendency to be more realistic, creative, and insightful.

Youngest children are often more protected than their older siblings. As a result, they are more likely to be dependent and controlling. They are often as creative as middle children, but usually more easygoing and social.

A child with no siblings, or an "only child," also exhibits some unique characteristics. While some parents worry that an only child will have difficulties socializing and making friends, studies show that an only child is just as intelligent, accomplished, and sociable as a child with siblings. In fact, some research indicates that being an only child has some benefits. These children tend to have better vocabulary, perform better at school, and maintain closer relationships with their parents than children with siblings.

Even though it is assumed that birth order dictates some personality traits, individuals can free themselves from the roles they played when they were young, but it can be difficult. According to Vikki Stark, family therapist and author of *My Sister, My Self*, change requires letting go of familiar ways of being and patiently asserting new behaviors that express one's true self.

# 2 Identifying Relative Clauses

## Grammar Presentation

| | |
|---|---|
| A relative clause modifies a noun and follows the noun it modifies. Identifying relative clauses provide necessary information about the noun. They are used in all kinds of academic writing, but they are especially useful in comparison and contrast writing to describe characteristics of elements that are being compared. | *Children* ***who/that have no siblings*** *are often very close to their parents. People gradually behave in ways* ***which/that are more consistent with their preferred self-image****.* |

### 2.1 Identifying Relative Clauses

| | |
|---|---|
| **A** An identifying relative clause modifies a noun. It begins with a relative pronoun: *that, which, who, whom,* or *whose.* (It is often called a *restrictive relative clause.*)<br><br>An identifying relative clause answers the question, "Which one?" It gives necessary information about the noun or noun phrase in the main clause. Without that information, the sentence would be incomplete. | IDENTIFYING RELATIVE CLAUSE<br>*People* ***who do not have children*** *may not be aware of differences in birth order.*<br><br>IDENTIFYING RELATIVE CLAUSE<br>*Creativity is a trait* ***that all middle children share****.* |
| **B** *Who, that,* and *whom* refer to people. Use *whom* for object relative clauses. In informal speaking and writing, the use of *who* for *whom* is common. | PEOPLE<br>*Researchers* ***who/that study families*** *have different views.*<br><br>*My siblings are the people in my life* ***whom I*** *will always trust.* |
| **C** *Whose* shows possession. It is followed by an animate or inanimate noun in academic writing. | POSSESSION<br>*Researchers* ***whose work focuses on families*** *disagree about the importance of birth order.*<br><br>*She cited a study* ***whose*** *results supported previous research.* |
| *Which* and *that* refer to things. In academic writing, *that* is often preferred to *which* in identifying relative clauses. | THINGS<br>*The study examines characteristics* ***that/which are common in firstborn children****.* |

## 2.1 Identifying Relative Clauses *(continued)*

**D** In a subject relative clause, the relative pronoun is the subject.

In an object relative clause, the relative pronoun is the object of the verb.

*Note:* The relative pronoun in object relative clauses can be omitted, but it is better not to do so in academic writing. The relative pronoun may not be omitted in subject relative clauses.

*Psychologists **who work with only children and their parents** can help the children learn to share attention.* (Who is the subject of the verb work in the relative clause.)

*There are several strategies **that parents use to help their only children**.* (That is the object of the verb use in the relative clause.)

*The research **(that) they just published on sibling order** was inconclusive.*

**E** A preposition can also come at the beginning of the clause, but this is only used in very formal writing.

*Note:* The relative pronoun may not be omitted in the formal version.

FORMAL WRITING: *An older sibling is someone **on whom** you can always rely.*

MORE COMMON: *An older sibling is someone **that/who** you can always rely **on**.*

*Researchers studied the ways **in which** parents interacted with their only child.*

### Data from the Real World

In academic writing, 75 percent of relative clauses with *whose* modify inanimate nouns.

*The report included the results of a study funded by an organization **whose** mission is to help children reach their potential.*

## 2.2 Using Identifying Relative Clauses

**A** Use identifying relative clauses in comparison and contrast writing to provide characteristics or information that shows the differences between the elements you are comparing.

*My friend **who lives in Boston** always remembers my birthday, but my friend **who lives in New Jersey** does not.*

*Some people like to play games **that involve competition**, while others like to play games **that encourage collaboration.***

**B** Relative clauses are similar to subordinate clauses in that they are fragments if they appear alone.

FRAGMENT: *A recent study reports that firstborns are generally smarter than siblings. **Who are born later.***

CORRECT: *A recent study reports that firstborns are generally smarter than siblings **who are born later.***

## Data from the Real World

In academic writing, the relative pronoun ***who*** is more commonly used than ***that*** to refer to people.

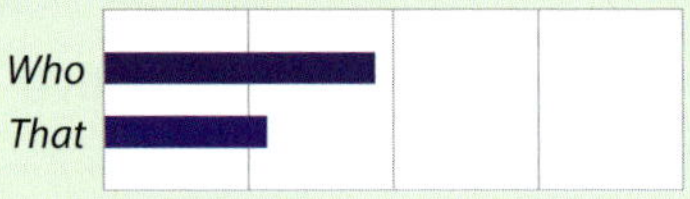


In speaking, the relative pronoun ***that*** is more commonly used than ***who*** to refer to people.

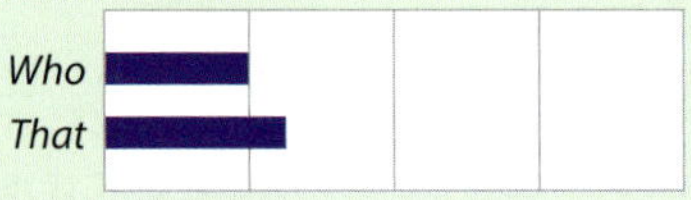


# Grammar Application

## **Exercise 2.1** Identifying Relative Clauses

**A** Read the paragraph about birth order. Complete each sentence with *that*, *who*, *whom*, or *whose*. Sometimes more than one answer is possible.

Birth order researchers have discovered some interesting information S *that* (1) can help us understand our colleagues better. Do you have a difficult boss ____________ (2) authoritarian personality makes your life difficult? If so, your boss might be a firstborn child. Children ____________ (3) are born first are often more authoritarian than their younger siblings. Do you have a co-worker ____________ (4) is passive, but particularly creative and insightful? This person may be a middle child. People ____________ (5) have both older and younger siblings are often passive because their older siblings were responsible for their well-being when they were young. The creativity ____________ (6) they exhibit might be the effect of their having spent a lot of time on their own due to having to share parental attention with their older and younger siblings. People ____________ (7) you work with ____________ (8) are controlling may be youngest children. These people are also likely to be more social than co-workers ____________ (9) are middle children. Of course, these are only generalizations. There are countless factors ____________ (10) help form people's personalities, but birth order research may shed some helpful light on people's behavior in the workplace.

**B** Look at the relative pronouns you wrote in A. Write *S* above each relative pronoun that is the subject of the clause, *O* above each relative pronoun that is the object of the clause, and *P* above each relative pronoun that shows possession.

## **Exercise 2.2** More Identifying Relative Clauses

**A** Combine each pair of sentences that describe opinions about parental behavior using an identifying relative clause.

1 Some parents often focus too much attention on their son or daughter. These parents have only one child.

*Some parents who have only one child often focus too much attention on their son or daughter.*

2 Parents put a lot of pressure on their children to do a lot of activities. These parents want their children to excel.

3 Children often feel a lot of stress. Their parents have high expectations of them.

4 Sports practice and music lessons are examples of activities. Some parents expect their children to do these activities after school.

5 Parents raise more independent adults. These parents give proper emotional support to their children.

6 Some children have behavioral problems at school. Their parents both work long hours.

**B** Pair Work **Tell a partner whether you agree or disagree with each opinion in A. Use identifying relative clauses where possible.**

A *I don't think it's true that parents who have only one child focus too much attention on that child. I was an only child, and I don't think that I received too much attention from my parents.*

B *I disagree. In my experience, parents who have an only child often want to give that child everything. The child doesn't realize what it's like to share, either.*

# 3 Comparatives with *As . . . As*

## Grammar Presentation

| | |
|---|---|
| Writers show similarities and differences in comparison and contrast writing by using *as . . . as*. | *Some people think that youngest children might not be* ***as mature as*** *their siblings.*<br>*Sometimes younger children do not get* ***as much attention as*** *their older siblings.* |

### 3.1 *As . . . As*

| | |
|---|---|
| **A** *As . . . as* can be used in the following patterns:<br><br>*(not) as + adjective/adverb + as* | ADJECTIVE<br>*Youngest children are not as* ***independent***<br>NOUN PHRASE<br>*as* ***their older siblings.***<br>ADVERB<br>*An only child socializes as* ***well*** *as children with siblings.* |
| *(not) as* + noun phrase + *as* | NOUN PHRASE<br>*An only child has as* ***many close friends*** *as children with siblings.* |
| **B** *As . . . as* can also be used to compare quantities with count and noncount nouns:<br><br>*(not) as much* + noncount noun phrase + *as*<br><br>*(not) as many* + count noun phrase + *as* | *Younger children sometimes don't get as* ***much attention*** *from parents as firstborn children.*<br><br>*Growing up as an only child has as* ***many advantages*** *as growing up in a large family.* |

### 3.2 Using *As . . . As*

| | |
|---|---|
| Use *as . . . as* in the following ways:<br>to emphasize two equal elements:<br>_____ *(just) as . . . as* _____ | *Only children usually turn out* ***just as well as*** *children from large families.* |
| to show that two things are slightly unequal:<br>_____ *almost/nearly/about/not quite as . . . as* | *Firstborn children are* ***almost as open to new experiences as*** *their younger siblings.* |
| to emphasize a difference:<br>_____ *not nearly as . . . as* _____ | *Genuine concern over sibling order may* ***not be nearly as widespread as*** *it seems at first glance.* |

# Grammar Application

## Exercise 3.1 Comparatives with *As . . . As*

**A** Complete the sentences about personality traits and birth order using the information in the chart and *as . . . as* phrases.

| | Firstborn Children | Middle Children | Youngest Children |
|---|---|---|---|
| **Responsible** | Very | Somewhat | Not Very |
| **Social** | Somewhat | Not Very | Very |
| **Creative** | Not Very | Very | Very |
| **Realistic** | Very | Very | Not Very |
| **Dependent** | Not Very | Not Very | Very |

1 Middle children *are not as responsible as* (responsible) firstborns.

2 Firstborn children ______________________ (social) youngest children.

3 Middle children ______________________ (creative) youngest children.

4 Youngest children ______________________ (realistic) middle children.

5 Middle children ______________________ (dependent) firstborn children.

6 Firstborn children ______________________ (realistic) middle children.

7 Firstborn children ______________________ (creative) youngest children.

8 Middle children ______________________ (dependent) youngest children.

**B** Look at the information in the chart in A about firstborn children, middle children, and youngest children again. Think about your birth order and the birth order of people you know. Does the information accurately describe your personality and their personalities? Why or why not? Give at least one example for each birth order.

*I'm a middle child and my brother is a firstborn child. According to the chart, I'm not as responsible as firstborn children, but actually, I'm much more responsible than my brother. Maybe it's because I was given the responsibility of taking care of everyone while my parents worked. I think I have always felt responsible for my siblings. I agree with the idea that youngest children are social. My younger brother is really outgoing and has a lot of friends . . .*

## Exercise 3.2 Comparatives with *As . . . As*

**A** Listen to the story of two famous sisters – Venus and Serena Williams. Complete the chart.

| | Venus Williams | Serena Williams |
|---|---|---|
| 1 Birth date | *June 17, 1980* | |
| 2 Height | *6'1"* | |
| 3 Year turned professional | | |
| 4 Wimbledon singles victories (individual years) | | |
| 5 U.S. Open singles victories (individual years) | | |

**B** On a separate sheet of paper, use the information from A and the cues below to write sentences with the following *as . . . as* phrases: *almost as . . . as*; *just as . . . as*; *not nearly as . . . as* and *not quite as . . . as*. Sometimes more than one answer is possible.

1 Serena / is / tall / Venus.

*Serena is not quite as tall as Venus.*

2 Serena / has / played / long / Venus.

3 Serena / is / old / Venus.

4 Serena / has / experience / Venus.

5 Serena / is / important to U.S. sports / Venus.

6 Serena / has / won / Wimbledon singles / Venus.

7 Venus / is / famous / Serena.

8 Serena / has had / Wimbledon singles victories / Venus has had.

9 Venus / has had / success in business / Serena. They are both successful businesswomen.

Serena and Venus Williams

**C** Pair Work Tell a partner about two people you know well. Compare them using *as . . . as* structures. Next, write five sentences about them using *as . . . as*. Use adjectives, adverbs, and noun phrases as well as phrases such as *almost, not nearly,* and *not quite* in your sentences where possible.

*Younsil does not have as many children as Victoria.*

*Younsil is not quite as shy as Victoria.*

# 4 Common Patterns That Show Contrast

## Vocabulary Presentation

Useful words and phrases that show contrast in academic writing include *difference(s)*, *differ*, *in contrast*, and *unlike*. These words are important in comparison and contrast writing.

*One **major difference** in some cultures is the role of adult children.*

***In contrast to** the past, more U.S. children now live with their parents into their early adulthood.*

### 4.1 Difference(s), Differ, In Contrast, Unlike

**A** A common pattern with the noun *difference* is:

*The difference between* ______ (NOUN PHRASE) *and* ______ (NOUN PHRASE) *is . . .*

*One **significant difference between** youngest children **and** their older siblings **is** that youngest children receive a lot of attention.*

**B** A common pattern with the verb *differ* is:

______ (NOUN PHRASE) *differ(s) from* ______ (NOUN PHRASE) *in that . . .*

*The results of current research **differ from** earlier results **in that** they show a definite relationship between birth order and personality.*

**C** Common expressions and patterns used with the phrase *in contrast* are:

*In contrast to* ______ (NOUN PHRASE), ______ (INDEPENDENT CLAUSE).

*In contrast,* ______ (INDEPENDENT CLAUSE).

***In contrast to** traditional American families, the Chinese have had several generations of one-child families.*

*Many children without siblings receive a lot of attention. **In contrast**, children with siblings often share their parents' attention.*

**D** A common pattern with the adjective *unlike* is:

*Unlike* ______ (NOUN PHRASE), ______ (INDEPENDENT CLAUSE).

***Unlike** firstborn children, youngest children are generally very creative.*

#### Data from the Real World

Adjectives and quantifiers that most frequently occur with *difference* are: *significant, major, important, many, large, small, some, minor, cultural, regional, individual.*

*There are many **cultural differences** in how parents treat their children.*

*One **major difference** between the siblings is that the older ones tend to be more confident.*

# Vocabulary Application

## Exercise 4.1 Vocabulary That Shows Contrast

**A** Complete the following sentences about children in the United States using the words and phrases in the box.

| | | |
|---|---|---|
| differ from | ~~major difference between~~ | unlike |
| in contrast | significantly different from | |

1 One *major difference between* children in the United States in 1900 and now is that children in the past didn't get a lot of individual attention from their parents, while children today get a lot of individual attention.

2 Another way that today's children are ____________________ children in the past is that in the past, children often worked to help their families, but children now often work for their own extra spending money.

3 Today's children also ____________________ children in 1900 in that they are required to attend school.

4 Children in the past often had large families with several siblings. ____________________, many children today have one or two siblings or are only children.

5 In 1900, children were very independent. ____________________ them, children today depend on their parents a lot.

**B** Pair Work **With a partner, draw a chart like the one below. Write five contrasting pieces of information about children in the 1900s and now in a culture that you are familiar with. Then present your information to the class, using vocabulary from A.**

| Children in the 1900s | Children Now |
|---|---|
| | |

*One major difference between young children in my native country today and in the 1900s is that in the 1900s, they used to work in factories. Today that's illegal.*

# 5 Avoid Common Mistakes ⚠

**1 Do not use *who* with inanimate nouns.**

*A study ~~who~~ that showed the benefits of being an only child was published last year.*

**2 Do not omit the relative pronoun in subject relative clauses.**

*Children ^who have older siblings tend to be somewhat dependent.*

**3 Remember that the subject and the verb must agree in relative clauses.**

*Children who ~~has~~ have siblings often become secure and confident adults.*

**4 Use *the same as*, not *the same than*.**

*Middle children often have the same level of creativity ~~than~~ as youngest children.*

## Editing Task

Find and correct eight more mistakes in this body paragraph from an essay comparing trends in families in the past and today.

Families Past and Present

A major way that families have changed is the number of families ^*that* have only one child. The number of families had only one child was low in the United States in the 1950s and 1960s. However, one-child families began increasing in the 1970s and are very common today. This is especially true in households who have only one parent. One reason families are smaller is the cost of living. It is not the same than it was 40 years ago. For example, it costs about 10 times more to send a child to college than it did 40 years ago. As a result, many parents choose to have only one child because they do not have enough money for more children. In addition, attitudes about only children are also not the same than attitudes about them in the past. In the 1950s and 1960s, people avoided having only one child. At that time, many people thought that children did not have siblings had many disadvantages. For example, people thought that they did not learn good social skills. However, recent studies who focus on only children show a different picture. These studies show that only children tend to have the same social skills than children who has siblings.

UNIT 6

# Comparison and Contrast 2: Complex Noun Phrases; Parallel Structure; Common Quantifiers

## Men, Women, and Equality

## 1 Grammar in the Real World

You will read an essay about how men and women are often treated differently in society. The essay is an example of one type of comparison and contrast writing, in which ideas are organized using the point-by-point method.

**A** Before You Read **Do you think men and women are treated differently in today's society? Read the essay. According to the writer, what are some ways that men and women are treated differently?**

**B** Comprehension Check **Answer the questions.**

1 According to the writer, what is gender inequality and where can it be found?

2 How does the writer say that women and men are treated differently in the workplace?

3 Give two examples of how boys and girls are treated differently in U.S. society.

**C** Notice **Follow the instructions below to find ways that the author uses parallel structure to contrast the differences in genders.**

1 Find the sentence on lines 23–24 that states how men are expected to behave in the workplace. Then look on lines 26–29 for the sentence that describes how women are expected to behave. How many adjectives describe men's expected behavior? How many adjectives describe women's behavior? What other similarities do the two sentences have?

2 Find the sentence on lines 42–45 in which the author compares the types of toys that boys and girls receive as presents. How many toys are mentioned for boys and how many for girls?

3 Find the sentence in the third paragraph that contrasts how boys and girls are expected to behave. How many adjectives describe boys' expected behavior? How many adjectives describe girls'? What other similarities do the two clauses in the sentence have?

# Gender Inequality

Although progress has been made in recent decades, it would be wrong to think that men and women today are treated equally in the United States or in other industrialized nations. Historically, men in the United States have always had more financial, legal, and political power and more job opportunities than women. However, since the 1960s, there has been a progressive increase in the number of women working outside the home, running their own businesses, and participating in political life. Nevertheless, despite women's increasing participation, gender inequality can still be found in the workplace as well as in cultural and social aspects of life.

Women and men are not always treated equally at work. The clearest sign of inequality in the workplace is at the top levels of management. For example, the vast majority of major corporations have male CEOs (Chief Executive Officers), and most of the top positions are filled by men. Another sign of gender inequality is the different expectations employers have of men and women in leadership positions. Men are usually expected to be assertive, confident, and decisive. When men take a dominant role, they are often rewarded by their employers. Assertive women, on the other hand, are often not well received in the workplace because they are expected to be flexible, cooperative, and deferential.[1] There are also significant differences in salary. According to the Institute for Women's Policy Research, women still make less than men even when they do the exact same job. For example, in 2016, full-time female employees made 80.5 cents compared to every dollar made by male employees or, in other words, a wage difference of 20 percent.

Gender differences are found in our cultural and social lives as well. Boys and girls are taught different gender roles and social expectations from birth. For example, in the United States many baby boys still receive blue clothes and blankets, while many girls receive pink ones. Boys are often given cars, trucks, and toy soldiers as presents, while girls often receive dolls, dollhouses, and toy ovens. In terms of behavior, in many cultures people tend to expect boys to be aggressive and dominant, whereas they generally expect girls to be emotional and subordinate.[2] As children grow up and become adults, these behavior patterns are usually reinforced through social interactions.

Gender inequality has existed in the United States and other industrialized countries for many years, and it will not disappear overnight. Progress has been made recently regarding the opportunities for women. However, both men and women should continue to work for equality to create a fairer environment for everyone.

[1]**deferential:** polite and showing respect
[2]**subordinate:** lower in position; following orders

# 2 Complex Noun Phrases

## Grammar Presentation

| | |
|---|---|
| Noun phrases include a noun and modifiers. Some modifiers, like adjectives, usually come before the noun, but there are other modifiers that can come after the noun. Complex noun phrases can have modifiers both before and after the noun. Complex noun phrases are common in academic writing because adding modifiers is an efficient way to present information. | Noun phrase modified with an adjective and a prepositional phrase:<br>*The **sensitive** issue **of gender inequality** has been discussed for many decades.*<br>Noun phrase modified with an adjective and an identifying relative clause:<br>*Sometimes **professional** women **who start their own businesses** have trouble getting loans.* |

### 2.1 Modifiers After Nouns

| | |
|---|---|
| **A** Common modifiers after a noun are:<br>relative clauses<br><br>prepositional phrases | RELATIVE CLAUSE<br>*New York has the most women **who own businesses**.*<br>PREP. PHRASE<br>*The organization provides advice for women **in business**.* |
| **B** Some relative clauses can be shortened by dropping the relative pronoun and the *be* verb.<br>*-ing* phrases<br>*-ed* phrases | *The number of women ~~who are~~ **starting their own businesses** is increasing.*<br>*Women ~~who are~~ **elected to Congress** are in the minority.* |

### 2.2 Using Noun Phrases

| | |
|---|---|
| **A** In academic writing, complex noun phrases can often replace other parts of speech, such as verb phrases. This process makes it possible to pack information into a sentence more efficiently by reducing the number of clauses. Writers also use complex noun phrases to connect ideas between sentences. | VERB PHRASE<br>*Recent research shows that there **are more mothers***<br>VERB PHRASE<br>***who are working**.* (2 clauses)<br>NOUN PHRASE<br>*Recent research shows **an increase in the number of working mothers**.* (1 clause)<br>*The **salary** of men and women **differ significantly** for the same job. This **significant difference** in **salary** is one indication of persistent inequality.* |

## 2.2 Using Noun Phrases *(continued)*

| | |
|---|---|
| **B** A complex noun phrase can often replace a verb (usually *be*) + adjective. The adjective from the verb phrase becomes part of the noun phrase. This makes it possible to include more information in one sentence. | VERB *BE* + ADJ.<br>*The rise of women in business* ***has been impressive****.*<br>*This indicates that traditional gender roles are being challenged.*<br>NOUN PHRASE<br>***The impressive rise of*** *women in business indicates that traditional gender roles are being challenged.* |
| **C** In comparison and contrast writing, noun modifiers are used to compare and contrast items in detail. | *The boy twin received a* ***blue blanket with white stripes****, while his twin sister received a* ***pink blanket with yellow stripes****.* |

# Grammar Application

### Exercise 2.1 Complex Noun Phrases

**A** Read the sentences about gender and careers. Underline the relative clauses. Circle the prepositional phrases that come after nouns.

1 A couple of decades ago, women who were interested in studying engineering were rare.

2 Today, there are more and more women in the field of engineering.

3 There didn't use to be many men who were attracted to the field of nursing.

4 Now the number of men who are working as nurses is growing.

5 Two fields that were once occupied only by men were law enforcement and firefighting.

6 These are two careers that are attracting many young women today.

7 Because of an increase in demand and services in data communications and home health-care aides, more men and women are choosing professions in these areas.

**B** Pair Work **On a separate sheet of paper rewrite each sentence from A that contains a relative clause. Shorten the relative clauses to *-ed* and *-ing* phrases.**

1. *A couple of decades ago, women interested in studying engineering were rare.*

## **Exercise 2.2** More Noun Phrases

**Read each sentence or pair of sentences about women in the workplace. Next, write the words in bold as a noun phrase in the sentence that follows. Change the form of the words as necessary.**

1 The number of women working outside the home has **increased significantly**.

There has been a _significant_ _increase_ in the number of women working outside the home.

2 It has not been easy for women to **achieve progress** toward equality in the workplace.

The ________________ of ________________ toward equality in the workplace has not been easy for women.

3 The **growing** number of women in management **is recent**. This indicates that gender differences are becoming less important.

The ________________ ________________ in the number of women in management indicates that gender differences are becoming less important.

4 In many companies the **roles** of men are **dominant**. This is still evident, although it is changing.

The ________________ ________________ of men in many companies is still evident, although it is changing.

5 The **struggle** for women in the workplace has been **long** and **difficult**. This has resulted in many more career opportunities in recent years.

The ________________ and ________________ ________________ for women in the workplace has resulted in many more career opportunities in recent years.

6 Women have **increasingly participated** in the workforce; nevertheless, gender inequality continues.

Although there is an ________________ in the ________________ of women in the workforce, gender inequality continues.

7 Current research shows that the number of women going to medical school and law school is **rising steadily**. This is expected to continue.

The ________________ ________________ in the number of women going to medical school and law school is expected to continue, according to current research.

8 **Women's enrollment** in college has been **higher** than men's since 2000. This is due in part to the fact that more men drop out.

________________ ________________ ________________ in college since 2000 is due in part to the fact that more men drop out.

9 In a recent survey, men **perceive** career advancement more **optimistically** than women. This supports the fact that men hold the majority of middle management positions.

Men's ________________ ________________ concerning career advancement supports the fact that men hold the majority of middle management positions.

# 3 Parallel Structure

## Grammar Presentation

| | |
|---|---|
| When each item in a list or comparison follows the same grammatical pattern, it is easier for readers to understand complex ideas. This is called *parallel structure.* | *In some cultures, men are expected to be* ***assertive****,* ***confident****, and* ***decisive****.*<br>*In some cultures, women* ***spend the day taking*** *care of the children, while* ***men spend the day working*** *outside the house.* |

### 3.1 Parallel Structure

| | |
|---|---|
| **A** Parallel structure applies to series of:<br>adjectives<br>noun phrases<br>verb phrases<br>clauses | ADJECTIVE / ADJECTIVE / ADJECTIVE<br>*Boys are encouraged to be* ***aggressive****,* ***outgoing****, and* ***strong****.*<br>*Many Vietnamese believe that marriage should promote the*<br>NOUN PHRASE / NOUN PHRASE / NOUN PHRASE<br>*interests of* ***the community****,* ***the family****, and* ***the couple****.*<br>VERB PHRASE<br>*A Brazilian bride and groom* ***say their wedding vows****,*<br>VERB PHRASE / VERB PHRASE<br>***kiss****, and* ***exchange rings****.*<br>*Many women struggle with cultural expectations*<br>CLAUSE / CLAUSE<br>***when they pursue a career*** *or* ***when they decide not to marry****.* |
| **B** Items in a series are often the same length. This makes the ideas easier to understand. | *Receptions for Brazilian weddings involve* ***delicious food****,* ***much laughter****, and* ***constant music****.* (The items listed are all about the same length – each noun is modified by one adjective.) |
| **C** Writers often use parallel structure to compare and contrast items in a series. | *Years ago, men* ***worked*** *outside the home, while women* ***cleaned*** *the house,* ***did*** *the cooking, and* ***cared for*** *the children.* |

## Grammar Application

### Exercise 3.1 Parallel Structure

Choose the best answer to complete the sentences about gender differences below.

1 Men and women working together can reduce inequality slowly, carefully, and *significantly* .
a with significance b significantly c significant

2 Unlike the past, these days women are often encouraged to go to college, have careers, and ______________ .
a invests in her future b investing in their future c invest in their future

3 Both men and women enjoy going to work, making money, and ______________ .
a provides for their families b providing for their families c they provide for their families

4 Traditionally, men have often been encouraged to become competitive, aggressive, and ______________ .
a unemotional b they are not emotional c they can't show their feelings

5 Companies that attract women tend to offer opportunities for advancement, flexible schedules, and ______________ .
a they have mentors for them b mentors c women need mentors

6 Unlike women, men are much more likely to ask for raises, bonuses, and ______________ .
a promote b promoting c promotions

### Exercise 3.2 More Parallel Structure

**A** Write answers to the questions below about men, women, and careers, using parallel structure. Use your own ideas or ideas that you have learned in this unit.

1 What are three things that women can do to decrease gender inequality in the workplace?
*Women can refuse to accept unfair treatment, make men more aware of their behavior, and continue to ask for what they want.*

2 What are three skills that many people thought in the past were women's skills?

______________

______________

3 What are two professions that men typically did in the past that are now also done by women?

______________

______________

4 What are three careers that women have traditionally gone into?

______________

______________

5 What are two different ways that some women react to having a female boss?

6 What are two possible ways that women are different from men in relationships?

**B** Write answers to the questions about men, using parallel structure. Use your own ideas.

1 What are three things that men can do to decrease gender inequality in the workplace?

*Men can be more aware of their behavior, honest in their interactions, and accepting of women as their equals.*

2 What are three skills that many people believe are more suited to men than women? Why do you think most people have this belief?

3 What are three professions that women did in the past that are now also done by men? What are your feelings about having men in these professions?

4 What are two professions that people still associate with men rather than women? What are possible reasons for this?

5 In your experience, what are two ways that some men react to having a female boss?

6 In your opinion, do men in their 20s and 30s have different perceptions of women in the workplace than men who are older? Why or why not? Give two reasons for your opinion.

**C** Group Work **Share your ideas for each item in A and B in a group. Tell if you agree or disagree and why.**

A *I say that women can refuse to accept unfair treatment, make men more aware of their behavior, and continue to ask for what they want. Those behaviors would decrease gender inequality.*

B *I don't agree with everything you say because first of all, I think that management must change and that change is difficult because it is like changing a culture's values and ideas.*

# 4 Common Quantifiers

## Vocabulary Presentation

| | |
|---|---|
| Quantifiers indicate the amount or degree of something. They can help a writer be more precise and avoid overgeneralizations. They are common in comparison and contrast academic writing. | ***Many*** *top positions are filled by men.*<br>***Few of*** *the top executives are women.* |

### 4.1 Quantifiers

| | |
|---|---|
| **A** Quantifiers are used before nouns. Examples include: *all, almost all, both, few, most, no, several, some.* | ***Most*** *toys are gender-specific.*<br>***Several*** *women hold important positions in that company.* |
| **B** Quantifiers also follow the pattern:<br>quantifier + *of* +:<br>*the/this/that/these/those/such* + noun phrase<br>possessive pronoun (*my, your,* etc.) + noun phrase<br>object pronoun (*it, them, us,* etc.)<br>*Note*: Use *none* instead of *no* in this pattern. | ***Many of the*** *women in my country have two jobs.*<br>***Most of my*** *friends are aware of traditional gender roles.*<br>***None of us*** *supports inequality in the workplace.* |
| **C** Use these quantifiers only before count nouns: *a few, a great many, both, few, many, several.* | *Only* ***a few*** *presidents of countries are women.*<br>***Both*** *boys and girls learn gender roles from an early age.* |
| Use these quantifiers only before noncount nouns: *a great deal of, a little, little, much.* | *The article contained* ***a great deal of*** *information about gender roles.*<br>*We have achieved* ***little*** *progress in gender equality.* |
| **D** Some quantifiers compare amounts: *fewer, less,* and *more.* | ***Fewer*** *men than women work as nurses.* |
| Adverbs such as *considerably, significantly, slightly,* and *substantially* are common before the comparative quantifiers. | *In the past, many men felt women could not succeed as executives.* ***Significantly fewer*** *men today believe that.*<br>*In the 1970s, most lawyers were men. Today there are* ***substantially more*** *female lawyers.* |
| **E** Use quantifiers to change overly general statements into qualified, more precise statements in comparison and contrast writing. | *Men are aggressive, and women are passive.* (Too general)<br>***Some*** *men are dominant and* ***some*** *women are passive.* (More accurate) |

# Vocabulary Application

## Exercise 4.1 Common Quantifiers

**A** The graph below shows the percentage of males and females across some of the major occupational groups in Canada. Write sentences by referring to the graph and using the cues in parentheses.

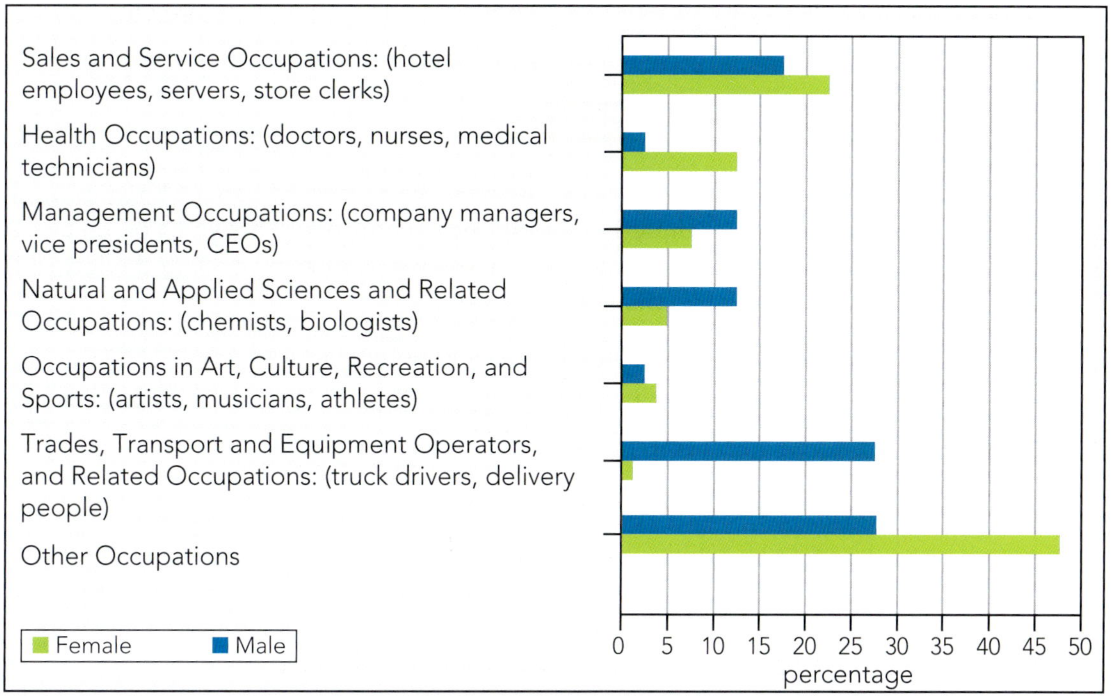


Source: Statistics Canada, Labour Force Survey. (www.statcan.gc.ca)

| | | |
|---|---|---|
| ~~a great deal of~~ | most of | a slightly higher number of |
| fewer | significantly fewer | substantially more |

1 *A great deal of* men are in the trades and transport areas.

2 ________________ men are in management occupations than in sales and service occupations.

3 There are ________________ men than women who are chemists and biologists.

4 ________________ women have occupations such as artists, musicians, and athletes than those of truck drivers and delivery people.

5 ________________ women than men have jobs in the trades, transport, and equipment operators sector.

6 ________________ the women have jobs in occupations not listed in the chart.

**B** Pair Work **Work with a partner. Create three sentences using the information in the chart in A. Use the words in the box in A and other quantifiers. Share them with another pair and give a possible explanation for the statement. Do they agree with the statements?**

*Significantly fewer men are in health occupations. I think this may be because there are usually more women in health-care occupations such as nursing.*

**C** Pair Work **Using your own knowledge and experience, write four sentences using quantifiers and adverbs about jobs and gender in your culture or community.**

*In my culture, significantly more women than men are teachers.*

## Exercise 4.2 More Common Quantifiers

**A** **You will listen to the results of a survey taken by the Bureau of Labor Statistics on the time that men and women in the United States spend on household activities on an average day. Before you listen, read each statement and guess the answer by circling the letter. Then listen and write the correct letter on the line.**

1 _____ percent of women spent some time doing general household activities.

a Seventy-four b Eighty-four c Ninety-four

2 _____ percent of men spent time doing general household activities.

a Twenty-seven b Forty-seven c Sixty-seven

3 _____ percent of women did some housework (cleaning or laundry).

a Twenty-nine b Forty-nine c Sixty-nine

4 _____ percent of men did some housework (cleaning or laundry).

a Five b Ten c Twenty

5 _____ percent of women prepared the food and cleaned up.

a Fifty-eight b Sixty-eight c Seventy-eight

6 _____ percent of men prepared food and cleaned up.

a Twenty-one b Thirty-one c Forty-one

Source: www.bls.gov

**B** **Compare the statistics in A. Write statements using the quantifiers in parentheses.**

1 (significantly fewer) *Significantly fewer men than women spent time doing housework.*

2 (substantially more) ______________________________

3 (some) ______________________________

4 (most) ______________________________

5 (both) ______________________________

# 5 Avoid Common Mistakes

**1 Remember to use parallel structure with two or more adjectives.**

*A study showed that elementary school teachers discriminated against children who were noisy, active, and ~~if they did not pay attention~~* ***inattentive****.*

**2 Remember to use parallel structure with two or more noun phrases.**

*Wedding guests include the friends of the bride, the bride's co-workers, and the bride's family ~~is also invited~~.*

**3 Remember to use parallel structure with two or more verb phrases.**

*The girls loved to play basketball, to wrestle, and ~~running~~* ***to run*** *races, just like the boys.*

**4 Remember to use parallel structure with two or more clauses.**

*These days most married women feel that they should continue working, have their own bank accounts, and ~~to~~ share household chores with their husbands.*

## Editing Task

Find and correct nine more mistakes in this body paragraph from an essay comparing women's roles in the past and in the present.

Women's Roles, Past and Present

Roles for women in the United States have changed in terms of the subjects that women study in college and ~~they choose careers~~ ***the careers that they choose***. Before the 1970s, most middle-class men were expected to attend college and pursuing careers that were both professional and they paid well. Men provided the main financial support for the family. Middle-class women, however, were expected to get married or, if they went to college, preparing for traditionally female professions, such as teaching or to be a nurse. Women were not expected to support a family. If a woman worked after college, she was expected to stop as soon as she got married or to have children. Because they did not expect to support a family or working for a long time, some women also studied non-career-oriented subjects such as literature or art history. Nowadays, in contrast, most women plan to work for most of their adult lives and they help support their families. Many women feel that they should prepare for a job, that they should move forward in their careers, and to find satisfaction in their work. Therefore, today, there are many more women studying career-oriented subjects such as business, accounting, and to work in law enforcement. In fact, many fields that were once thought of as for men only, such as law enforcement, now employ women. Although women still do not earn as much as men, they have come a long way since the 1970s in expanding their college and career opportunities.

UNIT 7

# Comparison and Contrast 3: Comparative and Superlative Adjectives and Adverbs; Articles; Common Expressions That Show Similarity

## Family Values in Different Cultures

## 1 Grammar in the Real World

You will read an essay about cultural differences between U.S. families from two cultural backgrounds: Latino and traditional U.S. The essay is an example of one kind of comparison and contrast writing in which the writer compares and contrasts aspects of two cultures.

**A** Before You Read **What does the term *family* mean to you? Read the essay. What are some ways that the writer defines *family*?**

**B** Comprehension Check **Answer the questions.**

1 How are the beliefs of Dr. Benjamin Spock related to the way many U.S. families raise their children?

2 Who might young Latino adults live with when they finish college? What about college graduates in traditional U.S. families?

3 What does the writer mean when he or she says that "it is wise not to stereotype cultures"? Do you think the writer avoids stereotyping cultures in this essay? Explain.

**C** Notice **Answer the questions below to help you notice the use of comparative adjectives and other ways to describe differences and similarities.**

1 Reread lines 24–25 in the second paragraph. What did Dr. Spock believe American children should become as they got older? Notice the two forms of the comparative. What determines which form is used?

2 What two things does the writer compare on lines 47–50?

3 Reread the last paragraph. How are traditional U.S. and Latino cultures the same? Underline the words the writer uses to show similarity.

# What Family Means:
## An Intercultural Perspective

**THE DEFINITION OF FAMILY** differs from culture to culture. These differences become more apparent when families from diverse cultures live in the same area. For example, with the increasing number of Latinos in the United States, diversity in the culture of U.S. families has become more noticeable. Differences include how family is defined, how children view themselves within the family, and what happens when children reach young adulthood.

Traditionally, in U.S. culture, when people refer to their family, they usually mean their immediate family, that is, their parents and their children. Many of these families follow the basic principles of Dr. Benjamin Spock, a famous pediatrician[1] in the mid-1900s. He wrote a popular book on raising children that changed the style of parenting from strict to more permissive. He believed that children should be free to set their own goals and choose their own career path. In Dr. Spock's view, as children get older they should become more independent. After finishing high school, American teenagers who go to college often move out of their parents' homes and live in a college dormitory or their own apartment. After college, many live on their own. Children who continue to live with their parents after high school or college might be asked to pay rent. In general, family takes on a smaller role as children enter adulthood.

In contrast, in many Latino cultures, when people refer to their family, they include extended family, such as aunts, uncles, cousins, and grandparents. Latino life centers on family. In fact, the largest component of Latino life is usually the family. Sociologists have suggested that each family member feels a moral responsibility to help other members of the family who may be experiencing problems such as poor health, financial concerns, and unemployment. It is common for Latino families to encourage longer visits from relatives, and they expect loyalty, sacrifice, and hard work from family members. Many Latino young adults live with their parents until marriage, and in some cases even after marriage. This is seen as more acceptable in Latino culture than in traditional US culture.

Beliefs about family relationships and expectations differ among traditional U.S. and Latino cultures. Despite these differences, traditional U.S. culture is similar to Latino culture in terms of the importance of family. Understanding the cultural background of others is valuable for people living in diverse communities, like in the United States. However, it is wise not to stereotype cultures. Not all Latino families stick together. Similarly, not all parents from traditional U.S. culture point to the door when their children turn 18. Cultural background plays a role in our relationships with family members, but culture is rarely the sole defining element for anyone.

[1]**pediatrician:** a doctor who treats children

# 2 Comparative and Superlative Adjectives and Adverbs

## Grammar Presentation

| | |
|---|---|
| Comparatives show how two things or ideas are different. Superlatives compare one thing or idea to others in a group. They are both important in comparison and contrast writing. | *In general, Asians are **less relaxed** about time **than** Latinos.*<br>*The **largest component** of Latino life is the family.*<br>*In general, sports fans in Latin America follow soccer **more intensely than** baseball.*<br>*People from traditional U.S. culture communicate **the most directly**.* |

### 2.1 Comparative Adjectives and Adverbs

| | |
|---|---|
| **A** Comparative adjectives are formed as follows:<br>Add *-er* to one-syllable and some two-syllable adjectives: *easier, greater, older.*<br>Add *more/less* before adjectives with two or more syllables: *more complex, less efficient.* | *Mexicans often have **larger** families **than** Chinese.*<br>*The concept of family is **easier** to define in some cultures **than** in others.*<br>*The extended family is **more important** in Latino families **than** in some other cultures.*<br>*The concept of family in the United States is **less rigid than** in other cultures.* |
| **B** Comparative adverbs are formed as follows:<br>Add *-er* to one-syllable adverbs: *harder, faster.*<br>Add *more/less* before adverbs of two syllables or more: *more quickly, less carefully.* | *Children from traditional U.S. culture usually leave home **earlier than** children in Latino culture.*<br>*Some people talk **more quickly than** others.*<br>*In general, the Japanese treat the elderly **more respectfully**.* |
| **C** Do not use *less* with one-syllable words. Use *not as . . . as.* | *The Asian population is **not as** large **as** the Latino population in the United States.*<br>NOT *The Asian population is ~~less large than~~ the Latino population in the United States.* |
| **D** Use a subject pronoun + an auxiliary verb (*be, have,* or *do*) after than in formal academic writing. The auxiliary verb is optional.<br>Use an object pronoun in informal writing and speaking. | FORMAL: *My family is more concerned about having dinner together **than I (am)**.*<br>INFORMAL: *My family is more concerned about having dinner together **than me**.* |

## 2.2 Superlative Adjectives and Adverbs

| | |
|---|---|
| **A** Superlative adjectives are formed as follows:<br>Add *the* + *-est* to one-syllable and some two-syllable adjectives: *easiest, greatest, oldest.*<br>Add *the most/the least* before adjectives with two or more syllables: *most common, least effective.* | *Latinos are currently one of* ***the largest*** *ethnic groups in the United States.*<br>*Solidarity is* ***the most significant*** *value for people of my culture.* |
| **B** Superlative adverbs are formed as follows:<br>Add *the* + *-est* to one-syllable adverbs: *hardest, fastest.*<br>Add *the most* before adverbs of two or more syllables: *the most quickly, the most significantly.* | *Researchers often debate about which groups work* ***the hardest****.*<br>*The Latino population in the United States has increased* ***the most significantly*** *of all ethnic groups in the country.* |

## 2.3 Using Comparatives

| | |
|---|---|
| **A** There are two common uses of comparatives:<br>Explicit: Both elements to be compared are included in the sentence. | COMPARED ITEM 1<br>*Independence is* ***more valued*** *in the United States than*<br>COMPARED ITEM 2<br>*in other cultures.*<br>COMPARED ITEM 1 COMPARED ITEM 2<br>*My sister and I are close, but my brother and I are* ***closer****.* |
| **B** Implicit: The comparison is with something already mentioned in the text, or with something outside the text but known to the reader. As a result, it is not necessary to repeat *"than* + the second element*"* after the verb. | *If people from traditional U.S. culture knew more about other cultures, they perhaps would be* ***more understanding*** (than they are). |

### Data from the Real World

In academic writing, comparatives with *-er* are more common than superlatives with *-est*. Writers tend to avoid making strong claims. Common adjectives include:

*best, better, earlier, easier, greater, greatest, higher, highest, larger, largest, lower, older, smaller, wider*

*The number of immigrants is* ***higher*** *in the United States than in Canada.*

## Grammar Application

### **Exercise 2.1** Comparative Adjectives and Adverbs

**A** Read each sentence or pair of sentences about traditional U.S. culture. Then complete the second sentence that is a restatement of the information. Use the comparative form of the adjective or adverb in parentheses. Include *than* when necessary.

1 Children from traditional U.S. culture are very assertive, compared to children from some other cultures.

Children from traditional U.S. culture are *more assertive than* (assertive) children from some other cultures.

2 Parents from traditional U.S. culture often allow their teenage children to work while they are in school. Parents from some other cultures want their children to focus only on education until they are out of school.

Parents from other cultures are much ________________ (likely) parents from traditional U.S. culture to allow their children to work while they are in school.

3 Children from traditional U.S. culture are often permitted to stay out late on weekends. Parents from some other cultures do not allow their children to stay out late.

Parents from traditional U.S. culture behave ________________ (strictly) parents from some other cultures.

4 Children from traditional U.S. culture speak informally to their elders. Children in most Asian families speak politely to their elders.

Children in most Asian families speak ________________ (politely) to their elders.

5 In traditional U.S. culture, elderly parents don't often live with their grown children like they do in other cultures.

While in many cultures elderly parents often live with their grown children, this is much ________________ (common) in traditional U.S. culture.

6 In many cultures, grandparents help to raise their grandchildren. This is not normally the case in traditional U.S. culture.

When it comes to their grandchildren's upbringing, grandparents from other cultures are often ________________ (involved) grandparents in traditional U.S. culture.

7 In traditional U.S. culture, the concept of family usually means parents and their children. In other cultures, *family* can mean parents, their children, the children's grandparents, and sometimes aunts, uncles, and cousins.

In traditional U.S. culture, the concept of family is ________________ (complex) in other cultures.

**B** Pair Work Work with a partner. Compare each statement in A to another culture that you are familiar with. Use words from the Data from the Real World chart as necessary. When you are finished, report your ideas to the class.

*I would say that Japanese children are less assertive than children from traditional U.S. culture because in Japanese culture it is more desirable to be part of a group.*

## Exercise 2.2 Superlative Adjectives and Adverbs

Complete the sentences with your ideas about cultural behaviors. Use the superlative forms of the adjectives and adverbs in parentheses.

1 One of *the biggest* (big) differences between my culture and *traditional U.S.* culture is *the way children speak to their parents* .

2 I think ______________ (important) thing to know about my culture is ______________ .

3 The ______________ (strange) thing I ever learned about a different culture is ______________ .

4 I think ______________ (difficult) thing to understand about ______________ culture is ______________ .

5 The ______________ (significantly) different thing between my culture and ______________ culture is ______________ .

6 The person in my family who works ______________ (hard) is ______________ .

7 The person in my family who behaves ______________ (patiently) is ______________ .

## Exercise 2.3 Comparative and Superlative Adjectives and Adverbs

**A** Listen to the lecture about ways that cultures differ. As you listen, check (✓) the correct columns in the chart.

| | High-Context | Low-Context | Collectivist | Individualist |
|---|---|---|---|---|
| 1 Communication is direct. | | ✓ | | |
| 2 Communication is indirect. | | | | |
| 3 Tone of voice, gestures, and status are important. | | | | |
| 4 The United States and European countries are examples of this type. | | | | |
| 5 Japan and South Korea are examples of this type. | | | | |
| 6 Africa, Latin America, and Asia are examples of this type. | | | | |
| 7 The group is valued. | | | | |
| 8 Family ties are strong. | | | | |
| 9 Merit and expertise are important. | | | | |
| 10 A person's goals are important. | | | | |

**B** **Complete the sentences about cultural behaviors with comparatives or superlatives. Use the information from the chart in A and the adjective or adverb form of the words in parentheses. Include *than* when necessary.**

1 There are a lot of important things to consider when working with people of different cultures. However, one of *the most important* (important) topics to learn about is communication style.

2 In high-context cultures like South Korea and Japan, the communication style is ______________ (direct) that of people in low-context cultures.

3 In low-context cultures like the United States and England, people communicate ______________ (direct).

4 For people in high-context cultures, words are not the only tool of communication. In low-context cultures, words are ______________ (essential) thing.

5 Facial expressions, gestures, and tone of voice are often ______________ (important) in low-context cultures.

6 Degree of individualism is one of ______________ (big) issues to consider when observing cultural differences.

7 In collectivist cultures, the group is valued ______________ (high) it is in individualistic cultures.

8 In individualistic cultures, an individual's goals are ______________ (valued) a group's goals.

9 Collectivist cultures consider a person's merit or expertise ______________ (important) family ties.

10 Communicating effectively with people from other cultures can be difficult. That's why ______________ (critical) important thing to do is to learn about cultural differences beforehand.

# 3 Articles

## Grammar Presentation

| | |
|---|---|
| Articles (*a/an, the*) or no article Ø precede nouns. Articles help writers distinguish between general and specific statements and shared knowledge. This is important in academic writing, including in comparison and contrast writing. | *In Latin America, **Ø** families include **a** mother, **a** father, **Ø** sisters, **Ø** brothers, **Ø** aunts, **Ø** uncles, and **Ø** cousins.*<br>*I have not met **the** family that lives across **the** street from my house.* |

### 3.1 Using the Definite Article

| | |
|---|---|
| **A** Use *the* when both the writer and the reader share common knowledge or information about the noun. | *In many cultures, it is important for families to eat meals together in **the** kitchen.* (The writer assumes the reader shares the knowledge that there is usually one kitchen in a house.) |
| **B** Use *the* when the noun was introduced earlier in the text and you give more information, or when the noun is related to a noun mentioned earlier. | *Each person in a family has a moral responsibility to aid other members of **the** family experiencing financial problems.* |

## 3.1 Using the Definite Article *(continued)*

| | |
|---|---|
| **C** Use *the* when you are writing about "which one" (when there is additional information that identifies the specific noun). | *Mexico is **the** country that is located south of the United States.* |
| **D** Use *the* with superlatives. | ***The** strictest family I ever met was from the United States.* |
| **E** Use *the* for:<br>abbreviations<br>(but usually not for acronyms)<br>groups<br>adjectives that refer to a category<br>when there is only one | <br>***the** CIA, **the** UN, **the** FBI*<br>*Ø NASA, Ø NATO*<br>***the** media, **the** military*<br>***the** rich, **the** elderly*<br>***the** president, **the** queen, **the** United States, **the** Alps, **the** moon, **the** equator* |

## 3.2 Using the Indefinite Article

| | |
|---|---|
| **A** Use *a/an* with a singular count noun when the noun is not specifically identified, or when it is first mentioned and new to the reader. | ***A** young Latino man is the new student in class.* (The man is not specifically identified.)<br>*The class read **an** article about cultural values.* (The reader does not know this article.) |
| **B** Do not use *a/an* with noncount or plural nouns. Use *some* or Ø. | *My cousin borrowed **some money** from me, but he has not paid me back yet.*<br>***Ø** Large **families** can be enjoyable but complicated.* |
| **C** Use *a/an* when introducing a count noun. | ***A** young Latina woman is the new student in my class. I found out that she is from Colombia.* |

## 3.3 Using Articles in Discourse

| | |
|---|---|
| **A** In academic writing, paragraphs and essays often begin with generalizations. Use the indefinite article when making generalizations:<br>Ø for noncount nouns and plural nouns<br>*a/an* for singular nouns | *"**Ø** Advertising is about **Ø** norms and **Ø** values, **Ø** aspirations and **Ø** prejudices." –Anil Ambani*<br>*In some cultures, **a** teenager is expected to move out of their parents' home and live in **a** college dormitory.* |
| **B** Use the definite article if it refers to a specific noun that is known to the reader. The reference may be:<br>direct | *Teens leave their parents' homes to live in a dormitory. **The** parents are often sad to see their children leave.* (Parents were already mentioned.) |
| clear from context | *Although **the** rooms are often very small, most teenagers do not seem to mind.* (Readers know that dormitories have rooms.) |

# Grammar Application

## Exercise 3.1 Indefinite and Definite Articles

**A** Read the article about how relationships are affected by mobility in the United States. Choose the best article (*a/an*, *the*, or Ø) for each item. Sometimes more than one answer is possible.

Mobility in the United States

The United States is a very mobile society. People frequently do not live in the same town for their entire lives. Often ___Ø___ (1) large corporations require their employees to move if they want to advance in ________ (2) company. Students typically do not go to ________ (3) college near their families. As a result, it is not uncommon for ________ (4) extended families to be separated by hundreds, if not thousands, of miles.

This mobility is probably one of ________ (5) most significant factors influencing ________ (6) relationships in the United States. For example, people tend to be very friendly on a casual basis and open to meeting many new individuals, but these interactions do not always result in ________ (7) close, lasting relationships. There is ________ (8) common tendency of people in ________ (9) United States to say things like, "Let's get together sometime," or "Let's have lunch," and then not follow through with ________ (10) invitation.

People who are not from ________ (11) United States sometimes see this informal style as superficial, and it can be confusing. If someone says, "Let's get together," ________ (12) visitor to the United States might expect the person to make ________ (13) call and suggest ________ (14) meeting time and place. This doesn't always happen. However, ________ (15) visitor who has this experience shouldn't be offended because ________ (16) expression "Let's get together" has almost ________ (17) same meaning as "hello" to many Americans.

**B** Group Work **Take turns explaining why you chose each answer in A.**

*I chose no article for item 1 because corporations is plural and here the writer is referring to all large corporations, not specific large corporations.*

## Exercise 3.2 More Indefinite and Definite Articles

**A** **Write sentences about cultural differences with the cues in parentheses. Use your own ideas. Use the correct articles.**

1 (a definition of *family*) *A family can consist of parents and children, or it can consist of parents, children, grandparents, and others.*

2 (a definition of *values*) ________________________________________

________________________________________

3 (a generalization about cultural differences – what they are) ________________________________________

________________________________________

4 (a description of one cultural difference concerning time, family, relationships, etc.)

________________________________________

________________________________________

5 (a detail about your difference in item 4) ________________________________________

________________________________________

6 (a statement about a cultural difference that you think is more confusing than any other)

_______________

_______________

7 (a generalization about groups and individuals in your culture) _______________

_______________

**B** Pair Work **Talk with a partner about your sentences in A. Which sentences are generalizations? Which contain specific nouns? Share your sentences with another pair. Ask the other pair to identify the reason why each article or no article is appropriate.**

*You used "a family" in this sentence because here you are using a singular count noun to make a generalization.*

# 4 Common Expressions That Show Similarity

## Vocabulary Presentation

| | |
|---|---|
| Some words and phrases are commonly used to show similarity in comparison and contrast writing. | *There are many **similarities** between Turkish and Brazilian cultures.*<br>*Japanese and South Koreans **have something in common**: they tend to avoid directly looking into someone's eyes while speaking.* |

### 4.1 Similar to, Similarities, Similarly, Likewise, Like

| | |
|---|---|
| **A** Use *be similar to* to compare two noun phrases. | *Mexican culture **is similar to** Spanish culture in many ways.* |
| **B** Use *the similarities between* ____ *and* ____ to compare two noun phrases. | *Many people believe that **the similarities between** the United States **and** Canada outweigh the differences.* |
| **C** Use *similarly* and *likewise* as transition words to connect sentences with shared features. Use a comma after the words. | *In Nigeria, social recognition is achieved through extended families. **Similarly,** a family's honor is influenced by the action of its members.*<br>*Chinese children enjoy playing video games. **Likewise**, American children find this an enjoyable activity.* |

## 4.1 *Similar to, Similarities, Similarly, Likewise, Like (continued)*

| | |
|---|---|
| **D** Use _____ *and* _____ *have + something/ one thing/a lot + in common* to introduce shared features of two nouns. | *Germany* **and** *Spain* **have something in common***: their people love coffee.* |
| **E** Use *Like* _____, before a clause to show how a noun is similar in one way to the subject of the clause. | ***Like*** *bedtime stories in the United States, the stories that Chinese parents tell their children send a strong message about values.* |

# Vocabulary Application

**Exercise 4.1** Words That Show Similarity

**A** **Complete the sentences about culture and online media with the appropriate word or expression from the box. Use each word or expression only once.**

| | | |
|---|---|---|
| in common | like | similarities between |
| is similar to | ~~likewise~~ | similarly |

1 A person who does business with people from different cultures should be aware of how cultures differ in communication styles. *Likewise*, website designers should be aware of how people from different cultures will respond to their designs.

2 People from different cultures communicate in different ways, but most have one important thing ____________________ . People in most cultures use the Internet on a daily basis.

3 Years ago, there were many ____________________ paper-based media and online media. Both included simple text and images that people read from top to bottom. Now, however, online media is much more interactive.

4 ____________________ a person engaging in face-to-face communication, a website designer must take into account another person's expectations and assumptions. Some users may expect direct communication, while others may want more indirect messages.

5 In terms of cultural expectations, face-to-face interaction ____________________ Internet interaction. Some cultures may expect a website to communicate information directly with headlines and clear text. Others may respond better to less text and more images.

6 In some cultures, the relationship between speakers is important in face-to-face communication. ____________________ some Internet users may respond better to websites that have animation or interactivity that imitates human interaction.

**B** Pair Work **With a partner, think of other ways that face-to-face communication and online communication are similar. On a separate sheet of paper, write five sentences using the expressions in A. Next, trade papers with another pair. Read their sentences. Share examples that illustrate their ideas.**

# 5 Avoid Common Mistakes

**1 Remember to use *more* or *-er* in comparisons. Do not use both.**
*Middle Eastern families tend to be ~~more~~ closer than families in other cultures.*

**2 Remember to use *best*, not *most*, before nouns.**
*In the 1960s, the ~~most~~ best-selling child-rearing book in the U.S. was* Raising an Independent Child.

**3 Do not use the definite article *the* with title/position + name.**
*~~The~~ Dr. Benjamin Spock wrote* Baby and Child Care *in 1946.*

**4 Remember to use *the* in the expression *the same as.***
*Child-rearing beliefs in one culture are rarely ^the same as child-rearing beliefs in another culture.*

## Editing Task

Find and correct eight more mistakes in the body paragraphs from an essay comparing the celebration of the new year in different cultures.

Women's Roles, Past and Present

The celebration of the New Year in South Korea is not ^the same as in the United States. First of all, South Koreans celebrate the Lunar New Year (the second new moon in winter), so the date is not same as in the United States, where the New Year is celebrated on the first day of the Gregorian Calendar (January 1). The New Year is more later in South Korea, usually in February. In addition, the South Korean New Year celebration lasts for three days and involves the entire family. According to the Dr. Sook-Bin Woo, this is because South Korean families tend to be more closer than traditional U.S. families. For example, South Korean families play special games with each other during this holiday. This family closeness may be the reason that many South Koreans report that their most childhood memories are of New Year's celebrations.

In the United States, the celebration of the New Year begins on the evening of the last day of the year and continues into the following day; it is therefore more shorter than the South Korean celebration. Traditionally, it tends to be primarily an adult celebration for many people. On New Year's Eve, many adults hire a babysitter for their children and go out to a restaurant or to a party to celebrate with other adults. Because U.S. celebrations often do not include children, most Americans are unlikely to say that their most childhood memories are of the celebration of the New Year. Sociologist the Dr. George Lee notes that this tradition is changing in the United States as more adults stay home and celebrate with their children.

UNIT 8

# Comparison and Contrast 4: Adverb Clauses of Contrast and Concession; Transition Words and Phrases That Show Contrast and Concession

## Intercultural Communication

## 1 Grammar in the Real World

You will read an essay about misunderstandings that can happen when people from different cultures attend business meetings together. The essay is an example of one kind of comparison and contrast writing.

**A** Before You Read **What are two cultural differences that might cause misunderstandings in business meetings with people from different cultures? Read the essay. What are assumptions that may cause misunderstandings?**

**B** Comprehension Check **Answer the questions.**

1 According to the essay, what are three main problems that businesspeople might have when they do business with people from different cultures?

2 Why do some cultures perceive the exchange of gifts as inappropriate in a business transaction?

3 According to what you have read in this essay, with whom would businesspeople from your culture possibly have misunderstandings? Explain.

**C** Notice **Answer the questions below to help you notice sentences in which two things are contrasted.**

1 In the second paragraph, find the words *in contrast* and the word *while* that both signal a contrast. Which one can only come at the beginning of a sentence? Which one is followed by a comma?

2 Find a word on line 37 that signals a contrast. Is it similar to *in contrast* or *while*?

3 Compare the use of the words *even though* and *however* in the fourth paragraph. Which word is similar to *while*? Which one is similar to *in contrast*?

4 *Even though* on lines 44–45 signals concession. This means that the information that follows is not only different from the preceding information, but is also unexpected. Explain why *even though* is more appropriate than *while* in this case.

# INTERNATIONAL Business Etiquette

Large companies want to remain competitive in today's global markets. To reach their goals, they are often required to take their businesses beyond the boundaries of their home countries. Consequently, they need to interact with individuals from other cultures. Cross-cultural business transactions can be challenging since the rules about what is considered appropriate and acceptable and what might be seen as rude vary across cultures. Some aspects of culture are likely to cause misunderstandings in multicultural business situations.

One aspect of culture that may be problematic during business interactions is the perception of time. People in countries such as the United States or Germany commonly pay close attention to schedules and meeting agendas. In those countries, it is impolite if someone habitually arrives late to meetings. In contrast, in countries such as Mexico and Brazil, people tend to see schedules simply as guidelines. They often see deadlines as being more flexible. A Brazilian businessperson, for example, might find it strange that a U.S. business meeting has an ending time that is nonnegotiable. In Brazil, the length of a meeting is generally dictated by the needs of its participants, while in the United States, a predefined length is often the norm.

The amount of emotion expressed during business interactions can be the cause of other potential cross-cultural problems. This can differ significantly from culture to culture. In some cultures, such as in parts of Italy, people express feelings more openly and argue more passionately about their points of view. For this reason, they may readily show emotion during critical parts of a negotiation, whereas this practice can come across as unprofessional in more emotionally neutral cultures, such as in Sweden. People in these cultures are generally more careful in controlling the feelings they display.

Understanding local customs can also be problematic for businesspeople. Some customs may seem inappropriate in some countries even though they are perfectly acceptable in others. For example, exchanging gifts between the parties involved in a business deal is a common practice in many parts of the world. However, this practice could be seen as inappropriate in other places, such as the United States or Britain. In those cultures, it could even be interpreted as being unethical since gift-giving may be seen as improperly influencing the outcome of the negotiation.

Doing business with people from different cultures can be challenging. When someone is conducting business abroad, it is important not to assume that what is considered polite in one culture is universal. Instead, it is essential to understand and respect other traditions and business practices. Being aware of those differences can give business professionals a competitive edge when conducting business abroad. It might make the difference between a deal's success or failure.

# 2 Adverb Clauses of Contrast and Concession

## Grammar Presentation

| | |
|---|---|
| Adverb clauses can show many different relationships. Adverb clauses of contrast and concession are common grammatical constructions in academic writing and are especially useful in comparison and contrast writing. | *In some cultures punctuality is important,* ***while in other cultures****, people arrive at events quite late.*<br>***Even though most companies train their executives****, cross-cultural problems still arise.* |

### 2.1 Adverb Clauses of Contrast

| | |
|---|---|
| **A** Adverb clauses of contrast are used mainly to contrast two things or ideas. | *The official language of Brazil is Portuguese,* ***while*** *in Colombia it is Spanish.* |
| **B** Adverb clauses of contrast are introduced by the subordinators *while* and *whereas*.<br>*While* is much more common than *whereas*. *Whereas* appears in academic writing, but it is rare in spoken English. | *In Mexico, the length of a meeting varies according to the needs of its participants,* ***while*** *in the United States, the time is generally set and unchanging.*<br>*Women in the United States work an average of 41 hours per week,* ***whereas*** *women in Europe work about 30 hours per week.* |
| **C** An adverb clause of contrast can come before or after the main clause. If it comes first, it is followed by a comma. However, it is more common for an adverb clause of contrast to appear second. Unlike other adverb clauses, a comma can come before an adverb clause of contrast when it appears second to emphasize contrast. | ***While*** *some countries are open to immigration, other countries have strict policies against it.*<br>*Some customs may be perceived as inappropriate in some countries,* ***whereas*** *they are perfectly acceptable in others.* |

### 2.2 Adverb Clauses of Concession

| | |
|---|---|
| **A** Adverb clauses of concession express a special kind of contrast. They show that the idea in the main clause is surprising or unexpected. | ADVERB CLAUSE OF CONCESSION<br>***Although*** *businesspeople are careful about cultural differences,*<br>UNEXPECTED INFORMATION<br>*misunderstandings sometimes occur during business transactions.* |

## 2.2 Adverb Clauses of Concession (*continued*)

**B** Adverb clauses of concession are introduced by subordinators: *although, even though, though,* and *while.*
A comma can precede an adverb clause of concession to emphasize the contrast.

*Note: While* can express general contrast as well as concession.

***Even though** face-to-face communication is preferred, sometimes business has to be conducted virtually.*

***The company is doing more business with South America, though/while** in the past, it conducted business more frequently with Europe.*

# Grammar Application

### Exercise 2.1 Adverb Clauses of Contrast

**A** Listen to an interview about possible differences between businesspeople in the U.S. and Mexico. Check (✓) the correct column for each opinion expressed by Dr. Julio Sanchez.

| | In the U.S. | In Mexico |
|---|---|---|
| 1 Most people are strict about time. | ✓ | |
| 2 Most people often arrive up to 30 minutes late for business meetings. | | |
| 3 It's polite to arrive on time to a dinner party. | | |
| 4 Most people share personal information in business meetings. | | |
| 5 Most people call each other by their first names as soon as they meet. | | |
| 6 Most people have a direct communication style. | | |
| 7 Most people may not tell you immediately when they can't attend an event. | | |

**B** Use the information from the chart in A and the interview to write sentences using *while* or *whereas.* Sometimes more than one answer is possible.

1 While *most people in Mexico are flexible about time, most people in the United States are very strict.*

2 Whereas ______________________________

3 ______________________________, whereas ______________________________

4 ______________________________, while ______________________________

5 While ______________________________

______________________________

6 ______________________________, while ______________________________

7 Whereas ______________________________

______________________________

**C Pair Work** Discuss with a partner your opinions of different behaviors of two cultures that you are familiar with. Write sentences that contrast these behaviors using adverb clauses of contrast, and then report your ideas to the class.

A *In Brazil, people are flexible about time.*

B *In my opinion, it's different in India. There, it's very important to be on time to meetings.*

*People are flexible about time in Brazil, while it's very important to be on time in India.*

## Exercise 2.2 Adverb Clauses of Concession

**A** Combine each pair of sentences about Chinese business culture using the subordinator in parentheses to show relationships of concession. Sometimes more than one answer is possible.

1 a It is not appropriate to treat a Chinese business colleague informally.

b Doing business in China often involves informal social gatherings where business is not discussed.

(even though) *It is not appropriate to treat a Chinese business colleague informally even though doing business in China often involves social gatherings where business is not discussed.*

2 a Rank is very important.

b Gender bias is not common.

(though) ______________________________

______________________________

3 a This lack of gesturing does not mean a lack of responsiveness.

b The Chinese do not gesture or show much body language.

(while) ______________________________

______________________________

4 a It is important to send written information about your company well before your arrival in China.

b Chinese businesspeople like to meet face-to-face rather than over the phone or by e-mail.

(although) ______________________________

______________________________

5 a Chinese business meetings are very formal affairs.

b The meetings may frequently be interrupted by the ringing of cell phones.

(even though) ______________________________

______________________________

6 a Chinese businesspeople are hardworking and serious.

b Chinese businesspeople have a great sense of humor.

(though) ______________________________

______________________________

7 a Some companies may be very successful in their own countries.

b Their success in China depends on a solid understanding of Chinese culture.

(although) ______________________________

______________________________

**B** Group Work **On a separate sheet of paper, write sentences about the customs of another culture. Use the subordinators of concession in A. Share your sentences with a group. Tell your group members about information that surprised you.**

*Even though Brazilian people are not very strict about time, it is necessary to schedule an appointment.*

*Although most business meetings in Morocco are conducted in French, sometimes English is used. Find out which language will be used before your meeting so that you can hire an interpreter if necessary.*

# 3 Transition Words and Phrases That Show Contrast and Concession

## Grammar Presentation

Another important way to signal differences or unexpected results in comparison and contrast writing is with transition words and phrases.

*Nodding means yes in some countries; **however**, this is not universal.*

*U.S. executives prefer time limits for meetings. **In contrast**, Greeks see them as less necessary.*

***Despite** their significant cultural differences, Mexico and China are strong trade partners.*

## 3.1 Transition Words and Phrases That Signal Contrast and Concession

| | |
|---|---|
| **A** Use transition words and phrases such as *conversely*, *however*, *in contrast*, *instead*, *nevertheless*, *nonetheless*, *on the contrary*, and *on the other hand* to signal differences. | *In some Asian cultures, it is impolite to arrive late at a meeting without an explanation.* ***In contrast****, in some European cultures, it is more natural to view schedules and start times as guidelines.* |
| **B** Transition words and phrases often begin a sentence and are followed by a comma and an independent clause.<br>Sometimes they are preceded by a semicolon, but this use is not as common. | *People in the United States usually smile when they greet other people.* ***On the other hand****, they don't always shake hands.*<br>*Some African cultures do not use the firm handshake common in the United States;* ***instead****, they prefer a gentle, slightly longer touching of hands.* |
| **C** Transition words and phrases can also come between the subject and the verb. In this case, commas go before and after it. | *In some Asian cultures, it is impolite to arrive late at a meeting without an explanation. In some European cultures,* ***in contrast,*** *it is more natural to view schedules and start times as guidelines.* |

## 3.2 Transition Words and Phrases: Differences in Meanings

| | |
|---|---|
| **A** *However* is the most common transition word that shows direct contrast. It is similar in meaning to *but*. | *In India, gift-giving is common.* ***However****, the gifts do not need to be expensive.* |
| **B** *On the contrary* rejects the statement that precedes it and then introduces an opposing idea. | *Adapting to another culture's customs is not a weakness;* ***on the contrary****, it builds stronger relationships and is simply good business.* |
| **C** *In contrast* presents two ideas that are different in some way. | *Table manners are informal in Canada.* ***In contrast****, Moroccan dining usually requires an understanding of a complex set of rules.* (These two cultures contrast in their table manners.) |
| **D** *On the other hand* presents contrasting aspects of one idea.<br>Note: Sometimes *in contrast* and *on the other hand* are used interchangeably. | *It is not common for people in Turkey to give gifts in a business relationship.* ***On the other hand****, they give gifts freely among family members.* (Giving gifts in Turkey contrasts in business and personal settings.) |

## 3.2 Transition Words and Phrases: Differences in Meanings *(continued)*

| | |
|---|---|
| **E** *Nevertheless* and *nonetheless* show unexpected facts or ideas. | *Learning about a new culture can be frustrating.* ***Nevertheless****, a little effort will lead to both personal and professional rewards.*<br><br>*Students may be anxious about studying abroad.* ***Nonetheless****, it is a once-in-a-lifetime chance that should be considered.* |

## 3.3 Prepositions That Show Contrast and Concession

| | |
|---|---|
| **A** Prepositions can also signal contrast or concession. Unlike transition words, prepositions are followed by a noun phrase. Often the noun phrase begins with a verb + *-ing*.<br><br>*Despite* and *in spite of* express an unexpected fact or idea. | NOUN PHRASE<br>***Despite / In spite of*** *their cultural differences, international students usually create close friendships.*<br><br>NOUN PHRASE (VERB + -ING PHRASE)<br>***Despite / In spite of*** *coming from different cultures, international students usually become very close friends.* |
| *Instead of* replaces one idea or thing with another.<br><br>*Note*: Don't confuse *instead* with *instead of*. | REPLACEMENT IDEA<br>*Some African cultures prefer shaking hands gently*<br><br>IDEA BEING REPLACED<br>***instead of*** *shaking hands firmly like in the United States.* |

## Grammar Application

**Exercise 3.1** Transition Words and Prepositions That Show Contrast and Concession

Read the email. Complete the sentences about cultural behaviors in different countries. Choose the correct transition words and prepositions.

Dear Professor Jones:

I am in your Anthropology 101 class. I really enjoyed your lecture today. I was not aware of how different other cultures can be. You asked us to e-mail the most interesting things we learned in Chapter 5. The aspects that really caught my attention were:

1 In many countries, shaking the head from side to side is used to indicate *no*. **Nonetheless, / However,** in India, individuals move their head from side to side to acknowledge what another person has said.

2 In many places, people greet by shaking hands. **In contrast, / Despite** people hug and kiss in informal circumstances in Latin America.

3 In Japan, the *OK* hand sign does not mean "fine" or "all right" as it does in the United States. **On the other hand, / Instead,** it means "money."

4 It's fairly common knowledge that bowing is a common practice in some Asian countries. **However, / Despite** this knowledge, not many people are aware that the way people bow depends on the social situation and the reason they are bowing.

5 Many businesses spend millions on cross-cultural training. **On the other hand, / Nonetheless,** embarrassing mistakes continue to occur.

6 Many Canadians can be very direct when sharing their opinions. **On the other hand, / In spite of** they can be vague when making social plans.

7 The tendency for many Canadians to be direct is not a sign of unfriendliness. **Nevertheless, / On the contrary,** they are very friendly people.

8 **In spite of / Instead,** the many opportunities for cultural misunderstandings, people continue to conduct business successfully across cultures.

I am looking forward to reading the next chapter.

Thank you,

Maria Yolanda Tavarez

# 4 Avoid Common Mistakes

**1 Use the correct preposition with *on the other hand.***

*In the United States, it is appropriate to send a thank-you letter after an interview. ~~In~~ On the other hand, a thank-you e-mail is also acceptable in some situations.*

*In some cultures, it is important to ask co-workers about their families. Asking too many personal questions, ~~at~~ on the other hand, could seem offensive.*

**2 Use *the other*, not *another* in *on the other hand.***

*On ~~another~~ the other hand, many young American businesspeople speak Chinese.*

**3 Remember to use a comma when transition words and phrases such as *on the contrary* and *in contrast* come at the beginning of a sentence.**

*Business meetings usually begin and end at specific times in the United States. In contrast, meeting times in some cultures are not always exact.*

**4 Do not use *but* in sentences with adverb clauses of concession.**

*Although many people in the United States speak other languages, ~~but~~ most international business meetings are conducted in English.*

## Editing Task

Find and correct seven more mistakes in the body paragraph from an essay comparing website differences in different cultures.

Although the use of corporate websites is universal, ~~but~~ corporate website design is another aspect of doing business that differs from culture to culture. The different website designs for Good Foods are one example. The company operates globally. It wants to appear as though it sells the same quality products everywhere in the world. On another hand, the company wants to appeal to the consumers in each country where it does business. Therefore, the look of its sites differs from country to country. For example, the website for Good Foods in the United States tends to use a limited number of colors. In contrast the company site in India tends to use a great deal of color. The Indian version uses bright colors, such as pink, red, orange, and purple, while the U.S. version of the site uses only shades of blue and gray. This is because the way people interpret colors is cultural. Bright colors suggest "fun" to people in the United States, while blue and gray suggest "importance." In another example, the Good Foods site in Switzerland shows the company's products; however it rarely shows people using or enjoying them. In the other hand, when it does show people, they are usually alone. In contrast the Good Food site for Mexico shows families shopping together and large groups of people enjoying the products. This is because people in Mexico tend to prefer being with others. However people in Switzerland value independence and solitude. Although the main purpose of a company's website is to present important information about the business, but the site must also address the cultural values of the people who view it.

UNIT 9

# Narrative 1: Past Perfect; Past Modals; Common Time Clauses

## The American Dream

## 1 Grammar in the Real World

You will read an excerpt from *The Pact: Three Young Men Make a Promise and Fulfill a Dream* (2003), a book about how three men raised in poverty achieved success. The excerpt is an example of narrative writing. Following that you will read a writer's response to the excerpt.

**A** Before You Read **In your opinion, what is the American Dream? Do you believe the American Dream is something that is worth aiming for? Read the essays. According to the writer, are people confident today that they can reach the American Dream? Why or why not?**

**B** Comprehension Check **Answer the questions.**

1 Why is the story of the three doctors remarkable?

2 What are some events that have negatively impacted or affected the American Dream?

3 According to Rodriguez, why is the American Dream important?

**C** Notice **Follow the instructions below to help you notice how the essay writer shows a sequence of past events.**

1 Read the two sentences on lines 46–49 again. Which came first: (a) people had considered the American Dream to be achievable or (b) the idea of the American Dream was damaged? What form of the verb gives you the answer?

2 Reread the sentence on lines 50–53 beginning with "In the late 1980s . . ." Which came first: (a) less job security for Americans or (b) more job security? What form of the verb does the writer use to show this?

# Excerpt from The Pact: Three Young Men Make a Promise and Fulfill a Dream (2003)

"WE TREAT THEM IN HOSPITALS EVERY DAY. They are young brothers, often drug dealers, gang members, or small-time criminals, who show up shot, stabbed, or beaten after a hustle[1] gone bad. To some of our medical colleagues, they are just nameless thugs,[2] perpetuating crime and death in neighborhoods that have seen far too much of these things. But when we look into their faces, we see ourselves as teenagers, we see our friends, we see what we easily could have become as young adults. And we're reminded of the thin line that separates us – three twenty-nine-year-old doctors (an emergency-room physician, an internist, and a dentist) – from those patients whose lives are filled with danger and desperation.

"We grew up in poor, broken homes[3] in New Jersey neighborhoods riddled with crime, drugs, and death, and came of age in the 1980s at the height of a crack epidemic[4] that ravaged communities like ours throughout the nation . . . Two of us landed in juvenile-detention centers[5] before our eighteenth birthdays. But inspired early by caring and imaginative role models, one of us in childhood latched on to[6] a dream of becoming a dentist, steered clear of[7] trouble, and in his senior year of high school persuaded his two best friends to apply to a college program for minority students interested in becoming doctors. We knew we'd never survive if we went after it alone. And so we made a pact:[8] we'd help one another through, no matter what" (Davis, Jenkins, & Hunt, 2003, pp. 1–2).

## Writer's Response

The excerpt from *The Pact: Three Young Men Make a Promise and Fulfill a Dream* might be described as a contemporary version of the American Dream. Simply stated, the American Dream is the belief that if people work hard and play by the rules, they will have a chance to get ahead. The American Dream is based on the belief that people have the same opportunity regardless of their race, creed, color, national origin, gender, or religion.

For middle-class Americans, the American Dream typically means that each generation will have more material possessions than the last. For some, achieving the American Dream means having a secure job and owning a home. For others, it is the promise that anyone may rise from poverty to wealth with hard work.

For many years, people had considered the American Dream to be achievable. Several decades ago, things changed. A number of events damaged the idea of the American Dream for the American middle class. In the late 1980s and early 1990s, housing costs increased dramatically, and job security, which had been assured for previous generations, became much less certain. As a result, many people believed that they would be worse off than their parents. Global events such as the Great Recession of 2008 further shook people's confidence about the likelihood of reaching the American Dream. More locally, natural disasters such as Hurricane Maria and Superstorm Sandy significantly affected many people's daily lives and, temporarily at least, shattered their hopes.

For some, it appears that the dream may have died, but does it really matter? *The LA Times* journalist Gregory Rodriguez would say yes. As he states, "The dream is the glue that keeps us all together . . . it's the fabled dream that fuses hundreds of millions of separate, even competing individual dreams into one national collective enterprise." Thus, it is the dream that reassures Americans that the factors for success – ability, strong work ethic, and education – will be rewarded. Like the three doctors who had grown up in such poverty before they achieved success, many people rely on the dream for encouragement as they work hard to create their own versions of the American Dream.

[1]**hustle:** the act of tricking people to cheat them out of money

[2]**thug:** a violent person, often a criminal

[3]**broken home:** a family where one parent has left

[4]**crack epidemic:** the widespread drug addiction to crack cocaine in some neighborhoods in the United States during the 1980s

[5]**juvenile-detention center:** a form of prison for young people who are not yet considered adults

[6]**latch on to:** grasp or hold on to

[7]**steer clear of:** avoid

[8]**pact:** a promise or an agreement to do something together in the future

# 2 Past Perfect and Past Perfect Progressive

## Grammar Presentation

| | |
|---|---|
| In academic writing, the past perfect and the past perfect progressive can be used to contrast earlier background events and information with other later events and information in the past. | *By the 1990s, housing costs* ***had increased*** *dramatically, and job security* ***had become*** *much less certain than for previous generations.*<br>*When Bob got his first job, his brother* ***had*** *already* ***been working*** *for several years.* |

### 2.1 Using Past Perfect

| | |
|---|---|
| **A** Use the past perfect to describe the first of two completed events in the past. Use the simple past for the later event. | EARLIER EVENT<br>*By midnight, he* ***had finished*** *most of his work,*<br>LATER EVENT<br>*so he* ***decided*** *to go to bed.* |
| **B** You can use the past perfect in sentences with time clauses with *when*, *by the time*, and *while*. The past perfect is often used in the main clause.<br>The use of the past perfect in sentences with time clauses with *before* and *after* is not necessary since the words indicate a clear time relationship.<br>*Note:* The use of the simple past in both the main clause and time clause with *when* shows a different time relationship.<br>Choose the past perfect to emphasize that one action was completed before the other. | LATER EVENT / EARLIER EVENT<br>*When she arrived, the class* ***had*** *already* ***started****.*<br>*By the time she registered for classes, the semester* ***had*** *already* ***begun****.*<br>*She started college after she* ***earned/had earned*** *enough money to pay for the first year.*<br>FIRST EVENT / SECOND EVENT<br>*When she arrived, the class started.* |
| **C** Use the past perfect to go back to an earlier time in a narrative or description. | *Nesreen was nervous on her first day of work. She****'d*** *never* ***had*** *a job before.* |
| **D** Use the past perfect in narrative writing, and in academic writing in general, to give background reasons and explanations for later past events. | *For years, many people* ***had considered*** *the American Dream to be achievable. Then the economy changed.* |

## 2.2 Past Events with Adverbs and Frequency Expressions

| | |
|---|---|
| Use adverbs of time with the past perfect to emphasize the earlier time period in the past:<br>*after, before, earlier*<br>*already, not . . . yet, still . . . not*<br>*ever, just, never, recently* | *No one in her family **had** ever **attended** college before.*<br>*She**'d** already **talked** to a few colleges, but she **hadn't applied** yet. She needed to find a way to pay the tuition.*<br>*They**'d** recently **applied** for a grant and were waiting for a final response.* |

## 2.3 Using Past Perfect and Past Perfect Progressive

| | |
|---|---|
| **A** Like the past perfect, the past perfect progressive can give background reasons or describe past events.<br>*Note:* As with other progressive forms, don't use past perfect progressive with stative verbs, such as *be, know,* and *seem.* | PAST PERFECT<br>*They **had experienced** many challenges, so they **decided** to make a pact.*<br>PAST PERFECT PROGRESSIVE<br>*They **had been experiencing** many challenges, so they **decided** to make a pact.*<br>*She **had known** that she wanted to be in education since she was a young girl.*<br>NOT<br>*She ~~had been knowing~~ that she wanted to be in education since she was a young girl.* |
| **B** Use the past perfect progressive to emphasize an ongoing past action leading up to a point in the past.<br>This action may have been occurring when another past action took place.<br>The past perfect progressive form is much less common than the past perfect. | *He**'d been talking about** applying to medical school for a long time. Finally, last January, he applied.*<br>FIRST EVENT<br>*They**'d been working** for about an hour*<br>SECOND EVENT<br>*when the bell rang.* |

# Grammar Application

## Exercise 2.1 Simple Past and Past Perfect

**A** Complete the sentences about an immigrant who came to the United States. Use the simple past or past perfect form of the verbs in parentheses.

1 Naresh ___had studied___ (study) English for three years in his native country, India, before he ___came___ (come) to the United States.

2 Naresh ____________ (arrive) in the United States six months ago to study. He ____________ (never/be) here before.

3 At first, he __________________ (stay) in a motel because he __________________ (neglect) to look for a place to live before arriving.

4 Naresh's parents __________________ (be) worried about him because after a month, he still __________________ (not find) an apartment.

5 They __________________ (contact) their friend Sam who was living in the United States. Naresh's parents __________________ (help) Sam 25 years earlier to adjust to living in India.

6 Sam and his wife, Lea, __________________ (be) good friends with Naresh's parents. They __________________ (go) to visit Naresh's family several times.

7 Naresh __________________ (hope) to live on his own, but after struggling so much, he __________________ (be) happy to accept Sam and Lea's offer to stay with them.

8 Sam and Lea __________________ (give) Naresh as much help as they could, just like Naresh's parents __________________ (assist) Sam 25 years earlier.

**B** Pair Work **Explain your answers in A to a partner. Do you agree?**

*First, Naresh studied English and second, he came to the United States. So we need to use the past perfect form* had studied *and the simple past form* came.

## Exercise 2.2 Past Perfect and Past Perfect Progressive

**A** **Complete the sentences about a South Korean woman who moved to the United States. Circle the past perfect or past perfect progressive form of the verbs. For some items, both forms are possible.**

1 Mi Young's mother **had planned / had been planning** to visit her daughter in the United States for several years, but by Mi Young's fifth year in New York, her mother still **hadn't visited / hadn't been visiting** her.

2 Mi Young's mother **had gone / had been going** to Los Angeles once before to visit her sister when she was much younger, and she **had wanted / had been wanting** to return ever since then.

3 At one point, it seemed as if Mi Young might come home because she **had lost / had been losing** her job and she **had looked / had been looking** for a new job for several months.

4 Mi Young **had thought / had been thinking** about moving back to South Korea when she got a job offer in Los Angeles. It was a company that a friend of hers **had just started / had been starting** to work for.

5 Mi Young's mom **had worried / had been worrying** about traveling all the way to New York, so she was happy when Mi Young moved to Los Angeles. The flight was a lot shorter!

6 Also, her mother **had had / had been having** a nice time in Los Angeles on her first trip, so she **had hoped / had been hoping** since then that Mi Young might get a job there.

**B** Pair Work Think of a major change in your life or in the life of someone you know, such as a move, a marriage, or a new job. Describe the events leading up to the change. Use the past perfect and the past perfect progressive where necessary.

*My boyfriend and I had been talking about getting married for over a year when he proposed to me. We'd been together for three years by that time. I'd known soon after we met that I was going to marry him, but I was still nervous about making the commitment. When I told my parents, they weren't surprised at all, but they thought I was too young. I was 21 at the time . . .*

# 3 Past Modals and Modal-like Expressions

## Grammar Presentation

| | |
|---|---|
| Past modals and modal-like expressions are used to give a perspective on events (whether the speaker or writer saw the event as possible, necessary, desirable, and so on). | *I* ***should have studied*** *French when I was in high school.*<br>*Joanna* ***could not finish*** *college in four years because she* ***had to*** *work full-time.* |

### 3.1 Past Modals and Modal-like Expressions

| | |
|---|---|
| **A** Use these modal-like expressions for past necessity and lack of necessity:<br>*had to* to say something was necessary in the past<br>*did not have to* to say something wasn't necessary in the past | *The three friends came from poor families, so they* ***had to*** *find a way to pay for their education.*<br>*They* ***did not have to*** *pay for their college education because they got scholarships.* |
| **B** Use these modals for past permission and prohibition:<br>*could* to say something was allowed or permitted in the past<br>*could not* to say something was not allowed or permitted in the past | *In the past, minority students* ***could apply*** *for special college grants.*<br>*Nonminority students* ***could not apply*** *for these special college grants.* |
| **C** Use these modals for disapproval or regret over an action taken or not taken:<br>*should have, should not have*, and *could have* | ***I should have applied*** *for a work study job.* (But I didn't, and I regret it.)<br>*She* ***shouldn't have missed*** *so many classes.* (But she did and now she's failing.)<br>*We* ***could have asked*** *for help.* (But we didn't and now we're sorry.) |

## 3.1 Past Modals and Modal-like Expressions *(continued)*

| | |
|---|---|
| **D** Use these modals for possibility or impossibility of a past action: | |
| *could/might have* to show possibility | *He* ***could/might have found out*** *about the job opening through the school's career center.* (It's possible because I know he went there.) |
| *could not have* to show impossibility | *We* ***could not have predicted*** *that the number of college applications would increase so much this year.* (It was impossible to predict.) |

## 3.2 *Would* and *Used To* for Past Habits

| | |
|---|---|
| **A** Use *would/used to* + base form of the verb to describe habits or routines that happened regularly in the past, but don't happen now. | |
| With *would*, a past time reference – such as a past time clause – must be used or understood. | *While I was living in my country, I* ***would go*** *for long walks.* |
| *Would* is more common than *used to* in academic writing. | *I* ***used to study*** *on the bus to school every day. Now I drive my car to school, so I can't study then.* |
| **B** Use *used to* with stative verbs (verbs like *have* or *be*) that describe states or conditions in the past. Do not use *would* to describe states or conditions in the past. | *I* ***used to be*** *a manager at a hotel, but now I work at a bank.*<br>*My brother* ***used to have*** *a bike. Now he has a car.*<br>*I* ***used to like*** *long walks in the country.*<br>NOT *I ~~would~~ like long walks in the country.* |

## 3.3 *Was/Were* + *Supposed To* and *Was/Were Going To* for Past Expectation

| | |
|---|---|
| Use *was/were* + *supposed to* and *be going to* + base form of the verb to describe required or planned actions in the past that did not take place.<br>They are often followed by *but* and a clause that explains why the action was not completed. | *The foundation* ***was supposed to provide*** *full funding for 30 students.*<br>*The students* ***were going to get*** *part-time jobs,* ***but there were none available****.*<br>*She* ***was supposed to start*** *classes this fall,* ***but she didn't have enough money for tuition****.* |

# Grammar Application

## Exercise 3.1 Past Modals and Modal-like Expressions

Complete the sentences about a woman who found success because of her hard work. Use the verbs in parentheses and a modal *(could, could have, had to, might have, should have)*. Use the cues at the beginning of the sentences to decide on the appropriate modal.

1 [necessary] Sarah *had to work* (work) when she was young because her father's salary wasn't enough for the family.

2 [not necessary] Every day, Sarah went to school and then went to work at a pizza shop. Her school and the pizza shop were close to home, so she ________________ (drive) or take the bus.

3 [possible] When Sarah finished high school, she wanted to go to college, but she didn't have enough money. She ________________ (win) a scholarship because she had high grades, but she never applied for one.

4 [regret] Later she realized that she ________________ (apply) for every possible scholarship.

5 [not necessary] Sarah decided that she could be a success even without a college education. Because she ________________ (go) to school anymore, she began working full time.

6 [possible] She worked 60 hours a week at the pizza shop and made a lot of money, yet she hardly spent any. Her thriftiness ________________ (be) the result of growing up in a poor household.

7 [not permitted] After a few years, the owner of the pizza shop decided he wanted to sell the shop. Sarah wanted to buy it. She didn't have enough money, so she tried to take out a loan at the bank, but she ________________ (get) a loan.

8 [allowed] The pizza shop owner really liked Sarah because she was such a hard worker. He told her that she ________________ (buy) the shop from him and pay him over five years.

9 [disapproval] The owner's friends thought it was a bad idea. They told him he ________________ (loan) her the money, but he knew he had made the right decision.

10 [possibility] Once Sarah had bought the shop, she made it more successful than it had ever been. No one ________________ (predict) how successful Sarah would be.

11 [impossibility] Sarah continued to work hard, and after 10 years, she bought five more shops. She herself ________________ (guess) that she would one day become such a successful businesswoman.

## **Exercise 3.2** *Used To and Would*

**A** Listen to the story about Rita and Edwin, a couple from the Dominican Republic. Write *T* if the statement is true or *F* if the statement is false.

1 __*F*__ Rita and Edwin used to live in New York.

2 _____ Every semester, they would enroll in the free English classes offered at schools.

3 _____ In his English classes, Edwin would always sit next to Spanish-speaking students.

4 _____ When she started classes, Rita wouldn't speak when the teacher called on her.

5 _____ She used to always start crying when she got nervous in class.

6 _____ Rita would often talk to her classmates.

7 _____ When he got a job at a hotel, Edwin would take a bus to get there.

8 _____ Rita and Edwin used to dream of a better life.

**B** Pair Work **Tell your partner about your past habits, and contrast them with your current life. Explain to your partner why your past habits have changed.**

*I used to work as a waiter in a restaurant, but now I'm a full-time student.*
*I realized that it was difficult to work and study at the same time, so I quit my job.*

## **Exercise 3.3** *Was / Were Supposed To and Was / Were Going To*

**A** The chart below shows expectations and plans that John and people who knew him had about his life and the reasons why the plans did not come true. Write sentences about John using the information in the chart and *was/were supposed to* and *was/were going to*.

| **Expectations** | **Reasons Why the Plans Did Not Come True** |
|---|---|
| 1 Everyone expected John to become a doctor. | Nobody knew that he couldn't stand the sight of blood. |
| 2 John planned to major in biology. | He changed his mind and decided to major in business instead. |
| 3 John and his friends planned to go into business together after college. | They didn't have enough money. |
| 4 John planned to move to California to find a job. | He was offered a job in Japan. |
| 5 Everyone thought John would marry his high school sweetheart. | He fell in love with a girl in Japan. |
| 6 John's parents planned to visit him this month. | His father broke his leg, so they postponed the trip. |

1 *John was going to be a doctor, but nobody knew he couldn't stand the sight of blood.*

2

3

4

5

6

**B** Pair Work Tell your partner about plans that you and others had that changed. Explain why they changed. Then tell your partner about plans that people you know had that changed and why they changed.

*I was going to major in computer science, but I decided I was more interested in history. My brother has always loved animals. We always thought he was going to be a veterinarian, but he ended up majoring in business. He said that he changed his mind when he started working at a bank. He really wants to own his own business some day.*

# 4 Common Time Clauses

## Vocabulary Presentation

Time clauses show time or sequence. It is common to use these constructions in longer, more complex sentences in a narrative.

***After** I finished high school, I had to find a job.*

*I started practicing interview skills **when** I heard that I had a job interview.*

### 4.1 Common Time Clauses

**A** Dependent clauses that show a time relationship begin with subordinators such as *after*, *as*, *before*, and *while*. They are sometimes called adverb clauses of time.

*Life in the U.S. was difficult at first. I did my English homework **while** my baby was sleeping.*

## 4.1 Common Time Clauses *(continued)*

| | |
|---|---|
| **B** Use these subordinators to show different aspects of time and sequence: | |
| *after* to show that the event in the time clause happened first | FIRST SECOND<br>**After** *he started working on campus, it was very difficult to keep up with his classes.* |
| *before* to show that the event in the time clause happened second | SECOND FIRST<br>**Before** *I moved to this country, I did not know how to cook.* |
| *every time* to show repeated events that are connected in either the past or present | **Every time** *they moved, the children had to adjust to a new school.* |
| *since* (often using the present perfect or past perfect in the main clause) to show when an action or state started in the past | *He's been working* **since** *he left high school.* |
| *once, when,* and *as soon as* to show that one event quickly followed another event | **Once** *I finished college, I started looking for a job.* |
| *when, while,* and *as* to show that both events happened at the same time | *He worked full-time at a grocery store* **while** *he was going to college.* |
| *until* to show a time frame that continues up to a certain time or event | *I had to work night shifts* **until** *I found a better job.* |
| *Before, when, until,* and *after* are the most frequently used subordinating conjunctions in academic writing. | |

# Vocabulary Application

### **Exercise 4.1** Common Time Clauses

**Combine the sentences about the author Stephen King using the subordinator in parentheses.**

1 Stephen King struggled a lot in his life. Then he became a famous author.
(before) *Stephen King struggled a lot in life before he became a famous author.*

2 He was two years old. His father left.
(when) ______________________________

3 His father left. Then his mother struggled to take care of him and his brother.
(after) ______________________________

4 He was 12. He became interested in writing horror stories.
(when) ____________________

5 He was in school. He wrote many stories.
(while) ____________________

6 He sold stories to his classmates. Then the teachers asked him to stop.
(until) ____________________

7 His first short story was published. Then he graduated college.
(before) ____________________

8 His mother died. Then his first novel, *Carrie*, was published.
(after) ____________________

## **Exercise 4.2** More Common Time Clauses

**A** **Complete the paragraph about the life of Dr. Martin Luther King, Jr. Circle the correct subordinators using information from the time line of events in his life.**

| |
|---|
| 1955 – Rosa Parks arrested on December 1 for refusing to give up her seat on a bus to a white passenger in Montgomery, Alabama; started a boycott on December 5 to stop segregation on Montgomery buses |
| 1956 – In June, segregation law declared unconstitutional; in December, bus segregation stopped |
| 1963 – King delivered "I Have a Dream" speech at the Lincoln Memorial in Washington, D.C. |
| 1968 – King assassinated at the Lorraine Motel in Memphis, Tennessee |
| 1986 – Birthday of Dr. Martin Luther King, Jr. declared a national holiday |
| 2011 – Memorial statue of King put up in Washington, D.C. |

**August, 1963, at the March on Washington**

Dr. Martin Luther King, Jr. was an influential leader in the 1950s and 1960s in the Civil Rights movement, a movement that ended segregation and discrimination of African Americans in American society. **After/While** (1) other leaders were considering violence as the way to bring about social changes in the early 1950s, King was urging people to use nonviolent means, such as boycotts and demonstrations. The movement did not become energized **until/as soon as** (2) Rosa Parks, a social activist, refused to give her seat on a bus to a white man. On December 1, 1955, black residents in Montgomery, Alabama, boycotted the buses and elected King as their leader. **Once/As** (3) the boycott continued into 1956, King's reputation as a courageous leader grew, and his outstanding speaking skills inspired many to join the movement. **Before/After** (4) the U.S. Supreme Court declared Alabama's segregation laws unconstitutional in June, segregation on Montgomery buses finally ended that following December. **Once / Since** (5) the Supreme Court made its decision, King ended the boycott. In 1963, King delivered his famous "I Have a Dream" speech. Just five years **since / after** (6) he delivered that speech, King was assassinated in Memphis, Tennessee. **Since / Until** (7) the Civil Rights Act of 1964 was passed, many people have benefited from it. Among other provisions, the act made it illegal to discriminate against someone based on race, religion, and gender. Dr. Martin Luther King, Jr. continues to be an icon for the civil rights movement. **As / Until** (8) more and more people recognized King's significant contribution to civil rights and equality over time, political figures began to ask for a day of remembrance. The first Martin Luther King Day of Service was observed in 1986. In 2011, a memorial was dedicated to King on the National Mall in Washington, D.C.

**B** Make a time line similar to the one in A with important events in your life or the life of someone that you admire on a separate piece of paper. Explain the events on your time line to a partner. Use time clauses.

*Since I was young, I've wanted to go to college to study math. Before I started college, I spent two years in the army. As soon as I got out of the army, I sent out applications for college.*

## 5 Avoid Common Mistakes ⚠

**1 Remember to use the past participle after *had* when forming the past perfect.**

*He had ~~went~~ gone to college, so he already had a degree.*

*Blanca's family had ~~came~~ come to the United States when she was still a child.*

**2 Remember to use the past perfect progressive, not the past progressive, in the main clause for an action that happens in an earlier time frame than the action in the *when* clause.**

*She ~~was taking~~ had been taking care of children for many years when she realized she needed an A.A. degree.*

*Ahmet ~~was working~~ had been working in a restaurant for a long time when he decided to go to college.*

**3 Remember to use the simple past, not the past perfect, for a single completed action or state. The past perfect is often used to describe a previous time before another past time.**

*I ~~had graduated~~ graduated from college last year.*

# Editing Task

Find and correct nine more mistakes in the use of the past perfect and past perfect progressive in the narrative paragraphs on changing careers.

### Changing Careers

Jessica had always loved photography, even as a child. She ~~was asking~~ *had been asking* for a camera for a long time when her father had gave her one on her tenth birthday. She would take her camera everywhere and record the small moments of everyday life that caught her eye: a cluster of leaves on the sidewalk, or a spider web on a garden fence. Jessica had always see photography as a hobby. Moreover, since she had came from a family that had endured economic hardships when she was growing up, she had always know that she had to choose a career that paid well and was secure. Therefore, after high school, she got a degree in landscape design. She was considering a job with the city during her last year of college, but when her uncle, the owner of a landscape company, asked her to work for him, she changed her mind. She had joined his landscaping business right after graduation. However, Jessica never lost her love of photography. She eventually bought herself a higher quality camera and continued to take pictures whenever she had the opportunity.

Jessica was working at the landscaping company for about two years when her uncle decided to build a website to advertise the business. He needed images of the company's best work to publish on the site and immediately thought of Jessica. She was taking photos of the company's projects the entire time that she had worked there. The website had been a success. More importantly, other companies saw it and wanted to know who the great photographer was. Soon, Jessica was working full time as a photographer. Her uncle missed Jessica's presence, but everyone was pleased that she was now earning a living doing something that she truly loved.

UNIT 10

# Narrative 2: Demonstratives; Common Time Signals

## Immigration

## 1 Grammar in the Real World

You will read an essay about the history of immigration in the United States. The essay is an example of a historical narrative.

**A** Before You Read **Why do people immigrate to the United States? What are some of the problems that immigrants encounter? Read the essay. How has the United States benefited from immigration throughout the years?**

**B** Comprehension Check **Answer the questions.**

1 Describe the immigrants who traveled to the United States in the seventeenth century.

2 When and why did the U.S. government start to restrict entrance into the United States?

3 Why does the writer say that the United States will continue to be built with the help of immigrants?

**C** Notice **Follow the instructions below to help you understand the use of demonstratives and time words to define different periods of time.**

1 On lines 20–23, notice the use of the word *these* in the sentence "Even though some of these immigrants . . .". What does *these* refer to?

2 On lines 27–28, notice the use of *that* in "During that period . . .". What does *that* refer to?

3 In the second paragraph, underline the words the writer uses to define two different periods of time.

# Immigration and the United States

SINCE THE SEVENTEENTH CENTURY, immigrants from all over the world have come to the United States in search of safety, freedom, and economic opportunities. Immigration patterns have varied over time, with distinct periods of immigration from different countries. In each of these periods, immigrants helped shape U.S. society and the economy. However, the flow of immigrants has also brought challenges that continue into the present.

The period from the seventeenth century through the early nineteenth century is the first and longest U.S. immigration wave. During this time, most immigrants came from Europe, including France and the Netherlands. The number of immigrants was small, and most of the newcomers became farmers. By the 1820s, this pattern started to change. From the 1820s to 1880s, approximately 15 million immigrants settled in the United States. Even though some of these immigrants decided to work in agriculture in the Midwest and Northeast, many more moved to big cities, such as New York City and Boston.

The immigration wave that took place between the 1890s and the beginning of the twentieth century is often referred to as the flood of immigrants. During that period, nearly 25 million immigrants arrived in the United States. They were mainly young Europeans from countries such as Italy, Greece, Hungary, and Poland.

Each group of immigrants presented distinct characteristics. Some groups were less formally educated and some were mostly young, for example. However, they all contributed to the growth of many industries, including steel, automobile, and textile. Because of them, the United States turned into one of the world's most powerful countries.

Over the course of the late nineteenth and early twentieth centuries, protests over immigrants grew. Many people were troubled by the new religions and customs that immigrants brought to the United States. As a result, in 1921 the government passed laws limiting the number of immigrants allowed to enter each year. Even though immigrants contributed to the economic growth of the United States, the country made it difficult for them to enter.

In the early 2000s, the immigration debate was reignited due to high numbers of immigrants, documented and undocumented. Opponents argued that immigrants took jobs away from people and that the cost of maintaining their welfare was a drain on the education and health care systems. Although the arguments continue to this day, it is important to remember that the country was and will continue to be built with the help of immigrants.

# 2 Demonstratives

## Grammar Presentation

| | |
|---|---|
| Demonstratives (*this, that, these, those*) are used in all kinds of writing to connect ideas or give coherence. | *In my neighborhood, there are people from all over the world. Most of **these** people have good jobs.*<br>*The article is about recent immigration. **That** topic always generates interesting conversation.* |

### 2.1 Demonstratives

| | |
|---|---|
| Use demonstratives (*this, that, these, those*) to show physical distance from the speaker or distance in time.<br>Use *this/these* to refer to people or things close in time and space to the speaker.<br>Use *that/those* to refer to people or things in a more distant time and space. | ***This** unit is about immigration. Let's look at the first page.*<br>*I remember **those** days when I'd been in this new country for only three weeks and didn't speak any English.* |

### 2.2 Demonstratives That Connect Ideas

| | |
|---|---|
| **A** Use demonstratives to connect ideas that are close to each other and to make the text cohesive. These are also called demonstrative adjectives. | *Immigrants came from all over Europe. Most of **these** immigrants opted for farming.* (These immigrants refers to the immigrants from all over Europe.)<br>*The flood of immigrants occurred between the 1890s and the beginning of the twentieth century. During **that** period, nearly 25 million immigrants arrived in the United States.* |
| **B** You can use demonstratives without a noun. When they stand alone, they are pronouns.<br>You can also use *it* for the same purpose. | *Climate change affects everyone. Indeed, **this** is the most important environmental issue of our time.* (**This** refers to climate change.)<br>*Climate change affects everyone. Indeed, **it** is the most important environmental issue of our time.* (It refers to climate change.) |
| **C** Use demonstrative pronouns to summarize or refer to a previously mentioned idea in the same paragraph. | *Economic disparity is widespread and increasing. **This** is an especially significant problem for developing countries.*<br>(This refers to the fact that economic disparity is increasing.) |

## 2.2 Demonstratives That Connect Ideas *(continued)*

| | |
|---|---|
| **D** Use a demonstrative with a noun that summarizes or clarifies what it refers to, for example:<br><br>*approach, aspect, development, experience, factor, reason, phenomenon, topic* | *Nearly 25 million Europeans traveled to the United States at the end of the nineteenth century and early twentieth century.* ***That development*** *changed the demographics of the country.* (*That development* refers to the idea of the previous sentence.) |
| **E** The summary word or phrase that follows demonstratives can reflect the writer's opinion about a previously described topic, for example:<br><br>*controversial argument, indisputable fact, questionable claim, undisputed fact* | *Some people believe immigration leads to increases in crime.* ***This controversial argument*** *has been challenged by many.*<br><br>*Millions of people have immigrated to the United States.* ***This undisputed fact*** *constitutes one of the central elements in the country's development.* |

# Grammar Application

## Exercise 2.1 Demonstratives

**A** **Read the sentences about immigration in Europe. Complete the sentences with the correct demonstratives. Sometimes more than one answer is possible.**

1 The European Union has expanded in recent years to include over two dozen countries. ___*This*___ has contributed to increased immigration all over Europe.

2 In 2004, ten countries joined the European Union. ________________ countries included Hungary, Poland, Lithuania, and Slovakia.

3 Citizens of European Union member nations have permission to live in any EU country where they work. ________________ makes it fairly easy for people to move from one EU country to another.

4 About 4.7 million people immigrated to one of the EU Member States in 2015 alone. ________________ figure includes not only people from outside the EU but also people moving between EU countries.

5 There are about five million immigrants living in Italy. ________________ people make up just over 8 percent of the population.

6 In 2017, 25,600 people wanted to immigrate to Sweden for asylum.[1] ________________ was 11.72 percent less than in 2016.

[1]**asylum:** protection or safety

**B** Pair Work **Take turns with a partner explaining what each demonstrative refers to in the sentences.**

*In sentence 1,* This *refers to the expansion of the European Union.*

## Exercise 2.2 More Demonstratives

**A** **Choose the correct word or words to complete the paragraphs that explain one writer's view of the challenges of immigration.**

Millions of people move to new countries every year. This phenomenon / reason (1) can cause challenges for both the residents of the host country and for the immigrants. Often, the people from the host country and the immigrants have difficulty relating to each other and understanding each other's customs. Also, the language of the host country and the immigrants' language are sometimes very different. If people cannot speak to each other, they cannot begin to understand each other. This fact / argument (2) may be the underlying cause of most misunderstandings between residents and immigrant groups. People often fear what they do not understand.

However, people disagree about which language immigrants should speak. This development / controversial issue (3) can produce very different responses. Some people believe that immigrants should stop speaking their native language and speak the host country's language, even in their homes. They feel that immigrants will be able to assimilate better if they adopt the host country's language. This questionable claim / aspect (4) is directly opposed to the opinion of those who believe that it is important for immigrants to continue to speak their own language while they learn the host country's language. Many believe that this second aspect / approach (5) is the best one for young children. These people / factors (6) argue that individuals who have a strong command of their own language are better able to learn a new language. This argument / topic (7) seems to have some validity since research shows that immigrant children who cannot read and write in their parent's language have trouble learning to read and write their adopted country's language.

**B** Pair Work **Discuss your answers in A with a partner. What do you think the writer's opinion is about immigrants and language? How do you know? Do you agree or disagree with the writer's opinion? Write a response of four to five sentences to the writer's opinions using demonstratives and the words in A. Present it to another pair or to the class.**

*The writer believes that immigration can cause problems for countries and immigrants. We understand that there are sometimes issues that need to be resolved, but we strongly feel that this phenomenon is actually, in the long run, good for both the countries and the immigrants because . . .*

# 3 Common Time Signals

## Vocabulary Presentation

Time signals are important to use in narrative writing to make the sequence of events or ideas easier to follow.

***Over the past twenty years***, *immigration has become a controversial issue in many European countries.*

*This is not* ***the first time*** *in U.S. history that immigrants have been criticized.*

### 3.1 Common Time Signals

| | |
|---|---|
| **A** The most common time signals are prepositional phrases such as: | |
| *by* + specific time | *The immigration situation changed* ***by*** *the mid 1800s.* |
| *from* + specific time + *through/to* + specific time | *The first and longest immigration era stretched* ***from*** *the seventeenth century* ***to*** *the early nineteenth century.* |
| *after/since* + specific time | ***After*** *the end of World War I (from 1914 to 1918), Congress changed the nation's basic policy about immigration.* |
| *over/during the course of* + specific time | ***Over the course of*** *the late nineteenth and early twentieth centuries, the government took measures to slow down immigration.* |
| *over the past/next/last* + time period | ***Over the last/past*** *20 years, immigration has increased.* |
| *in the past/next/last* + time period | ***In the next*** *10 years, immigration is likely to decrease.* |
| *for* + time period | *The high rate of immigration continued* ***for*** *almost one hundred years.* |
| **B** Time adverbs are also considered time signals:<br>*already, always, ever, just, lately, never, now, recently, since, yet, the first/last time.* | *We've* ***always*** *lived in this neighborhood.*<br>*I will* ***never*** *again feel so helpless.*<br>*I* ***now*** *work in a clinic that serves immigrants.*<br>*It felt great* ***the first time*** *I realized I could make my own choice.*<br>*The debate over immigration has heated up* ***recently****.* |
| *Note:* Use the present perfect with the expression *this is the first time.* | INCORRECT: ***This is the first time*** *I ~~read/am reading~~ about immigration issues.*<br>CORRECT: ***This is the first time*** *I've read about immigration issues.* |

## 3.1 Common Time Signals *(continued)*

| | |
|---|---|
| **C** Use *every day*, *once* (*once more*/*once again*/*once or twice*), and *twice* to indicate frequency. | ***Every day***, *I'm amazed by how far I've gone.*<br>*By 2000, the United States had* ***once again*** *become a nation of immigrants.* |
| **D** Use time + *later*/*earlier* to indicate when something happened in relation to another event. | *I left my neighborhood when I was just 11.* ***Years later***, *I returned to Boston to go to medical school.* |

# Vocabulary Application

## Exercise 3.1 Time Signals

**You will listen to an essay written by a Vietnamese immigrant to the United States. Listen and write the missing words. Then listen and check your answers.**

I was born in Vietnam. My family moved to the United States ___when I was eight___ (1). ____________ (2), I lived in San Jose, California. All our neighbors were immigrants. ____________ (3) a new immigrant family arrived, we helped them settle. We lived there ____________ (4).

____________ (5), I studied very hard in school. My parents taught me to value education even though they were poorly educated. Then ____________ (6), I went to college and ____________ (7) to medical school. I ____________ (8) work in a hospital in the same neighborhood that I grew up in, and ____________ (9) I feel happy that I can give back to my community.

Vietnamese American Tet Festival in San Jose, California

I am very grateful for the life I have now. Even though it is ____________ (10) that I arrived, sometimes that first day here seems like yesterday. ____________ (11) I still remember how terrified I felt ____________ (12) I took the bus to school. ____________ (13) I wait for my young son's school bus to arrive and watch him get on the bus. The freedom that I still cherish is normal for him. ____________ (14) I intend to teach my son about the values of hard work and the sacrifices that his grandparents made so that he can enjoy the world he lives in.

## Exercise 3.2 More Time Signals

**A** Complete sentences about yourself. Write about your life, for example, important events in your past and present and your hopes for the future.

1 I ______________________________ for the first time in

______________________________

2 By the time I was ______________________________

I ______________________________

3 Years later, I ______________________________

4 After I ______________________________

I ______________________________

5 Over the past few years, I ______________________________

6 I recently ______________________________

7 Every day, I ______________________________

8 In the next few years, I hope to ______________________________

**B** Pair Work Share your sentences with a partner. Give more details.

*I flew in a plane for the first time in 2002. I was 16 years old. I flew from Taiwan to Australia to see my aunt who had immigrated there. We spent a few days at a beach. It was so beautiful. We also went to a national park, and I saw koalas and kangaroos.*

# 4 Avoid Common Mistakes ⚠

**1 Remember to use this/that with singular nouns and these/those with plural nouns.**

These
*~~This~~ ideas about immigrants are common.*

**2 Remember to use *the* in time signals such as *over the past year* and *in the next five years*.**

the
*In ^ last five years, our neighborhood has become less diverse.*

**3 Remember that frequency adverbs are usually placed before the main verb but after the verb *be*.**

never
*He ~~never~~ has ^ seen so much traffic.*

always
*The traffic ~~always~~ is ^ bad.*

He usually
*~~Usually he~~ arrives late.*

## Editing Task

**Find and correct eight more mistakes in the paragraph about an innovative device for the developing world.**

The lack of clean drinking water is a problem in many parts of the world, but even when people have a source of water, collecting it can be arduous. Every morning, Isha gets water for her family. It always ~~Always it~~ takes her 30 minutes to get to the well and about an hour to walk back with a heavy clay container of water balanced on top of her head. By time she returns, her body is aching from the weight of the water. She has been bringing water home like this for last 20 years. Isha lives in Niger, a country in West Africa. In Africa, women, and sometimes children, often are the ones responsible for collecting their family's water, and these responsibility takes a toll on their bodies. For some women, the journey to a water source is very long. This women have to walk up to 18 miles (30 kilometers) a day for water. Hans Hendrikse, a native South African, wanted to do something about this problem. Working with his engineer brother, Pieter, he created a new way of transporting water. It is called the Q-Drum. The Q-Drum is lightweight, durable, and affordable, and it can hold 50 liters of water. While this features alone make the product appealing, the most groundbreaking feature is its doughnut shape. When a rope is looped through the hole in the Q-Drum, the container can be rolled along the ground like a wheel. The Q-Drum's unique design allows even a young child to pull water for several miles, so the women never will have to carry the water solely on their heads. Over next decade this invention will have a major impact on the lives of the people of Africa, especially the women.

UNIT 11

# Classification and Definition 1: The Passive; Common Words and Phrases Used to Classify

## Job Interviews

## 1 Grammar in the Real World

You will read an essay describing different types of job interviews. This essay is an example of a classification essay, which classifies information into groups or categories.

**A** Before You Read **Have you ever gone on a job interview? What was the experience like? Read the essay. How does the writer classify different types of job interviews?**

**B** Comprehension Check **Answer the questions.**

1 According to the writer, what are the main differences between remote and face-to-face interviews?

2 Why is an audition considered a less conventional type of interview?

3 Do you agree with the writer's conclusions in the final paragraph? Why or why not?

**C** Notice **Find sentences in the essay that mean the same as the sentences below and write the number of the line on which each sentence is located. Compare the underlined verbs below with the verbs in the sentences in the essay. What do you notice about the form of the verbs the writer used? Why do you think the writer uses this form?**

1 It is possible to divide interviews into two types. ________

2 You can classify face-to-face interviews as either collective or sequential. ________

3 A single interviewer screens multiple candidates in a group interview. ________

4 Interviewers might ask a candidate for a marketing job to persuade them to buy a fictitious product. ________

# Job Interviews

Interviews are a familiar process for anyone entering the job market. They are by far the most common method used by companies to recruit new employees. All job interviews have the same goals – getting to know the job candidate better and giving the candidate a chance to learn about the job. However, they can take several different forms depending on geographic location and format.

Depending on the geographic location of the candidates, interviews can be divided into two types: remote[1] and face-to-face. In remote interviews, candidates are geographically separated from the interviewers. This type of interview is usually the preferred method for initial screening,[2] as it eliminates traveling expenses. These interviews can be conducted over a teleconferencing system or over the phone. Face-to-face interviews, in contrast, require the physical presence of the candidate. They are normally reserved for candidates who have already gone through a first round of remote screening.

Face-to-face interviews can be classified as either collective or sequential, depending on the number of people interacting with the candidate. Collective interviews can have two possible structures: team interviews and group interviews. In a team interview, multiple interviewers interact with the candidate. In a group interview, multiple candidates are screened by a single interviewer. Sequential interviews, on the other hand, involve private, one-on-one conversations between the candidate and several interviewers, one after another.

As far as the format is concerned, interviews can be divided into two categories: structured and unstructured. In a structured interview, the same list of questions is rigidly followed with all candidates. Companies sometimes use this format to ensure equal treatment among interviewees. It also makes it easy for recruiters to directly compare how two candidates responded to the same question. Conversely, unstructured interviews have a less strict format. Candidates might be asked more open-ended questions that encourage them to lead the discussion. For example, the interviewer could start by asking candidates to talk about themselves. Interviewers could also ask them to describe their professional experience.

Finally, there are a few less conventional types of interview formats. One example is an audition. In this type of interview, recruiters might ask candidates to perform a task that simulates the actual duties of that job. For example, a candidate for a computer programming position could be required to write a small piece of computer code. Candidates for a marketing job might be asked to persuade their interviewers to buy a fictitious product, and interviewees applying for a teaching job may be invited to prepare and deliver a mini-lesson.

Despite their possible variations, interviews should be seen as almost always having two main objectives. First, they are a way for the employer to test the potential employee. Second, but equally important, they are an opportunity for candidates to learn more about the company and to evaluate their interest in the job. Being aware of the different types of interviews will help job seekers to be more prepared to accomplish those goals.

[1]**remote:** not near, at a distance, far away

[2]**screening:** the process of sorting something into different groups

# 2 The Passive

## Grammar Presentation

The passive focuses on the action rather than the person or thing that receives the action. In academic writing, the passive can also improve text cohesion by making connections across sentences.

*Candidates* ***are asked*** *several questions during the interview. The interview questions* ***are created*** *by a hiring committee.*

### 2.1 Forming the Passive

AGENT: The committee; OBJECT: the results of the survey

The committee presented the results of the survey at the meeting. (Active).

The results of the survey were presented by the committee at the meeting (Passive).

### 2.2 The Passive

**A** Passive and active sentences have similar meanings, but a different focus.

In active sentences, the subject is the agent – the person or thing that performs the action of the verb.

In passive sentences, the subject is the receiver – the person or thing that receives the action of the verb.

AGENT: HR; RECEIVER: the candidates

Active: *HR* ***screens*** *the candidates*.

RECEIVER: Candidates; AGENT: by HR

Passive: *Candidates* ***are screened*** *by HR* .

**B** Passive sentences consist of a form of *be* and the past participle.

Simple present: *Remote interviews* ***are considered*** *to be effective.*

Present progressive: *The candidate* ***is being interviewed***.

Present perfect: *The final candidates* ***have*** *already* ***been selected***.

Simple past: *Candidates* ***were expected*** *to send a thank-you note after the interview.*

Past progressive: *The candidate* ***was being interviewed*** *when his cell phone rang.*

Past perfect: *Several candidates* ***had*** *already* ***been interviewed*** *when I arrived for my interview.*

## 2.2 The Passive *(continued)*

| | |
|---|---|
| **C** The passive can also be used with modals. | *By Friday, several candidates* ***will have been chosen****.*<br>*Candidates* ***may be asked*** *difficult questions.*<br>*The candidates* ***should have been asked*** *more questions about their problem-solving skills.* |
| **D** Some verbs that usually occur in the passive are followed by prepositions:<br>*associated with, based on, compared to/with, involved in, linked to, related to* | *Interview questions* ***should be based on*** *job requirements.* |
| **E** The passive is often followed by infinitives with verbs for speaking and thinking. Common verbs are:<br>*ask, believe, expect, find, know, say, think, understand* | *Approximately 100 people* ***are expected to apply*** *for the job.*<br>*Auditions* ***are known to be*** *effective job interview tools.* |

### Data from the Real World

| | |
|---|---|
| The following verbs are commonly used in the passive in academic writing:<br>*analyze, argue, carry out, conduct, consider, discuss, estimate, examine, explain, find, illustrate, include, note, observe, perform, present, study, suggest* | *Personal questions about age and marital status* ***are*** *never* ***included*** *in the interview process.*<br>*Job responsibilities* ***are discussed*** *with the candidates at the interview.* |

## 2.3 Using the Passive

| | |
|---|---|
| **A** Use the passive when the agent is not known, not obvious, or not important. | *Many types of interview formats* ***have been used*** *at the research lab.*<br>*Some candidates* ***are required*** *to perform a task.* |
| **B** Use the passive to improve the flow of ideas across sentences. | *In the group interview, multiple candidates* ***are screened*** *by a single interviewer. The interviewer asks a set of questions on standard topics. These questions* ***have been chosen*** *by the managers.* |

## 2.3 Using the Passive *(continued)*

| | |
|---|---|
| **C** Use the passive to describe a process. Common verbs are: *classify, compare, develop, examine, measure, study, test* | *In many community colleges, interview questions* ***are*** *carefully* ***developed*** *and* ***tested*** *before they are used.* *Face-to-face interviews* ***can be classified into*** *several different types.* |
| **D** Use the passive to report news events. | *According to a government report, fewer people* ***were hired*** *by companies in June than in May.* |

# Grammar Application

## Exercise 2.1 The Passive

Rewrite the tips and information about job interviews by changing the parts of the sentence in bold from active to passive. Leave out the agent when it is not important, is unknown, or is obvious.

1 Occasionally **a member of the human resources staff will observe an interview**.

*Occasionally an interview will be observed by a member of the human resources staff.*

2 **A company may not even consider you** for the job if you arrive late to the interview.

3 During the interview, **the interviewer will ask you questions** about your résumé.

4 **Interviewers may conduct interviews** over the phone.

5 One question you could ask is "What **training programs does the company offer**?"

6 **Employers often base the decision to employ someone on** a person's behavior during an interview.

7 **Federal and state laws prohibit employers** from asking certain questions about race, religion, and age.

8 **People have known some employers** to give tests during interviews.

9 If you do well, **an interviewer might ask you** to come in for a second interview.

______________________________________________

10 Interviewers often see more than one candidate in a day, so **they will probably compare you** with other candidates.

______________________________________________

## Exercise 2.2 More on the Passive

**A** Complete the email below about recent interviews at a software company. Use the correct passive form of the verbs and, where appropriate, modals in parentheses.

To chen_kim@cup.org
From campbell_peter@cup.org
Subject The search for project managers

Hi Kim,

Our search for new project managers is going very well so far. Ten interviews *have been conducted* (1) (conduct) this week so far. The following procedures ______ (2) (follow) each time. First, the interviewees all had individual interviews during which they ______ (3) (ask) about their previous work experience. Then the interviewees ______ (4) (divide) into two groups: those with project management experience and those without that experience. After that, each interviewee ______ (5) (give) a problem-solving test. The test items ______ (6) (base) on the kinds of problems that project managers might encounter. My experience has shown me that a lot ______ (7) (can / learn) about a candidate through a problem-solving test.

Then the interviewees ______ (8) (give) a short writing test. They ______ (9) (tell) when they applied that they might have to do some writing. After the writing test, the interviewees went home. The tests ______ (10) (should / evaluate) by Friday, and three interviewees ______ (11) (will / choose) to come in for second interviews.

Let me know if you have any questions.

Peter

**B** Pair Work **Discuss with a partner your experiences or experiences of people you know with job or college interviews. Use the passive where possible.**

*When I went to the interview for my current job, I was interviewed by my manager first. Then I was asked to take a test. After that, they told me they would call me if they were interested. They called, and I went in, and I talked to someone in the personnel department.*

# 3 Common Words and Phrases Used in Classification Writing

## Vocabulary Presentation

| | |
|---|---|
| There are common words and phrases that writers use to organize or classify ideas in classification writing. | *Colleges **can be classified** into different types.*<br>*Most colleges offer the most popular majors, which **include** business administration and psychology.* |

### 3.1 Classification Words and Phrases

| | |
|---|---|
| **A** Use the following common verbs and phrases (listed from most to least frequent) to classify ideas: | |
| *involves _____* | *The job **involves** a lot of traveling.* |
| *involves not only _____ but also _____* | *Preparing for an interview **involves not only** physical preparation **but also** mental preparation.* |
| *can be classified into _____* | *Interviews **can be classified into** two types.* |
| *is a combination of ____, ____, and ____* | *A strong cover letter is **a combination of** confidence, preparation, **and** curiosity.* |
| *consists of _____* | *A typical job application **consists of** a cover letter and a résumé.* |
| *is made up of _____* | |
| *can be/is/are divided into _____* | *A résumé **is divided into** several key sections.* |
| *is composed of _____* | |
| **B** Use the following common nouns to describe groupings:<br>*categories, classifications, divisions, factions, groups, kinds, parts, sections, sets, types, units* | *Job interviews can be divided into two **categories**.*<br>*Interviews can be divided into two **kinds**: remote and face-to-face.*<br>*There are two main **types** of interviews.* |

## 3.1 Classification Words and Phrases *(continued)*

| | |
|---|---|
| **C** Use these common phrases to develop topics:<br><br>TOPIC, *which are* A *and* B.<br>TOPIC, *which include* A *and* B.<br>TOPIC, *such as* A *and* B.<br>TOPIC: A, B, *and* C.<br>TOPIC, *including* A, B, *and* C.<br>TOPIC. *These are* A, B, *and* C.<br><br>Notice the use of commas in these structures. | TOPIC<br>*There are two main types of interviews,*<br>A AND B<br>***which are*** *remote* ***and*** *face-to-face.*<br><br>TOPIC<br>*The field of health care provides many opportunities:*<br>A B AND C<br>*therapy, outpatient care,* ***and*** *home health care.* |
| **D** Use these common phrases to introduce the criterion (method) for classification:<br><br>*according to, based on, depending on, on the basis of* | TOPIC PHRASE<br>*Job interviews can be classified* ***according to***<br>CRITERION<br>*their structure.*<br><br>PHRASE CRITERION<br>***Depending on*** *the number of participants,*<br>TOPIC<br>*job interviews can be divided into two categories.* |

## Vocabulary Application

### Exercise 3.1 Classification Words and Phrases

Choose the best word or words to complete the sentences about work.

1 A successful job search _____ determination, networking, and luck.
  a can be divided into  b involves  c can be classified

2 Job descriptions on websites often _____ job titles, salaries, and benefits.
  a are divided into  b can be classified into  c consist of

3 Succeeding in an interview _____ both preparation and an ability to adapt quickly to a situation.
  a involves  b is composed of  c is made up of

4 Some companies prefer interviewing people in _____ .
  a types  b parts  c groups

5 Most people want a job that _____ interesting opportunities, challenging tasks, and nice co-workers.
a is a combination of  b can be divided into  c can be classified into

6 Most businesses _____ several divisions.
a can be classified into  b are composed of  c involve

7 There are three _____ of a small business owner's job: managing employees, handling the finances, and marketing the business.
a kinds  b sets  c parts

8 Data Technician and Social Worker I are two _____ of government jobs listed online.
a classifications  b sections  c sets

## Exercise 3.2 More Classification Words and Phrases

**Read the questions below. Then listen to a lecture about higher education in the United States. Take notes as you listen. Then write the answers to the questions in complete sentences. Use the classification nouns and phrases in parentheses in your answers.**

1 How many categories can higher education in the United States be divided into?

(can be divided) *Higher education in the United States can be divided into five categories, which are universities, community colleges, liberal arts colleges, vocational-technical and career colleges, and special interest colleges.*

2 What are the main criteria for determining whether an institution of higher education is a community college or a university?

(classified / according to) ______________________________

______________________________

3 What are the three degree programs in a university?

(is composed of / generally ) ______________________________

______________________________

4 What is another way that schools can be divided?

(can be divided by) ______________________________

______________________________

5 How many funding classifications of schools are there?

(which are) ______________________________

______________________________

6 What are the types of publicly supported schools?

(can be subdivided into) ______________________________

______________________________

7 What are the advantages of attending a community college?

(including) ______________________________

______________________________

## Exercise 3.3 More Classification Words and Phrases

**A** Write sentences about job interviews using the words below and your own ideas.

1 a job interview involves

*I think a job interview involves not only talking about your experience but also making a good impression on the interviewers.*

2 interviews can be classified into

______________________________

3 a successful job search is a combination of

______________________________

4 the perfect job involves

______________________________

5 a good résumé consists of

______________________________

6 I answer job advertisements on the basis of

______________________________

**B** Pair Work Share your ideas with a partner. Decide which of your answers are the best. Report your best answers to the class.

*I said that a job interview involves talking about your experience and making a good impression. My partner said that it involves finding out about job requirements. We agreed that my answer was probably the better answer because it's very competitive, so people need to sell themselves very well.*

# 4 Avoid Common Mistakes ⚠

**1 Remember to place the adverb after the modal in passive sentences.**

*Leadership skills can* often *be ~~often~~ determined in group interviews.*

**2 Remember to use the correct preposition in the phrase *based on*.**

*The company's hiring decisions are based ~~in~~* on *candidates' interview behavior.*

**3 Remember to use the correct preposition in the phrase *involved in*.**

*The company vice presidents are rarely involved ~~on~~* in *hiring decisions.*

## Editing Task

**Find and correct seven more mistakes in the introduction and body paragraph from an essay on ways to pay for a college education.**

**Funding Options for Higher Education**

There are many issues involved ~~on~~ in choosing an institution of higher education. A prospective student's choice might be based in the location of the institution, or it might be based in the reputation of the academic programs and the faculty. However, for many students, the process of choosing a university may be often determined by economics. A college education may be one of the greatest expenditures an individual will make in his or her lifetime. If money is an issue in a student's choice, there are several funding options.

One funding option available to low-income college students is a grant. A grant is a sum of money that does not have to be paid back. Government programs are the primary source of education grants. In addition to government sources, grants may be sometimes awarded by private organizations and companies. The main factor involved on the awarding of government grants is income level. Private grants may often be based in additional factors, such as ethnicity, grades, or other academic achievements. As reporting one's income is always involved on the process of applying for a grant, a good place to begin is with the U.S. Department of Education's Free Application for Federal Student Aid (FAFSA). The FAFSA application simplifies the income-reporting process and matches the applicant's income with several grant opportunities. Grants are often the first and best choice for students who cannot afford a college education on their own.

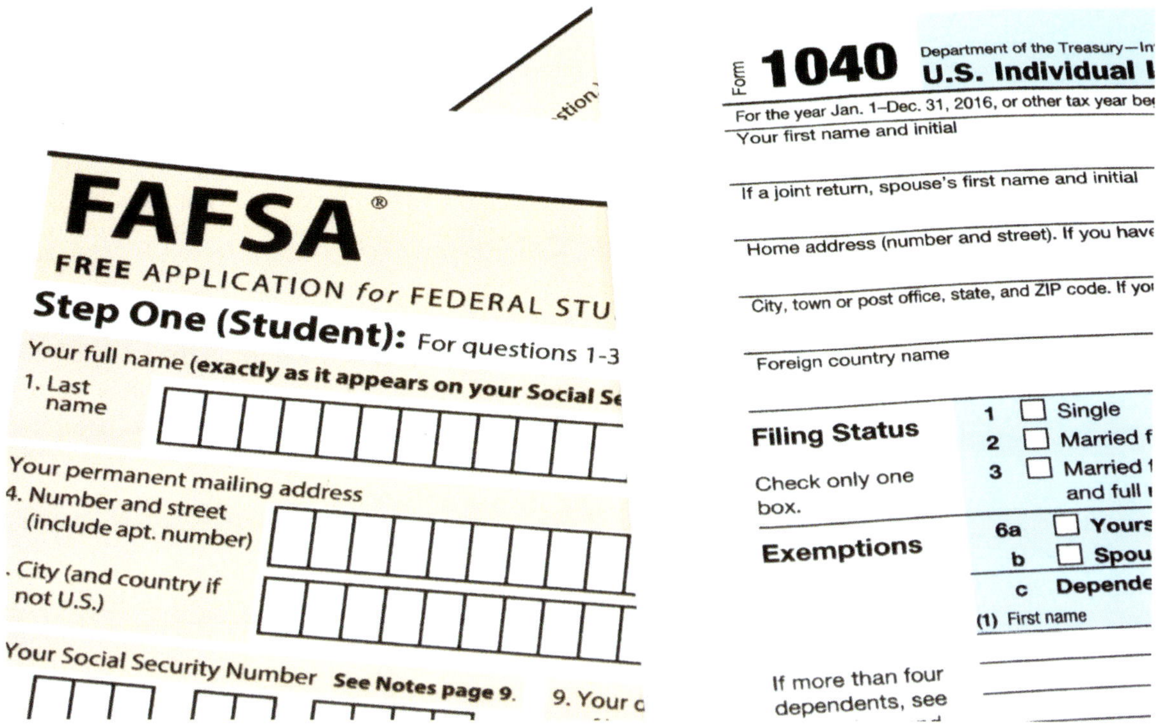

UNIT

# 12 Classification and Definition 2: The Language of Definition; Appositives

## Your Ideal Job

## 1 Grammar in the Real World

You will read an essay that examines the theories of vocational psychologist John Holland. The essay is an example of classification and definition writing that shows how Holland categorizes people according to their personalities.

**A** Before You Read **How would you describe your personality? Do you think that your personality influences your decision in careers? Read the essay. What are the six personality types?**

**B** Comprehension Check **Answer these questions.**

1 Why are people's career choices so important for success?

2 According to the essay, how will understanding one's vocational personality type be helpful?

3 Based on this essay, what is your personality type? Why?

**C** Notice **Find the sentences that contain the definitions of the personality types that follow to notice the grammar the writer uses to introduce the definitions. Underline the verb phrases used in each definition.**

1 Artistic personality type on lines 11–13.

2 Investigative personality type on lines 13–15.

3 Realistic personality type on lines 17–18.

4 Social personality type on lines 20–21.

# Matching Personality Type and Work Environment

Most people spend over a third of their waking hours at work. Because work is such an enormous part of people's lives, their career choices are critical for personal and professional success. Vocational[1] counselors, who are trained to help with these choices, use many tools to help people find the best jobs. One tool is the use of personality tests to suggest job choices that could lead to greater job satisfaction. The most popular of these tests was created by John Holland, a leading researcher in vocational psychology. He developed six categories of personality type – *Artistic, Investigative, Realistic, Social, Enterprising*, and *Conventional* – which are used to help identify the best job choices. Understanding these personality types can help identify an appropriate job for one's personality.

Each personality type has defining characteristics. An Artistic personality type refers to a person who enjoys creative activities like art, dance, or creative writing, and who generally avoids highly structured or repetitive activities. A person with an Investigative personality type, on the other hand, is defined as someone who likes to study and solve math or science problems. People who fall into the Investigative personality type generally see themselves as scientific and intellectual. Having a Realistic personality type means valuing practical work, such as jobs that require technical or manual skills and are productive. A person with a Realistic personality type particularly values environments where they produce goods or use machines. Other people have good skills at teaching, counseling, nursing, or giving information. They are referred to as Social personalities. People with Enterprising personalities are good at leading people and selling things or ideas. Many entrepreneurs fall into the Enterprising category. Finally, people who have a Conventional personality type are able to work with written records and numbers in a systematic way. These people are usually very detail-oriented and value structure and planning.

[1]**vocational:** relating to a job, career, or profession

Holland's personality types can provide insights into compatible jobs and work environments where people can best use their abilities. For example, Realistic personality types would look for environments that allow them to use tools or machines and generally avoid those that require a lot of interaction with people. Artistic people are more likely to find satisfaction and success in an artistic environment, such as an arts center or theater. Someone with an Investigative personality type would be best suited for a job in an investigative field, such as medicine or mathematics. Figure 1 provides examples of jobs that match each personality type. Holland believed that people who look for jobs that suit their abilities are more likely to find environments in which they can succeed and be satisfied.

**Figure 1. Holland Personality Types and Career Examples**

| ARTISTIC | INVESTIGATIVE | REALISTIC | SOCIAL | ENTERPRISING | CONVENTIONAL |
|---|---|---|---|---|---|
| Architect | Mathematician | Auto Mechanic | Nurse | Flight Attendant | Accountant |
| Dancer | Professor | Cook | Teacher | Lawyer | Cashier |
| Musician | Scientist | Electrician | Therapist | Salesperson | Secretary |

Matching someone's personality type with a work environment is actually a more complicated process because people are often a combination of two or three personality types. This means that the range of suitable jobs can actually be quite diverse. For example, a person may have a Realistic personality type but also have characteristics of an Enterprising personality type and a Social personality type. This person would likely be suitable for a job as an electrician, a salesperson, or a nurse. Discovering one's major personality types involves using assessment tools that identify skills and strengths.

For many people, it is often a difficult task to decide on a career. Realizing that much of one's life will be spent doing a certain kind of work can make the decision stressful. Many people use tools like Holland's personality types to help make their decisions. Information about personality types can be interesting and useful. Holland's theory is a valuable guide for people in choosing satisfying jobs and careers.

# 2 The Language of Definition

## Grammar Presentation

Definitions are very common in academic writing. Writers define key terms in the text so that readers will understand the exact meaning of the concepts being described. Definitions usually use the simple present form of *be*, the verb *means*, or the passive of certain verbs.

*Having a Conventional personality type* ***means*** *being good at working with written records and numbers in a systematic way.*
*A person with an Investigative personality type* ***is defined as*** *someone who likes to study and solve math or science problems.*

### 2.1 Definitions

| | |
|---|---|
| **A** A definition generally follows the pattern:<br>term + *be* + general noun + defining details | TERM / IS/ARE / GENERAL NOUN<br>*Realistic personality types* ***are*** *people*<br>DEFINING DETAILS<br>*who value practical work.* |
| A general noun names a larger category for the term being defined. It is more general than the term being defined. | DEFINED TERM / GENERAL NOUN<br>*A Realistic person is a* ***person*** *with practical skills.*<br>*Visual learning means* ***learning*** *by seeing.* |
| The defining details are often in the form of an identifying relative clause or a prepositional phrase. | IDENTIFYING RELATIVE CLAUSE<br>*A headhunter is a person* ***whose job is to find qualified people to take high-paying jobs.***<br>PREPOSITIONAL PHRASE<br>*A chief executive officer is the person* ***with the most important position in a company.*** |
| **B** You can also use the verb *mean* to define terms. | *Conventional* ***means*** *standard, predictable, or normal.* |
| **C** Avoid gender-specific singular pronouns in definitions. | SINGULAR NOUN: GENDER-SPECIFIC<br>*A general practitioner is a doctor who provides basic medical services to* ***his*** *patients.* (This assumes the doctor is a man, not a woman.) |
| Make the noun plural and use *their*. | PLURAL NOUN: GENDER NEUTRAL<br>*General practitioners are doctors who provide basic medical services to* ***their*** *patients.* |
| OR<br>Keep the noun singular and use *his or her* or *his/her*. | SINGULAR NOUN: NEUTRAL<br>*A general practitioner is a doctor who provides basic medical services to* ***his/her*** *patients.* |

## 2.2 The Passive in Definitions

| | |
|---|---|
| You can use the verbs *call*, *define*, *know*, and *refer* in the passive when defining a term.<br>With *is/are defined as*, the definition comes last.<br>With *is/are known as*, *is/are called*, and *is/are referred to as*, the definition comes first. | TERM<br>*A certified public accountant (CPA)* ***is defined as***<br>DEFINITION<br>*a person who has passed a state accounting exam.*<br>DEFINITION<br>*A person who has passed a state accounting exam*<br>TERM<br>***is known as*** *a certified public accountant (CPA).*<br>DEFINITION<br>*A person who instructs or trains others, especially in a*<br>TERM<br>*school,* ***is called*** *a teacher.* |

## 2.3 Using Definitions

| | |
|---|---|
| **A** Place the term being defined at the end of the sentence to make a stronger connection to the subject of the next sentence. | *People who are skillful at occupations such as nursing, teaching, and counseling are known as Social types.*<br><br>*The types of people in this group like to work in social environments.* (The link between the term *Social types* and the next sentence is stronger.) |
| **B** Break more complex definitions into two sentences. Use a pronoun in the second sentence to create cohesion. | *Some people are good at jobs that require working with numbers and following strict procedures.* ***They*** *are called Conventional personality types.* (The definition of *Conventional personality types* is in the previous sentence.) |

# Grammar Application

## Exercise 2.1 Identifying the Parts of Definitions

**A** **Unscramble the sentences below and find definitions of different types of jobs.**

1 who repairs / water pipes, baths, / is / a person / a plumber / and toilets

*A plumber is a person who repairs water pipes, baths, and toilets.*

2 who designs / is a person / certain that they / new buildings and makes / an architect / are built correctly

______________________________

3 sell merchandise / who work / are sometimes referred to / people / as sales associates / in stores and

______________________________

4 is called / a musician / who / someone / is skilled / in playing music

______________________________

5 out of materials / sculptors / make art / are artists / like clay, marble, and metal / who

______________________________

6 as stylists / fashionable clothing, / who / hairstyles, and makeup / are known / people / help their clients choose

______________________________

**B** Rewrite items 1–6 in Part A using the cues below.

1 (is called) *A person who repairs water pipes, baths, and toilets is called a plumber.*

2 (is referred to as) ______________________________

3 (are people who) ______________________________

4 (is defined as) ______________________________

5 (are known as) ______________________________

6 (are people who) ______________________________

**C** Pair Work Think of definitions for other jobs. Ask questions and test your partner to see if he or she knows the name of the job. Use different defining language in your questions.

A *What do you call someone who flies an airplane?*

B *A person who flies an airplane is called a pilot.*

## Exercise 2.2 Writing Definitions

**A** Listen to two students who are studying for a criminal justice test. As you listen, match the terms with the correct definition.

| Field | Noun | Noun | Verb | Verb | Adjective + Noun |
|---|---|---|---|---|---|
| law | testimony | bankruptcy | to appeal | to sentence | ~~admissible evidence~~ |

1 *admissible evidence* : the kind of evidence that juries or judges can consider in civil and criminal cases

2 ______________ : a system of rules that a community recognizes as regulators of behaviors and actions of people

3 ______________ : evidence presented orally by witnesses during trials or before grand juries

4 ______________ : to ask a higher court to review a decision after a trial to determine if it was correct

5 ______________ : to announce a punishment to someone convicted of a crime

6 ______________ : a legal procedure for dealing with debt problems of individuals and businesses

**B** Write definitions for the terms in A using the verbs in parentheses.

1 (define) *Evidence that juries or judges can consider in civil and criminal cases is defined as admissible evidence.*

2 (be) ______________

3 (know) ______________

4 (means) ______________

5 (call) ______________

6 (refer) ______________

# 3 Appositives

## Grammar Presentation

To provide additional information about a noun or noun phrase in academic writing, you can use an appositive: a noun phrase that either defines, restates, or gives important additional information about the noun phrase it follows.

*John Zappa, **president of Sylvania Community College**, believes that instructors should always be aware of different learning styles.*

*People with Enterprising personalities, **personalities that have leadership traits**, are good at leading people and selling things or ideas.*

## 3.1 Appositives

| | |
|---|---|
| **A** An appositive is a noun phrase that refers to the same person or thing as the noun it follows.<br><br>A sentence with an appositive is similar in meaning to one with a nonidentifying relative clause. The only difference is the relative pronoun and *be* verb are left out. | MAIN NOUN / APPOSITIVE<br>*John Holland, **a leading researcher in vocational psychology**, developed a theory about career choices.*<br>(*John Holland* and *a leading researcher* refer to the same person.)<br><br>NONIDENTIFYING RELATIVE CLAUSE<br>*John Holland, **who is a leading researcher in vocational psychology**, developed a theory about career choices.* |
| **B** You usually set off an appositive with commas.<br><br>You can also use dashes or parentheses to set off an appositive. | MAIN NOUN / APPOSITIVE<br>*Enterprising personalities, **personalities that have leadership traits**, are good at leading people and selling things or ideas.*<br><br>MAIN NOUN / APPOSITIVE<br>*Kinesthetic learners – **people who learn through moving, doing, and touching** – prefer actively exploring the physical world around them.*<br><br>MAIN NOUN<br>*Workers with the Enterprising personality type*<br>APPOSITIVE<br>***(people who are energetic, ambitious, and sociable)*** *often work in real estate agencies and law firms.* |
| **C** You can also place an appositive before the noun that it refers to. | APPOSITIVE<br>***A leading vocational psychologist**, John Holland developed a well-known list of personality types.* |

## 3.2 Using Appositives

| | |
|---|---|
| **A** You can use an appositive to provide a definition or description of a proper noun. | APPOSITIVE ADDING DESCRIPTION<br>*Ben Cohen, **co-founder of Ben & Jerry's Ice Cream**,*<br>APPOSITIVE PROVIDING A DEFINITION<br>*is a good example of a "Healer," **a business leader who provides nurturing harmony to a business**.* |
| **B** You can use an appositive to refer to tables or figures and citations, or when you use an acronym (a word formed from the first letters or parts of other words) or an abbreviation.<br><br>References to tables and acronyms are usually in parentheses.<br><br>These uses are very common in academic writing. | *To illustrate his theory, Holland created a model of*<br>APPOSITIVE<br>*personality types **(Figure 1)**.*<br><br>*Federal data are now collected using the North*<br>APPOSITIVE<br>*American Industrial Classification System **(NAICS)**.* |

# Grammar Application

## Exercise 3.1 Appositives

The items below contain information about remarkable people and organizations. Rewrite each sentence or pair of sentences to make a sentence containing an appositive.

Michael Pollan

Bono

Howard Gardner

1 Michael Pollan is the author of *Food Rules* and *The Omnivore's Dilemma*. Michael Pollan believes we should all examine our eating habits.

*Michael Pollan, the author of Food Rules and The Omnivore's Dilemma, believes we should all examine our eating habits.*

2 Steve Jobs, who was a driving force in technology, had an enormous impact on the way we use technology on a daily basis.

3 One supporter of the nonprofit housing organization Habitat for Humanity is Jimmy Carter. Jimmy Carter is a former U.S. president.

4 Desmond Tutu is a Nobel Peace Prize laureate and retired South African archbishop. Desmond Tutu has promoted peaceful conflict resolution for many years.

5 Dr. Douglas Schwartzentruber and Dr. Larry Kwak are cancer researchers. Dr. Douglas Schwartzentruber and Dr. Larry Kwak are both working separately to find a vaccine against cancer.

6 Bono is a famous singer with the band U2. Bono works to improve health and nutrition throughout the world.

______________________________________________

______________________________________________

7 Howard Gardner proposed nine types of intelligences. The nine types of intelligences are in Table 1.

______________________________________________

______________________________________________

8 The Ronald McDonald House Charities help families of children who are receiving medical treatment for serious diseases. The abbreviation for the organization is RMHC.

______________________________________________

______________________________________________

**Exercise 4.2** More Appositives

On a separate sheet of paper, write five sentences about people, places, or organizations that you know about, using appositives. Try to use different punctuation – commas, dashes, and parentheses – in your answers.

*Jules Yakakao, an expert in English language learning, works at a major university in Côte d'Ivoire.*

*Human Rights Watch – an organization dedicated to defending human rights – is well respected.*

# 4 Avoid Common Mistakes

**1** **Remember to use singular and plural nouns correctly in definitions.**

*Artistic types are ~~a person~~ people who ~~enjoys~~ enjoy creative activities.*

**2** **Remember to use the correct verb form in the passive when giving definitions.**

*Sometimes, emergency medical technicians are ~~refer~~ referred to as paramedics.*

**3** **Remember to use the correct pronoun in relative clauses. Specifically, remember to use *who* only with animate nouns.**

*A résumé ~~who~~ that does not include dates is called a functional résumé.*

*People ~~which~~ who are energetic and sociable often work in sales.*

**4** **Make sure your pronoun use is clear so that it can only refer to one preceding noun. Otherwise, use more precise words, not pronouns, to refer to previously mentioned nouns.**

*Julio and Luis are creative people. They work in an art studio making large murals.*

*The murals are very expensive. Many people come to see ~~them~~ the artists to learn about ~~them~~ their work.*

# Editing Task

Find and correct seven more mistakes in the introduction and body paragraph from an essay about a personality test.

### The Myers-Briggs Personality Type Indicator

The Myers-Briggs Type Indicator, MBTI, is a personality assessment tool ~~who~~ *that* has increasingly gained popularity in the workplace. It is based on a psychological theory developed by Carl Jung. Jung proposed that there are two basic categories of thinking styles: rational and irrational. Rational functions involve thinking and feeling. Irrational functions involve sensing and intuition. Jung further proposed that there are two basic types of people, introverts and extroverts. While there are several personality qualities who psychologists associate with each type, introverts are usually define as people who are more interested in ideas and thinking. In contrast, extroverts are define as people who are more action-oriented. The MBTI has taken these four basic Jungian personality categories and types and established four sets of opposing pairs: extrovert/introvert, sensing/intuition, thinking/feeling, and judgment/perception. While individuals use all of these thinking styles, their MBTI results indicate their thinking-style preferences. They can help match individuals to careers and help managers understand how to best work with these employees.

One of the MBTI personality types, ISTJ (Introvert, Sensing, Thinking, Judgment), illustrates the way in which the MBTI assessment tool can match individuals to appropriate working environments. ISTJ personality types are a person who tends to be quiet. They prefer to be alone. They attend to details rather than to the Big Picture. They prefer thinking to feeling. This means that they use logic when making decisions. ISTJ personality types like controlled, organized environments. They are concrete, ordered, and predictable. They are more in tune with facts than with other people's feelings. ISTJs do well as accountants and in law enforcement. Managers of ISTJ types who are having difficulty getting along with others need to take action. They can be placed in situations where they can work alone, for example. Other remedies for unhappy ISTJs might include moving them to a more organized work group.

UNIT 13

# Problem–Solution 1: Present Perfect and Present Perfect Progressive; Noun Phrase Structures

## Food and Technology

## 1 Grammar in the Real World

You will read an essay about genetically modified food. The essay is an example of problem–solution writing, in which the writer poses a problem and then suggests some possible solutions.

**A** Before You Read **Do you worry about the safety of the food you buy from supermarkets? What information do you think should be on the labels of packaged foods? Read the essay. What information does the writer want to see on food labels?**

**B** Comprehension Check **Answer the questions.**

1 According to the writer, what is the problem with GM foods?

2 Give two reasons why food is genetically modified, according to the essay.

3 In the third paragraph, the word "enhanced" is in quotation marks. Why do you think the writer used quotation marks around this word?

**C** Notice **Follow the instructions below to help you notice and understand how the writer uses the grammar to explain the problem.**

1 Read the second paragraph again.

a Do the verbs *have entered* and *has been done* describe a period of time up to now or a specific time in the past?
b How does the meaning of the verb *has been warning* differ from the meaning of the verbs in a? Which form of the verb emphasizes that the action is potentially still continuing, the present perfect or present perfect progressive?

2 Reread the sentence starting on line 29 beginning with "Statistics have revealed" Why do you think the writer used the present perfect form (*have revealed*) instead of the past form of the verb "reveal" (*revealed*) in this sentence?

# Genetically Modified Foods

Any time humans make technological advances, they have the potential to do great harm and great good. Genetically modified (GM) foods, which are foods that have had changes made to their DNA, are no exception. Many people believe that there are possible advantages to genetically modifying plants, for example, to improve their nutritional value or protect them from pests as they grow. So far, scientists have added a cattle growth hormone to fish for faster growth and high starch to potatoes so that they absorb less oil when fried. Despite these alleged[1] benefits, there are some scientists and consumer groups that fiercely question the safety of these foods for human consumption and the environment. Peter Katel, a writer for CQ Researcher (a publication that reports on congressional news), has claimed that more independent tests are needed in order to conclude whether GM foods are suitable for consumption by the general public. Researchers must continue to thoroughly test GM foods to verify their safety, and consumers need to educate themselves and demand that food companies be more open in their identification of food sources.

According to The Center for Food Safety, GM foods have entered nearly every sector of the food market. This shift means that a majority of the public is consuming GM foods as part of their regular diet. Statistics have revealed a little known fact: Up to 92 percent of U.S. corn has been genetically engineered, along with 94 percent of cotton. Current estimates are that 75 percent or more of prepared foods in a typical supermarket in the United States contain GM ingredients. However, not enough research has been done concerning the existence of any short- or long-term side effects. Larry Trivieri, author of several books on alternative medicine, has pointed out that the U.S. Food and Drug Administration does not require independent safety tests on GM food. Because of the lack of conclusive research, Neal Barnard, a well-known physician and promoter of plant-based diets, as well as other researchers, has been warning us that potential health risks may be associated with the consumption of these foods.

As consumers, we must make informed choices in the food we buy for the sake of our health. To do that, we need to educate ourselves on the issues surrounding GM foods so that we can choose whether to buy this "enhanced" food or not. Even though research has been inconclusive as to the effects of eating GM foods, there is some evidence that it may result in increased food allergies. Currently, foods with genetically modified ingredients are not always labeled as such. One way to address the problem is by systematically labeling all foods. Almost two decades ago, Eli Kintisch, a writer for *The New Republic* (a well-known magazine of politics and arts), suggested that the few remaining products should be simply labeled "GM-free." Currently, confusion arises from the number of different labels given to GM foods. These include the term *bioengineered*, often abbreviated to "BE," which few people fully understand. Likewise, legislation in the U.S. allows for symbols instead of words, which causes further confusion and misunderstanding.

[1]**alleged:** said to be true, but without proof that it is true

# 2 Present Perfect and Present Perfect Progressive

## Grammar Presentation

| | |
|---|---|
| In problem–solution writing, the present perfect is used to describe situations, recent research, or trends that have an impact on a problem. The present perfect emphasizes a time in the past up to now. The time period may or may not be completed but in both cases there is a connection to the present. The present perfect progressive describes an action that started in the past and emphasizes that it is still going on. | *Genetically modified food* ***has been*** *available in grocery stores for many years.*<br>*Researchers* ***have been studying*** *the impact of GM foods on our health.* |

### 2.1 Using Present Perfect

| | |
|---|---|
| **A** Use the present perfect to describe an event that started at an unknown or unspecified time in the past. This event may be completed, or it may continue into the future.<br>*Note:* Do not use the present perfect for events that happened at a specific time in the past. | *Some researchers* ***demonstrated*** *that genetically modified foods may cause damage to humans.* (completed event)<br>*The consumption of GM foods* ***has increased*** *significantly in the last ten years.* (the event may continue)<br>SIMPLE PAST<br>*Sales of GM foods* ***increased*** *dramatically between 2001 and 2011.* |
| **B** Use the present perfect to indicate that a past event relates to the present – it is still important *now*. These are often recent events.<br>These events may include general experiences up to now. | *Researchers* ***have discovered*** *recently that some GM foods may cause health problems.* (The discovery is important and relevant now.)<br>*It is true that most people* ***have not noticed*** *any difference after eating GM foods.*<br>*The research team* ***has received*** *several grants for GM food research.* |
| **C** Use the present perfect to introduce general ideas and provide background information about a problem.<br>Then use the simple past to fill in the details that led to the problem. | *The farming of GM foods* ***has increased*** *in recent years.*<br>*In 2010, Brazil dramatically* ***increased*** *the use of land for farming GM crops.* |

## 2.1 Using Present Perfect *(continued)*

| | |
|---|---|
| **D** The adverbs *already, ever, never,* and *yet* often occur with the present perfect. | *Many farmers **have** already **seen** enormous gains in productivity using GM crops.*<br>***Has** any technological advance ever **been accepted** immediately?*<br>*They **haven't finished** the research yet.* |
| **E** Use the present perfect in academic writing to refer to earlier parts of a text.<br>You can also use the present perfect to refer to other research. | ***As we have seen**, there is no easy answer to the problem of our nation's food shortage.*<br>***Swanson has argued that** labeling foods may be the only short-term solution to the problem of GM foods.*<br>***Critics have examined** the situation carefully but have not proposed any definitive solution to the problem.* |

## 2.2 Using Present Perfect Progressive

| | |
|---|---|
| **A** Use the present perfect progressive to describe actions that started in the past and to emphasize that they continue to the present and may continue in the future.<br>As with other progressive forms, do not use the present perfect progressive with stative verbs. | *Researchers **have been warning** us for many years that GM foods have potential health risks.*<br>*This group **has been studying** the effects of GM foods since 2001.* (They are still studying them.)<br>*Some scientists **have believed** for years that GM foods are unsafe. not*<br>NOT *Some scientists ~~have been believing~~ for years that GM foods are unsafe.* |
| **B** Use the present perfect progressive with time expressions to emphasize how long an action has been going on:<br>Use *all (semester), for (years), in (months), not . . . in (a long time),* to show the duration of the action or event.<br>Use *since (2010)* to show the starting point of the action or event. | *He**'s been collecting** data all semester.*<br>*They**'ve been interviewing** consumers for three months.*<br>*Stores **have not been carrying** that product since 2010.* |
| **C** The present perfect progressive often has no time expression associated with it. | *What **has** your research group **been working on**?*<br>*We**'ve been studying** GM crops.* |

## 2.2 Using Present Perfect Progressive *(continued)*

| | |
|---|---|
| **D** The present perfect and the present perfect progressive can often have the same meaning and can be used interchangeably. | *The number of farms that grow GM foods* ***has increased*** *since 2005.*<br>*The number of farms that grow GM foods* ***has been increasing*** *since 2005.* |

# Grammar Application

## Exercise 2.1 Present Perfect Forms or Simple Past?

**A** Complete the paragraph about one farmer's story about switching to organic farming. Use the passive where appropriate. Sometimes more than one answer is possible.

Since 1990, *I've been farming* (1) (farm) using conventional methods and ________ (2) (get) good results. However, after my first daughter ________ (3) (be) born, I ________ (4) (start) to think of the world that she would live in and to consider organic farming. It means making a lot of changes, though. I ________ (5) (always / apply) chemical fertilizers to promote plant growth, but that will change. For years, I ________ (6) (spray) insecticides to reduce pests and disease, but that will change, too. Starting next year, I will use birds, insects, and traps to do that. For the entire time I ________ (7) (live) on the farm, chemical herbicides ________ (8) (use) to kill weeds. Once in 2006, I ________ (9) (use) natural herbicides, but they ________ (10) (not work) well, so I ________ (11) (stop) using them, and I ________ (12) (go) back to using chemical herbicides. However, starting next year, I will rotate crops to manage weeds.

**B** Pair Work **Role-play a discussion between two people with different views on genetically modified foods. Use the present perfect and present perfect progressive forms where appropriate.**

**Student A** You are skeptical about the farming of GM foods and think that not enough research has been done. You do not trust food companies and you wish that more information about GM foods were available. You believe that the use of the foods may harm the ecosystem. Your solution: There should be more research done on GM foods.

**Student B** You are enthusiastic about GM foods. You have read some research on the foods and are convinced that they are not harmful and that our bodies will adapt to eating them. You think that the use of technology to create new foods will allow people to be healthier and potentially reduce starvation worldwide. Your solution: There should be more GM foods.

A *The farming of GM foods is a problem. The research on GM foods has suggested that they could be harmful, so I don't feel confident that the foods are good for society.*

B *I disagree. We've been eating these foods for years now with no ill effects, and it seems the advantages outweigh the disadvantages . . .*

## **Exercise 2.2** More Present Perfect Forms or Simple Past?

**Complete the sentences. Use the present perfect, present perfect progressive, or simple past of the verbs in parentheses. Use the passive forms when necessary. Circle any time markers that help you decide which form is correct. Sometimes more than one answer is possible.**

1 From 2000 to 2007, the value of GM crops *increased* (increase) considerably.

2 For the past 20 years, researchers ________________ (track) the areas used to grow GM crops in the world.

3 Over the past 15 years, the number of GM crops ________________ (grow) significantly.

4 Over 457 million acres of land ________________ (use) for GM crops in 2016 compared to 444 million in 2015.

5 Many people are not even aware that farmers ________________ (begin) growing GM crops in the mid-nineties.

6 Statistics show that the global area of GM crops ________________ (increase) steadily since the mid-nineties.

7 In 2017, 18 million farmers from 28 countries, including the U.S., Brazil, and China, ________________ (plant) GM crops.

8 The effects of GM foods on people ________________ (not/determine), and scientists continue to do research.

9 Research ________________ (not/show) yet that GM foods have a negative effect on our health and environment.

10 Until there is definite proof that GM foods are not harmful, some people ________________ (decide) to avoid them.

Source: Genetically modified plants: Global cultivation on 134 million hectares. (2010). GMO Compass. Retrieved from www.gmo-compass.org

## Exercise 2.3 More Present Perfect Forms and Simple Past

Read the statements below. Then listen to the radio program about urban gardening. As you listen, decide if the statements are true or false. Circle *T* or *F*.

T/(F) 1 Residents of urban areas such as Los Angeles grow vegetables in their apartments.

T / F 2 Mark Johnson started a rooftop garden five years ago.

T / F 3 Mark Johnson no longer has a rooftop garden.

T / F 4 The neighborhood swap in Mark's neighborhood started four years ago.

T / F 5 Emily Ling regularly brought cooked food to the neighborhood swap.

T / F 6 Emily Ling goes every week to the neighborhood swap.

T / F 7 Emily and her neighbors never buy vegetables from stores anymore.

T / F 8 Neighborhood gardens have been popular for a while in Emily's city.

T / F 9 Annie Suarez started to grow food in her local neighborhood garden in 2010.

T / F 10 Annie Suarez currently writes a gardening blog.

# 3 Common Noun Phrase Structures

## Vocabulary Presentation

In academic writing, certain noun phrase structures (sometimes called *shell nouns*) are used to identify and restate more complex ideas. They generally refer to information already mentioned or that will follow in the text. In problem–solution writing, these structures can be used to define a problem and explain its importance.

*It is important to identify* ***the causes of*** *famine.*

*Research needs to be done because of* ***the fact that*** *more and more people are consuming GM foods.*

## 3.1 Noun Phrases with *Of*

| | |
|---|---|
| **A** Some noun phrases with *of* explain, label, or define a concept. For example:<br>*the basis of, the concept(s) of, the definition of, the essence of, the idea of, the meaning(s) of, the notion of* | *It is important that the public understands* ***the concept of*** *genetic engineering and its implications.*<br>***The definition of*** *organic farming is agriculture that relies on natural methods and limits the use of chemical fertilizers and pesticides.* |
| **B** Some noun phrases with *of* express consequences and outcomes. For example:<br>*the cause(s) of, the consequence(s) of, the effect(s) of, the result(s) of* | *Consumers need to be aware of* ***the potential consequences of*** *GM foods on their health.*<br>*No one has studied* ***the effects*** *of GM foods on babies.* |
| **C** Some noun phrases with *of* express goals. For example:<br>*the aim of, the benefit(s) of, the goal(s) of, the purpose(s) of* | ***The aim of*** *the program is to reduce reliance on pesticides.*<br>***The purpose of*** *food labeling is to help consumers make more informed decisions.* |
| **D** Some noun phrases with *of* express the importance of a concept. For example:<br>*the core of, the heart of, the importance of* | *Sustainability is* ***the heart of*** *organic farming.*<br>***The importance of*** *organic farming is sustainability – not harming the environment and managing it well.* |
| **E** Some noun phrases with *of* indicate measure and quantity. For example:<br>*the amount of, the frequency of, the majority of, a number of, the number of, the rest of*<br>Note: *A number of* means "several" or "many" and is followed by the plural form of a verb. *The number of* refers to a specific number and is followed by the singular form of a verb. | *Consumers need to be aware of* ***the amount of*** *GM foods that they eat.*<br>***The majority of*** *GM products come from crops such as soybeans, corn, and cotton.*<br>***A number of*** *people* ***have asked*** *about the benefits of organic farming.*<br>***The number of*** *consumers who buy GM foods* ***is increasing***. |

## 3.2 Noun Phrases with *That* Clauses

| | |
|---|---|
| **A** Noun phrases with *that* clauses are used to: | |
| express a fact: *conclusion, fact* | ***The fact that*** *the population continues to increase makes efficient food production essential.* |
| express an idea: *claim, idea, notion* | *New research may support* ***the notion that*** *modifying food has a negative impact on health.* |
| express a view: *belief, doubt, sense, view* | *Many governments hold* ***the view that*** *genetically modified food has successfully fed many hungry people.* |
| express a claim that is not yet proven: *assumption, hope, hypothesis, impression, observation, possibility, suggestion* | *Many people are concerned about* ***the possibility that*** *GM foods can be dangerous.* |
| **B** Noun phrases with *that* clauses can appear anywhere noun phrases appear (for example, as a subject or object). | SUBJECT<br>***The claim that GM foods can be beneficial*** *is true.*<br><br>SUBJECT<br>***The fact that conventional agricultural products can have an "organic" label*** *has created skepticism in consumers.*<br><br>OBJECT<br>*I support* ***the idea that GM foods should be labeled****.* |
| **C** *The fact that* and *the idea that* are especially common expressions in academic writing.<br><br>*The fact that* often introduces ideas that are generally accepted. You can use *the fact that* to persuade. A reader is less likely to challenge a statement that follows *the fact that*. It suggests that the information is not an opinion. | *The writer cites* ***the fact that*** *no long-term studies have been done on the effects of GM foods.*<br><br>*Not all consumers agree with* ***the idea that it is necessary to label foods****.* |

# Vocabulary Application

## Exercise 3.1 Noun Phrases with *Of*

**A** Complete the sentences about genetically modified foods with an appropriate noun phrase from the box. Sometimes more than one answer is possible.

| | | | | |
|---|---|---|---|---|
| a number of | the basis of | ~~the concept of~~ | the heart of | the number of |
| the aims of | the benefits of | the effects of | the majority of | |

1 *The concept of* genetic modification is not new.

2 One of ________________ modifying food genetically is to produce enough food, especially corn, rice, and soybeans, for people all over the world.

3 However, ________________ genetic modification of food are still not completely understood.

4 In a recent study, ________________ people surveyed were uncomfortable with the idea of GM foods. In fact, ________________ them avoided the foods.

5 At ________________ their concern is the fact that researchers don't really know whether GM foods are completely safe.

6 ________________ GM foods produced every year is steadily growing.

7 Proponents of this technology talk about what ________________ this technology will be; however, only time will tell if they are correct to be so optimistic.

8 Opponents of GM foods do not think that the government should allow more GM foods on ________________ inconclusive findings.

**B** Group Work Work in a group to answer the questions about GM foods. Use the noun phrases from the word box in A in your answers. Then present your answers to the class.

1 What are some reasons why scientists created GM foods?

2 What are some advantages and disadvantages of GM foods?

3 What do you think the majority of people know about GM foods? What do they base their understandings on? What are some of their concerns?

## Exercise 3.2 Noun Phrases with *That* Clauses

**A** Read about the benefits of eating locally grown food and circle the correct phrases to complete the sentences.

Among the many current food trends, one is based on the belief that / the fact that (1) it is better to eat locally grown food than food exported from far away. The doubt that / The notion that (2) local food is better for you is based on a few facts.

First, the idea that / the fact that (3) food has only traveled a few miles to get to your supermarket means that the food is probably fresher than meat or produce that has been shipped from the other side of the world. There is a conclusion that / possibility that (4) produce that has traveled a long way may have lost some of its nutrients or begun to deteriorate during the trip.

Second, people who prefer local food might hold the view that / the conclusion that (5) eating locally grown food is good for the community. For example, buying this food supports local farmers and other food producers, like cheese manufacturers and bread bakers.

Third, the doubt that / the hope that (6) eating locally grown food will help protect the environment – because less fuel is required to transport the food – might motivate some people to follow this trend.

Ironically, locally grown food can sometimes be more expensive than exported food even though it doesn't have to travel very far. This is often due to the impression that / the fact that (7) local food producers usually consist of small businesses with high overhead costs and low levels of production.

**B** Pair Work **What is your opinion of eating locally grown foods? What are the benefits? What are some possible disadvantages? Talk with a partner and explain your opinion. Use nouns phrases with *that*.**

*The possibility that exported food may be less nutritious is surprising to me. I didn't realize that food could lose nutritional value like that. I think the fact that locally grown food might be more nutritious is a strong argument for eating food that is produced near my home.*

# 4 Avoid Common Mistakes ⚠

**1** **Remember that noncount nouns such as *advice, equipment, evidence, information, knowledge,* and *research* do not have plural forms.**

*We do not have enough ~~informations~~ information on the health effects of GM foods.*

**2** **Remember to use *the fact that,* and not *this fact that.***

*Many people are not aware of ~~this~~ the fact that many snack foods contain GM ingredients.*

**3** **Remember that *a number of* takes a plural count noun and plural verb.**

*A number of ~~expert agrees~~ experts agree that GM foods may help solve world hunger.*

## Editing Task

Find and correct eight more mistakes in the body paragraph from an essay on environmental problems associated with food production.

### Engineered Food and the Environment

A number of animal rights ~~activist thinks~~ activists think that laboratory-generated meat, also known as cultured meat, provides a solution to the negative environmental effects of food production. Cultured meat is grown in a laboratory from animal tissue cells. There are many benefits of cultured meat. First, animals do not have to be killed for food. According to Compassion in World Farming, 70 billion farm animals are farmed and killed for food worldwide each year. This fact that cultured meat would virtually eliminate animal suffering is not in dispute. Additionally, most people are aware that raising animals for food is harmful to the environment. This is because processing meat requires large amounts of resources such as land and water. There is also a great deal of informations on this fact that raising animals for meat contributes to greenhouse gases and pollutes water, air, and land. Recent researches on the environmental impact of cultured meat is very promising. A number of environmentalist agrees that cultured meat would greatly reduce greenhouse gas emissions. There is also evidences that cultured meat might be healthier and safer. A number of scientist is continuing to do researches on cultured meat. Many of these experts predict that we will see cultured meat in supermarkets within five to ten years. It seems clear that relying more on engineered food products may someday help to solve some of the environmental problems that we face today.

UNIT 14

# Problem–Solution 2: Reporting Verbs; Adverb Clauses and Phrases with *As*; Vocabulary for Describing Information in Graphics

## Children and Health

## 1 Grammar in the Real World

You will read an essay that focuses on the problem of childhood obesity. The essay is an example of problem–solution writing, in which the writer describes the problem and the reasons why the problem exists. At the end of the essay, the writer voices a need to find a solution to the problem.

**A** Before You Read **In what ways have the lifestyles of children changed in the past 20 years? How have these changes affected their health? Read the essay. According to the author, what are the main causes of childhood obesity?**

**B** Comprehension Check **Answer the questions.**

1 According to the essay, what are some health issues that result from children being overweight or obese?

2 What are the social concerns for children who are overweight or obese?

3 Why does the author say, "It is clear that the reasons for the rise in childhood obesity are complex"?

**C** Notice **Find the verbs that the writer uses to report ideas and information from sources. Write them on the blank lines.**

1 The Centers for Disease Control and Prevention *state that* . . .

2 Former President Bill Clinton ______________ . . .

3 Finally, other studies of obese children and teens ______________ . . .

4 Researchers ______________ . . .

5 Parents, doctors, scientists, and policy makers all ______________ . . .

# Fighting Childhood OBESITY

**CHILDHOOD OBESITY IS A MAJOR CONCERN** in the United States and in many other countries around the world. Obesity in U.S. children has more than tripled since the late 1970s. The Centers for Disease Control and Prevention state that an overweight child has a Body Mass Index (BMI, a measure of weight in relation to the child's age, sex, and height) above the 85th percentile and less than the 95th percentile for his or her age and sex. As an example of this,a second grader whose weight is above the 85th percentile would weigh 95 pounds or more. An obese child has a BMI at or above the 95th percentile. While it appears that the rates of obesity are falling for younger children, this trend is still likely to persist and perhaps worsen in the future for older children.

Many high-profile people are concerned about this epidemic. Among those people is former President Bill Clinton, a supporter of stronger policy on childhood obesity. Clinton asserts that the causes of this health crisis range from overworked parents, with no time to prepare healthy food, to a lack of sidewalks and safe outside play areas for children. Another contributing factor is the marketing of inexpensive large-portion meals at fast-food restaurants. Companies make these meals for children even more attractive by giving away small toys and prizes with each meal.

Doctors are concerned about increased childhood obesity because of its health-related consequences. One consequence of obesity is cardiovascular disease.[1] Certain risk factors, such as high blood pressure, high cholesterol, and high blood sugar, are present in people who develop this disease. Several studies of obese children and adolescents has shown that obesity in childhood is associated with a higher chance of disability and dying prematurely.

There are additional health risks associated with being overweight or obese. Though less common, they are serious health issues. They include asthma, sleep apnea (when breathing stops during sleep for at least 10 seconds), and Type 2 diabetes. While Type 2 diabetes has been a common health consequence of adult obesity, in recent years it has become a problem among children and adolescents. Finally, other studies of obese children and teens have indicated that these young people are more likely to develop certain cancers in later life.

Apart from physical issues, childhood obesity can also generate social problems. Researchers note that overweight and obese children are often discriminated against socially, and that this can cause stress and low self-esteem. These feelings are likely to have an impact on children's academic and social lives.

Parents, doctors, scientists, and policy makers all believe that childhood obesity is a critical issue. It is clear that the reasons for the rise in childhood obesity are complex. Therefore, the solution must involve everyone – parents, doctors, the media, as well as the community. A committed response now will ensure that the obese child of today will not grow up to be an obese adult.

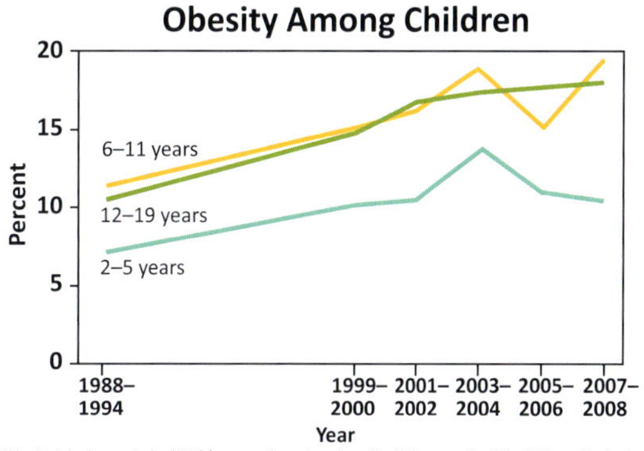


NOTE: Obesity is body mass index (BMI) for age and sex at or above the 95th percentile of the CDC growth charts.
SOURCE: CDC/NCHS *Health, United States, 2010*, Figure 13. Data from the National Health and Nutrition Examination Survey.

[1]**cardiovascular disease:** heart disease

# 2 Reporting Verbs

## Grammar Presentation

| | |
|---|---|
| Academic writers use reporting verbs to report ideas or findings from a source. | *Bill Clinton* ***provides*** *several reasons for the increase in childhood obesity.*<br>*The study* ***illustrates*** *several possible consequences of childhood obesity.* |

### 2.1 Reporting Verbs

| | |
|---|---|
| **A** Reporting verbs have the pattern:<br>the source + a reporting verb + *that* + clause with source's information. | SOURCE / REPORTING VERB<br>*Researchers* ***point out that***<br>CLAUSE WITH SOURCE'S INFORMATION<br>*obese children are targets of social discrimination.* |
| **B** In less formal writing, *that* can be omitted after a reporting verb.<br>It is better to keep *that* in academic writing. | INFORMAL: *Many parents* ***believe*** *children should avoid junk food.*<br>FORMAL: *Doctors* ***believe that*** *children should avoid junk food.* |
| **C** Many reporting verbs, such as *illustrate*, *point out*, *show*, and *suggest*, can also be followed by a noun phrase. | NOUN PHRASE<br>*Figure 1* ***illustrates*** *the three levels of influence on children's health.* |
| **D** Some reporting verbs can only be followed by noun phrases and never by *that* clauses, for example:<br>*describe, display, evaluate, give, investigate, present, summarize* | *Chart 1* ***describes*** *seven parental influences on children's health.*<br>NOT *Chart 1 describes* ~~*that there are*~~ *seven parental influences on children's health.*<br>*Figure 1* ***gives*** *eight community influences on children's health.* |

#### Data from the Real World

| | |
|---|---|
| Common reporting verbs that take *that* clauses are (in order of frequency):<br>*say, show, assume, suggest, complain, announce, argue, add, declare, explain, imply, mention, point out, propose, recommend, remark, report, state, write, warn* | *A recent government report* ***suggests that*** *obesity is a problem for all ages, but it is most significant among children.* |

## 2.2 Using Reporting Verbs

| | |
|---|---|
| **A** Most reporting verbs are neutral in tone. Use them to report facts. | *Research* ***demonstrates that*** *the consumption of fast food has increased in the last 10 years.*<br>*The authors of the study* ***conclude that*** *childhood obesity can be very harmful.* |
| **B** Use certain reporting verbs to report a point of view, for example:<br>*believe, emphasize, predict, recognize, recommend, suggest* | *The U.S. Department of Health and Human Services* ***believes that*** *people should read food labels carefully when shopping.*<br>*Doctors* ***recommend that*** *people get 30 minutes of exercise daily.* |
| **C** Use certain reporting verbs to report results, for example:<br>*conclude, demonstrate, estimate*<br>*Note:* The verbs *demonstrate* and *estimate* can also be followed by a noun phrase, but the meaning is different. | *The U. S. Department of Health and Human Services* ***concluded that*** *consumers should read ingredient lists carefully.*<br>*The workshop* ***demonstrated*** *ways for children to improve their health.* |
| **D** Use *allege* and *claim* when you doubt or are unsure of the truth of the original author's statement. | *Ramirez* ***claims that*** *the number of fast-food restaurants in the world has increased.*<br>*The attorney general* ***alleges that*** *the problem started with a complaint from parents in the public schools.* |
| **E** Use *propose* and *suggest* when the author presents information as likely but still uncertain. | *Davidson* ***suggests that*** *the consumption of fast food has increased.* |

# Grammar Application

### Exercise 2.1 Reporting Verbs

**Underline the reporting verbs in the letter to a newspaper about the problem of childhood obesity.**

Dear Editor,

I want to bring your readers' attention to the issue of childhood obesity in the United States. Recent studies show that 37 percent of children and adolescents in the United States are overweight. Doctors claim that unhealthy childhood weight can affect adult weight. Some reports estimate that children who are overweight before the age of 15 are 80 percent more likely to be obese at 25 than children with healthy weights.

Experts suggest that some of the main causes of childhood obesity are a lack of parental influences, a lack of nutritious foods available in the home, and availability of fast-food restaurants. However, we should also consider the role that school plays in influencing a child's diet and weight. Because students spend a large part of their day at school, that is where they do much of their eating. Research indicates that children get as much as 50 percent of their daily calories while they are at school. This statistic suggests a link between school lunches and childhood obesity. In addition, most students these days have to do a lot of homework. Some parents estimate that their children have to do more than three hours of homework a night. This keeps them from spending their after-school time engaging in physical activities. I don't want to blame schools for childhood obesity, but I do think we should all work together to help our children be healthy.

Sincerely,

A concerned parent

## Exercise 2.2 More Reporting Verbs

**A** Complete the sentences with the appropriate reporting verbs. Remember to write *that* after the verb.

1 A report from the Dietary Guidelines for Americans *suggests that* people should "eat fewer calories, be more active, and make wiser food choices."

a suggests b complains c demonstrates

2 The Centers for Disease Control and Prevention (CDC) ______________ one way to fight childhood obesity is to remove high-calorie, low-nutrition snacks.

a emphasizes b illustrates c warns

3 Former President Bill Clinton ______________ many parents are overworked and don't have time to prepare healthy food for their children.

a describes b believes c estimates

4 A report by the Centers for Disease Control and Prevention ______________ a child whose body mass index is above the 85th percentile is overweight.

a states b recommends c warns

5 The Dietary Guidelines for Americans ______________ people can reduce the risk of many chronic diseases, including cancer, through better nutrition.

a assume b predict c point out

6 A spokesperson from the American Academy of Pediatrics ______________ it is unhealthy to allow children age two or younger to watch television.

a recommends b mentions c claims

7 The results of various studies ________________ overweight children are often bullied and teased by their peers.

a evaluate    b demonstrate    c believe

8 Several states have had court cases in which the state ________________ childhood obesity is a form of child abuse.

a has emphasized    b has alleged    c has recommended

**B** Pair Work **Talk with a partner and explain your choices in A.**

*I think* suggest *is the best answer for item 1 because the Dietary Guidelines are not forcing people to do anything, but telling people what might be a good thing for them to do. The guidelines are certainly not complaining about anything or demonstrating something.*

**Exercise 2.3** Using Reporting Verbs

Pair Work **Talk with a partner about one of the topics below or a topic approved by your teacher. Take notes on your partner's answers, and then report your partner's ideas to the class. Use reporting verbs in your report.**

- At what age should children have cell phones?
- At what age should children be allowed to join social networks?
- At what age should children have their own computers?
- At what age should children have TVs in their rooms?

*Monica argues that children under 10 should not have cell phones. She points out that cell phones are expensive and young children could easily break them. She also believes that children under 10 should always have an adult present, so they wouldn't need their own phones.*

# 3 Adverb Clauses and Phrases with *As*

## Grammar Presentation

| | |
|---|---|
| Use adverb clauses and phrases with *as* to refer to a source of information. | ***As seen in Figure 1**, the number of fast-food restaurants in the country has increased significantly.*<br>***As researchers point out**, there is a variety of reasons related to the increase in childhood obesity.* |

## 3.1 Adverb Clauses and Phrases with *As*

| | |
|---|---|
| **A** Use adverb clauses with *as* to refer to information from a chart, graph, or other sources.<br>Common verbs in *as* clauses are:<br>*demonstrate, illustrate, point out, and show* | ***As Figure 1 illustrates****, eating habits have changed recently.*<br>***As a recent study points out****, a key issue is the stigma of obesity.* |
| *Use a comma after the clause.* | ***As Dr. Jarolimova illustrates,*** *there are many things that children can do every day to become healthier.* |
| **B** You can also use adverb phrases with *as* in the passive, for example:<br>*as demonstrated in/by _____, as illustrated in _____, as seen in _____, and as shown in/by _____* | ***As demonstrated in Table 1****, there is a positive trend in the results.*<br>***As shown by Professor Green****, there are actions that can effectively address the problem.* |
| **C** You can use the passive with modals, for example:<br>*as can/may be seen in __________* | ***As can be seen in Graph 1****, a higher percentage of boys has become overweight in the past several decades.* |

# Grammar Application

## Exercise 3.1 Using Adverb Clauses with *As*

**A** Answer the questions about the results of the Virginia Childhood Obesity Survey. Use adverb clauses with *as* and the correct form of the verb in parentheses. Use the passive with modals where appropriate.

Chart 1

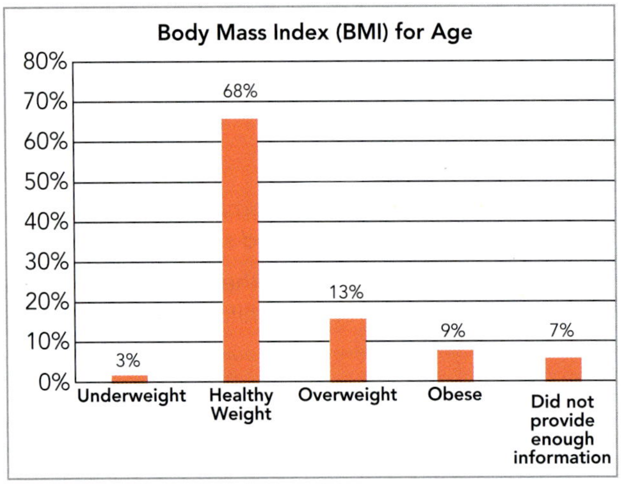


Chart 2

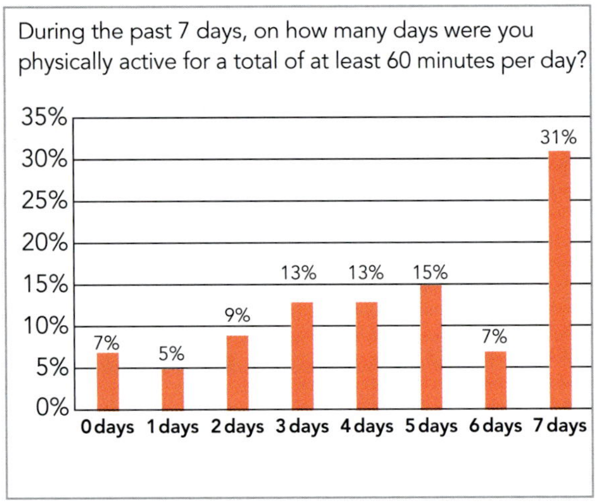

1 What percentage of Virginia youth are physically active at least twice a week?

(demonstrate) *As demonstrated in Chart 2, / As Chart 2 demonstrates, 88 percent of Virginia youth are physically active at least twice a week.*

2 What percentage of Virginia youth are obese?

(show) ______________________________

3 Are the majority of Virginia children overweight?

(illustrate) ______________________________

4 Are most Virginia youth active at least four days a week?

(point out) ______________________________

5 What percentage of Virginia youth are not at a healthy weight?

(demonstrate) ______________________________

6 What percentage of Virginia youth are physically active less than two days per week?

(see) ______________________________

**B** Pair Work **Compare your answers with a partner. Then create two more questions and answers with the information in the chart.**

## Exercise 3.2 Using Adverb Phrases with *As*

Answer questions about the information from the Virginia Childhood Obesity Survey. Use adverb phrases with *as*.

Chart 3

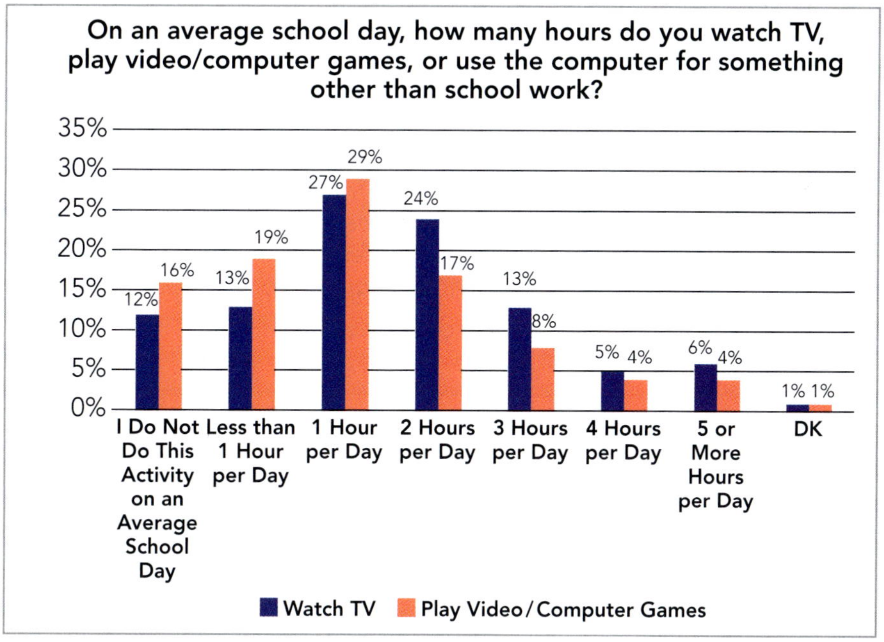

1 Compare the percentage of Virginia youth who watch TV for two or more hours per day with those who spend two or more hours playing video games.

*As Chart 3 shows, Virginia youth spend more time watching TV than playing video and computer games.*

2 Compare the percentage of Virginia youth who don't watch TV with those who don't play video / computer games.

3 Compare the percentage of Virginia youth who spend one hour or less watching TV per day with those who spend one hour or less playing video / computer games.

4 Compare the percentage of Virginia youth who spend three hours per day playing video games with those who spend one hour playing video games.

5 Compare the percentage of Virginia youth who don't watch TV or play video / computer games with those who spend five or more hours watching TV and playing video / computer games.

# 4 Common Vocabulary for Describing Information in Graphics

## Vocabulary Presentation

Graphics (tables, charts, graphs) provide helpful visual support for ideas in writing. There are common words and phrases that are used to introduce the graphic and direct readers to specific information in it.

***It can be seen from Figure 1 that*** *the number of girls and young women in sports has* ***increased dramatically*** *in recent decades.*

***Chart 2 shows*** *that overall participation in physical education has* ***declined***.

## 4.1 Common Vocabulary for Describing Information in Graphics

| | |
|---|---|
| **A** Refer to a graphic by first identifying it and then highlighting specific information that you want readers to notice.<br>*Chart 1 shows _____ .*<br>*The graph shows (that) _____ .* | IDENTIFY GRAPHIC HIGHLIGHT INFORMATION<br>***Chart 1 shows that*** *most students watched one hour or less of TV per average school day.*<br>***The graph shows*** *how many hours a day individuals from certain countries spend watching television.*<br>***The graph shows that*** *there is a relationship between weight and amount of exercise.* |
| **B** You can use passive forms to identify a graphic.<br>*From _____, it can be concluded/estimated/inferred/seen that _____ .* | *From the chart,* ***it can be concluded that*** *individuals in the United States are getting much less exercise than a few decades ago.*<br>*From the chart,* ***it can be inferred that*** *individuals in Switzerland maintain active lifestyles and healthy weights.* |
| **C** You can use these nouns to describe change:<br>↑ *increase, rise*<br>↑↓ *fluctuation*<br>↓ *decline, decrease, drop, fall* | *There was* ***an increase*** *in girls' participation in team sports from 2016 to 2018.*<br>*Figure 1 shows* ***the fluctuation*** *in funding for physical education in the last three decades.*<br>*There was* ***a decrease*** *in students' participation in physical education between ninth and tenth grades.* |
| **D** You can use the following adjectives to describe the intensity of a change:<br>*slight, slow*<br>*gradual, steady*<br>*dramatic, rapid, sharp, steep, sudden* | *There was a* ***slight*** *rise in physical activity among ninth graders between 2015 and 2018.*<br>*There was a* ***gradual decline*** *in physical education participation during high school.*<br>*There was* ***a sharp drop*** *in physical education participation between ninth and tenth grades.* |
| **E** You can use the following verbs to describe a change:<br>*decline, drop, fall, increase, reduce, rise* | *Participation in sports* ***fell*** *in three grades in the last few years.*<br>*Participation has* ***increased*** *only for ninth graders.* |
| **F** You can use the following verbs to indicate no change:<br>*remain, stay, maintain* | *The hours students spent in physical activity each week has* ***remained*** *steady for the past few years.* |

## Vocabulary Application

### Exercise 4.1 Vocabulary to Describe Chart Information

**A** The principal at Cascades High School developed a program last year to address students' low energy levels. As you listen to the principal describe the program and its results, fill in the missing information in the line graph below.

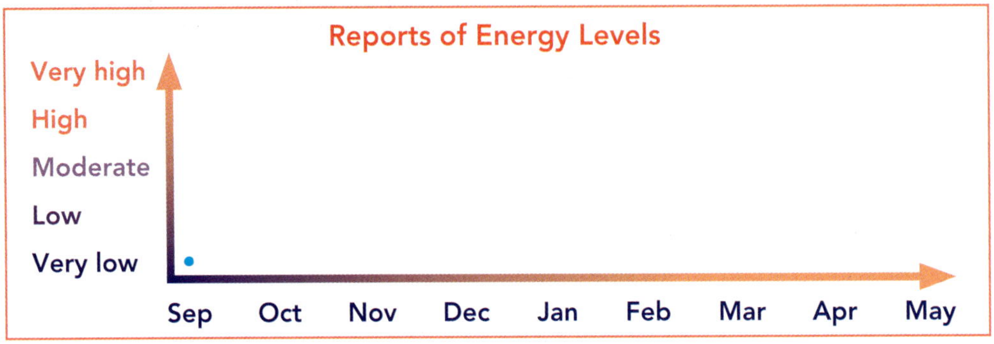


**B** Pair Work Describe the information in the chart in A using the common vocabulary to describe chart information.

### Exercise 4.2 More Vocabulary to Describe Chart Information

On a separate sheet of paper draw a chart similar to the one in Exercise 4.1. Imagine one year of reports of flu or colds among schoolchildren and create a line graph similar to the one in A. Describe your chart to a partner. Use the common vocabulary to describe charts.

*As shown in the chart, the number of colds remained low from September through October. Then in November there was a sharp rise. This was probably a result of the fluctuation in temperature during the day and cold winds . . .*

# 5 Avoid Common Mistakes

**1 Remember to use the base form of *be* after modals in the passive.**

*be*
*From the chart, it can ^ inferred that simple lifestyle changes result in major health gains.*

**2 Remember that reporting verbs such as *demonstrate, illustrate,* and *show* can be followed by a *that* clause or by a noun phrase. Be careful to use these two correctly.**

*there is*
*Table C shows that ^ an increase in weight loss.*
*Figure 8 illustrates ~~that~~ the results of increased exercise over a three-week period.*

**3 In general, when referring to a numbered chart, graph, figure, or other source with *As . . . ,* do not use an article.**

*As ~~the~~ Chart 1 shows, the number of hours participants engaged in physical activity per week had a direct effect on their body weight.*

## Editing Task

Find and correct eight more mistakes in the body paragraph from an essay on the problem of obesity.

Genetics and Obesity

Several studies have shown ~~that~~ a connection between genetics and obesity. As the Smith's study shows, people who have access to exactly the same foods will use those calories differently. Figure A demonstrates that the differences. It shows how a controlled diet and exercise program affected a group of 50 participants: some people in the group gained weight, others maintained their weight, and a small percentage even lost weight. From this study, it can inferred that these different responses to the same situation are primarily genetic. Wu's research provides further support for the genetic connection to obesity. Her long-range study on body weight and family history clearly demonstrates that a genetic link to obesity. As the Figure B illustrates, there was very little variation in body weight among three generations of ten families. Finally, several studies have shown that a connection between a gene called FTO and obesity. These studies also demonstrate that a relationship between FTO and diabetes and other diseases. From these and other studies, it can argued that genetics plays a role in body weight.

UNIT 15

# Problem–Solution 3: Adverb Clauses and Infinitives of Purpose; Reduced Adverb Clauses; Vocabulary to Describe Problems and Solutions

## Health and Technology

## 1 Grammar in the Real World

You will read an essay about people who use the Internet to diagnose themselves and find information about illnesses. The essay is an example of problem–solution writing.

**A** Before You Read **How often do you or people you know use the Internet to diagnose symptoms? Read the essay. According to the writer, what are some concerns that doctors have?**

**B** Comprehension Check **Answer the questions.**

1 What is cyberchondria?

2 What concerns do doctors have when patients use the Internet to self-diagnose?

3 What is the solution suggested in the essay?

**C** Notice **Follow the instructions below to notice how the author uses adverb clauses and phrases to express purpose or reason.**

1 Find the last sentence in the first paragraph. Which phrase in the sentence explains the purpose of the parts of the solution?

2 Find the sentence that starts with *while* in the second paragraph. What form of the verb follows *while*? What is the understood subject of the phrase with *while*?

3 Find the sentences that contain *when* on lines 62–64 beginning with "When searching . . . " and on lines 73–75 beginning with "However, when health-care website providers . . . " How is the use of *when* in these two sentences different in structure?

# Doctor–Patient Relationships in the 21st Century

There was a time when a person with a medical problem would ask a family member, friend, or neighbor about their symptoms before visiting a doctor. Now, many people gather a great deal of information before their first visit. Their first source for this information is now the Internet. In fact, a survey by Pew Research Center's Internet & American Life Project (2011) found that 80 percent of American adults use the Internet for health-related information. This increased use of the Internet for health purposes has led to a new phenomenon, *cyberchondria*. Cyberchondria is a situation in which people with no medical background diagnose themselves by reviewing symptoms and other information online and determine that their situation is worse than it really is. Educating patients about using online information, identifying changes doctors could make, and using online medical information more effectively are all necessary in order to solve this problem of cyberchondria.

The term *cyberchondria* is based on the term *hypochondria*, a belief that one has a serious disease even though there is no medical confirmation. After gathering information online, cyberchondriacs often conclude that they have a disease or health issue that is worse than the one that their doctor diagnoses. While not being a real physical condition, cyberchondria can lead to problems. For example, patients often find it difficult to accept their doctor's diagnosis, causing friction[1] between patients and doctors.

With patients self-diagnosing more often, a shift has occurred in the patient–doctor relationship. For example, patients may challenge doctors more aggressively and spend more time discussing topics that they had researched online. Another concern is that patients do not always use credible websites. As a result, they may find information that is based on out-of-date research. Most importantly, doctors are concerned that patients will scare themselves when reading symptoms online. As Brazilian cardiologist Dr. Fernando Botelho explains, "Patients read non-contextualized information and do not know how to process it. This situation can bring anxiety."

While acknowledging these concerns, many doctors also see the benefit of having more actively engaged patients. Dr. Igor Barrios, a surgeon in Venezuela, believes that these changes will lead to better care. He feels that doctors will have to become more effective communicators. Doctors should become more sensitive to patients' more active role and learn to accept that they will have to be able to provide explanations for patients' questions about information they find on the Internet.

Using medical information available on the Internet wisely can also address the problem of cyberchondria. Health-care websites must state clearly that their information should be in addition to, rather than a replacement of, a consultation with a doctor and medical treatment. For doctors, while it may be difficult, they need to acknowledge that the old rules have changed – they are no longer the only source of information. They should educate their patients on how to evaluate the health information they find on the Internet so that the process of diagnosing becomes collaborative rather than adversarial.[2] Finally, the last part of the solution involves patients. When searching for information on the Internet, patients should remember that no website can replace a doctor's physical exam. Before approaching their doctor, they should check that the information they have is up-to-date and credible. In this way, they can avoid wasting time during appointments.

This cooperation will not be easy to implement. It will be difficult to persuade health-care website providers to change information online. It will also be challenging for doctors and patients to change their roles, especially without additional training about these new relationships. However, when health-care website providers, doctors, and patients all realize that these changes will benefit health care, they will be more likely to collaborate. This cooperation will help create a stronger twenty-first-century model for patient–doctor relationships.

[1]**friction:** unpleasant feelings caused by differences of opinion
[2]**adversarial:** opposing each other, like enemies

# 2 Adverb Clauses of Purpose and Infinitives of Purpose

## Grammar Presentation

| | |
|---|---|
| Adverb clauses of purpose and infinitives of purpose express the purpose, or reason, for an action or idea. They usually follow the main clause and are often used in problem–solution writing to explain the reasons for a proposed solution. | *Some clinics have computer stations* ***so that*** *patients can go online in the waiting room.*<br>*She researched the disease on the Internet* ***in order to*** *learn more about it.* |

### 2.1 Adverb Clauses of Purpose

| | |
|---|---|
| **A** An adverb clause of purpose is a dependent clause that answers the question *why?* | *Doctors should educate their patients about how to evaluate medical information on the Internet* ***so that the process of diagnosing becomes collaborative rather than adversarial****.* |
| **B** *So that* is the most common way to introduce clauses of purpose. Sometimes it is reduced to *so*. | *He cut down on fatty food* ***so that*** *he could lose weight.*<br>*He cut down on fatty food* ***so*** *he could lose weight.* |
| **C** The adverb clause of purpose usually comes after the main clause. | COMMON: *The clinic provided training for using online medical reference information* ***so that patients would feel less anxious****.*<br>LESS COMMON: ***So that patients would feel less anxious****, the doctors provided training for using online medical reference information.* |

## 2.2 Infinitives of Purpose

| | |
|---|---|
| **A** When the subject of the main clause and the adverb clause of purpose are the same, you can use *in order* or *so as* with an infinitive (*to* + verb) of purpose. For example:<br>*in order to* + verb<br>You can omit the words *in order* when the meaning is clear.<br>*so as to* + verb | *Doctors place brochures on medical conditions in their waiting rooms (**in order**) **to provide** patients with valuable information.*<br>*Doctors should discuss treatment options with patients **so as to address** any concerns.* |
| **B** You can also use these forms in the negative. The *not* comes before the infinitive:<br>*in order not to* + verb<br>*so as not to* + verb | *A patient might not say anything about what he or she reads on the Internet **in order not to** make the doctor angry.*<br>*Patients should avoid the use of unqualified medical websites **so as not to make** false assumptions about their medical issues.* |
| **C** When an infinitive is followed by an infinitive of purpose, you should use *in order to* or *so as to* for clarity. | UNCLEAR: *Some patients write a list of questions to ask **to use** time efficiently during medical appointments.*<br>CLEAR: *Some patients write a list of questions to ask **in order to** use time efficiently during medical appointments.* |

### Data from the Real World

The 10 most common verbs that follow *in order to* are (in order of frequency):

*be, make, get, obtain, keep, determine, avoid, see, protect, provide*

*Why can't we email our doctor **in order to make** an appointment?*

---

The 10 most common verbs that follow *so as to* are (in order of frequency):

*avoid, be, make, provide, have, create, form, maintain, preserve, give*

*Ari made his next appointment before he left the doctor's office **so as to avoid** having to do it later.*

# Grammar Application

## **Exercise 2.1** Adverb Clauses and Infinitives of Purpose

Read the magazine article about how a mother used the Internet to diagnose a disease. Underline seven more examples of adverb clauses and infinitives of purpose.

Before the invention of the Internet, people would visit their doctors in order to find out what was wrong with them. These days, when people begin to feel ill, they often turn to the Internet to diagnose themselves. Many medical professionals agree that self-diagnosis by the Internet can often cause unnecessary and unwarranted fears. However, once in a while, the patient's hunches are correct.

Take the case of Alison Chambers. Alison has a 10-year-old son named Miles. When Miles was about two years old, he began getting fevers on a regular basis. She took him to a doctor to get help, and her doctor told her that children often get fevers and it was nothing to worry about. The doctor told Alison that Miles should stay home from day care when other children were ill so as not to get sick. He also said that Miles should wash his hands often so that he would not pick up other children's germs as readily. Although Alison was very careful to follow the doctor's advice, Miles continued to get a fever about once a month. She took Miles to three more doctors so that she could get other opinions, but they all agreed with her doctor's diagnosis.

Alison began to get very frustrated and started researching Miles's symptoms online so as to find out some information for herself. She read about a rare disease whose symptoms sounded like Miles's symptoms. She visited Miles's doctor to ask his opinion. He thought it was unlikely that Miles had the disease, but he agreed to test him for it. The test showed that Miles did have the rare disease. Alison was scared but relieved to know what was wrong with her son. Miles received treatment and stopped getting fevers soon after. It can be dangerous to rely on the Internet for medical information, but in Alison and Miles's case, it paid off.

### **Exercise 2.2** More Adverb Clauses and Infinitives of Purpose

**A** Listen to the podcast interview about using digital tools for health. Then write answers to the questions using adverb clauses of purpose and infinitives of purpose.

1 Why did Cindy interview people?

*Cindy interviewed people to understand how they used digital tools to monitor and improve their health.*

2 Why did a writer for the *New York Times* use Twitter?

3 Why does Pam use an app to take pictures of her food?

4 Why does Pam use a running app?

5 Why do people need to commit to using digital resources?

6 Why do we need to arrive at the doctor's office armed with knowledge?

7 Why might doctors have to change their relationships with patients?

8 Why does Jeff want Cindy to tell one more piece of advice?

**B** Pair Work With a partner discuss the apps that people used in the interview. Would they work for you? Why or why not? Which app seemed the most helpful to you? Why? What other apps have you heard about to improve health or break bad habits? What kind of app would you invent to improve your health and your life?

*I liked the app that calculated calories based on pictures. I'd use it with my boyfriend so that I could persuade him to make better choices too. I don't run, but I'd like an app to motivate me and to remind me of my goals. I'd love someone to invent an app that I could easily use to describe symptoms and conditions in English so as to make it easier to communicate with doctors.*

# 3 Reducing Adverb Clauses to Phrases

## Grammar Presentation

| | |
|---|---|
| You can reduce adverb clauses to adverb phrases. The adverb phrase modifies the subject of the main clause. Adverb phrases can describe problems and solutions. | *Sometimes patients become frightened* ***when they read symptoms online****.*<br>→ *Sometimes patients become frightened* ***when reading symptoms online****.* |

### 3.1 Adverb Phrases

| | |
|---|---|
| **A** You can reduce adverb clauses to phrases when they begin with *when, while, before,* and *after* and when the subject of the main clause and the adverb clause are the same. | ADVERB CLAUSE<br>*Joanna tried various home remedies* ***before she saw the doctor****.*<br>ADVERB PHRASE<br>*Joanna tried various home remedies* ***before seeing the doctor****.* |
| **B** If a clause contains a present progressive or past progressive verb, you can reduce the adverb clause by deleting the subject and the form of *be*. | ***When I am dieting****, I never eat sugar or red meat.*<br>***When dieting****, I never eat sugar or red meat.*<br>***While Tran was searching*** *the Internet, he found positive reviews about his doctor.*<br>***While searching*** *the Internet, Tran found positive reviews about his doctor.* |
| **C** If a clause contains a simple present or simple past verb, delete the subject and change the verb form to the *-ing* form. | ***Before they see*** *a doctor, many patients use the Internet to find information about their symptoms.*<br>***Before seeing*** *a doctor for an appointment, many patients use the Internet to find information about their symptoms.*<br>*In the past* ***before they saw*** *a doctor, people would ask for advice from family and friends.*<br>*In the past* ***before seeing*** *a doctor, people would ask for advice from family and friends.* |
| **D** If a clause contains a verb in the present perfect or past perfect, delete the subject of the adverb clause and change *have* or *had* to *having.* | ***After you've read*** *multiple articles online, you'll have a better understanding of your doctor's diagnosis.* ***After having read*** *multiple articles online, you'll have a better understanding of your doctor's diagnosis.*<br>***After he'd read*** *multiple articles online, he had a better understanding of his doctor's diagnosis.*<br>***After having read*** *multiple articles online, he had a better understanding of his doctor's diagnosis.* |

# Grammar Application

## Exercise 3.1 Reducing Adverb Clauses

**A** Complete the excerpt from a blog entry for evaluating the information in health-related websites. Reduce each adverb clause to an adverb phrase. Remember to use commas.

A few months back, I was plagued with headaches and fatigue.
*Before going to the doctor,* (1 before I went to the doctor) I decided to read up on possible diagnoses. ______ (2 after I'd visited a few sites) I was frantic. My long list of ailments included migraines, Lyme disease, and one deadly disease. ______ (3 while she was looking at the list) my wife kept shaking her head and frowning. She asked me where I found the information. I didn't remember. Then she emailed a friend of hers who is a nurse practitioner and we got the following advice on how to use the Web wisely for research:

- ______ (4 when you do research) look for websites with the domains .gov and .edu, which tend to be more credible.
- Also, ______ (5 when you consider which websites to go to) look for websites that are operated by hospitals, universities, and recognized medical institutions.
- ______ (6 after you've read an article that interests you) search for the name of the author (if there is one) to find out his / her credentials.
- Be extra critical ______ (7 when you visit websites that try to sell you products). A lot of advertising might mean that the objective of the website is really to sell merchandise.
- ______ (8 after you collect all the information) make a list of questions about it to ask your doctor.
- ______ (9 after you've been diagnosed) if something doesn't feel right, you should tell your doctor and continue your research because you never know when you'll come across important new therapies and medicines for you and your doctor to discuss.

**B** Pair Work **With a partner, explain how you or someone you know uses the Internet for medical or health purposes. Use adverb phrases.**

*After hearing or reading about some new research on health that I'm interested in, I'll look it up on the Internet and find out more about it. While searching, I try to go to a variety of sites so that I can find out a few opinions of the information.*

## Exercise 3.2 Adverb Phrases

Combine each pair of sentences about online support groups. Use the appropriate adverb phrase with *when*, *while*, *before*, and *after*, depending on the sequence of the actions.

| | FIRST ACTION | SECOND ACTION | SIMULTANEOUS ACTIONS |
|---|---|---|---|
| 1 | Some people discover they have a serious illness. | Some people find help through online support groups. | |
| 2 | | | ■ People go through treatment.<br>■ People find it comforting to communicate with others diagnosed with their disease. |
| 3 | People talk with others about their illness. | People don't feel so alone. | |
| 4 | People should read the messages that members post to make sure the group is supportive. | People choose a group to join. | |
| 5 | | | ■ Leaders monitor members' messages.<br>■ Leaders should encourage positive participation. |
| 6 | Members notice that a member is going through a difficult time. | The members of good groups offer encouragement and advice. | |
| 7 | Members of good groups receive the support they asked for. | Members of good groups stay with the group and give others support. | |

1 *After discovering they have an illness, some people find help through online support groups.*

2 ______________________________

3 ______________________________

4 ______________________________

5 ______________________________

6 ______________________________

7 ______________________________

# 4 Common Vocabulary to Describe Problems and Solutions

## Vocabulary Presentation

There are several common words and phrases that are useful in problem–solution writing.

***The most important problem is** finding the right doctor to treat your illness.*

***There are several ways to address the problem of** cyberchondria.*

***One solution for** cyberchondria **would be to** avoid unreliable websites.*

### 4.1 Phrases to Introduce Problems

Use the following phrases to introduce a problem:

*The key/main/primary/most important problem is _____ .*

*A/The secondary issue/problem is _____ .*

*While _____ are issues/problems/factors, the most important/urgent/pressing/critical issue/problem is _____ .*

*For doctors, **the main problem is** the extra time they spend arguing with ill-informed patients.*

***A secondary issue is** the patients' increased stress.*

***While** wasted time and patient stress **are factors, the most urgent issue is** misinformation on the Internet.*

### 4.2 Phrases to Introduce Solutions

**A** Use the following phrases to introduce solutions:

*The solution to the problem lies in _____ .*

*There are several ways to address the problem of _____ .*

*One solution to/for _____ would be to _____ .*

*The problem of _____ can be solved by _____ .*

*_____ is a possible solution to the problem of _____ .*

***The solution to the problem lies in** medical websites, doctors, and patients.*

***There are several ways to address the problem of** cyberchondria.*

***One solution to** cyberchondria **would be to** educate patients.*

***The problem of** cyberchondria **can be solved by** reorganizing information on medical websites.*

*Educating patients **is a possible solution to the problem of** cyberchondria.*

**B** Use the following phrases to make recommendations for possible solutions:

*is needed*

*is necessary*

*should be/may be/might be/must be considered*

*A definite decision by the government **is needed**.*

*Based on the results, it **will be necessary** to make changes to the treatment.*

*An individual's caloric needs **should be considered** before starting any diet.*

# Vocabulary Application

## **Exercise 4.1** Phrases to Introduce Problems and Solutions

Complete the sentences about the patient–doctor relationship using phrases to introduce problems and solutions.

| | | |
|---|---|---|
| a secondary issue | one solution for the first problem | the problem of |
| can be solved by | ~~the most important problem~~ | |

*The most important problem* (1) when communicating with doctors is that sometimes they don't understand exactly what a patient is feeling. ______ (2) is the fact that patients don't always ask the right questions. ______ (3) would be to require doctors to use checklists when discussing symptoms so that there is more discussion of feelings. ______ (4) asking the right questions ______ (5) providing patients with frequently asked questions about their illness to help them come up with questions.

| | |
|---|---|
| are issues | there are several ways to address the problem of |
| is necessary | while |
| the most urgent issue is | |

The patient–doctor relationship has changed in recent years and new issues have arisen. Patients come to appointments with a great deal of information and strong opinions. Doctors can feel uncomfortable with their patients' new assertiveness, and patients can feel mistrustful and even skeptical of their doctor's opinions. ______ (6) patients' mistrust and skepticism ______ (7), ______ (8) the antagonistic relationship that can develop. ______ (9) antagonism. One way is for doctors to help their patients use the Internet more discerningly and discuss findings. In sum, a change in the patient–doctor relationship ______ (10) in order to adapt to the current information age.

## **Exercise 4.2** Phrases to Introduce Problems and Solutions

**A** Pair Work **With a partner, rank the three problems below that doctors have with patients from 1 (the most serious) to 3 (the least serious).**

- Some patients believe inaccurate information.
- Some patients don't follow advice.
- Some patients are unwilling to admit the seriousness of their health issues.

**Next, decide on a possible solution for doctors to each problem. Use the phrases below or others in Chart 4.2 on page 177. Then share your ideas with another pair.**

| | |
|---|---|
| *The primary issue with patients is . . .* | *One solution to the problem might be . . .* |
| *The secondary issue with patients is . . .* | *. . . is a possible solution to the problem of . . .* |
| *The last issue with patients is . . .* | *The problem of . . . can be solved by . . .* |

*In my opinion, the primary issue with patients is that they don't follow their doctor's advice. I think that one solution to the problem might be for doctors to ask the patient to follow up and call after a week or two to report how he or she is doing. This will motivate the patient to follow the advice and avoid getting sicker.*

**B** Group Work **Work with a group and choose one of the problems concerning health issues below. Brainstorm possible solutions to the problem. Write one sentence describing the problem and three to four sentences describing possible solutions. Use the common phrases to introduce problems and solutions. Present your ideas to the class.**

- You are sick and you disagree with your doctor's diagnosis.
- You have insomnia.
- You have a friend who is a cyberchondriac.
- Present a different problem that your teacher approves.

*There are many things you can do if you feel sick and you disagree with your doctor's diagnosis. One solution would be to . . .*

# 5 Avoid Common Mistakes ⚠

**1** **Remember that *for example* is always singular, even when several examples follow.**

*There are many solutions to the problem of cyberchondria. For ~~examples~~ example, using credible websites or avoiding the Internet altogether are ways to solve cyberchondria.*

**2** **Remember that the phrase *The problem of* is not followed by *the*.**

*The problem of ~~the~~ Internet addiction can be solved by limiting time spent online.*

**3** **Remember not to confuse *so that* (to express purpose) and *so* (to express result). Do not use a comma before *so that*.**

*The physician provided her patients with a list of credible medical ~~websites, so~~ websites so that they would stop arguing with her about their symptoms.* (purpose)

*The patient stopped consulting medical ~~websites so that~~ websites, so he argued much less with his physician.* (result)

# Editing Task

**Find and correct eight more mistakes in the body paragraph from an essay on the problem of cyberchondria.**

Cyberchondria

A solution to the problem of ~~the~~ cyberchondria is to help individuals become informed Internet users. The Internet can be a useful source of information, but only if people use it wisely. Individuals need to know how to evaluate search results, so they can avoid misleading information. For examples, a website may be out of date, or it may not be published by a credible medical source. Users should look for a date somewhere on the site, so they know that content is updated regularly. The solution to the problem of the unreliable medical websites is to establish the validity of sites. For examples, users should avoid sites with URLs ending in ".com" and sites that do not have scientific or medical sponsors. A commercial website that looks like a medical source may actually be a business selling products. However, medical sites with URLs ending in ".gov" or ".edu" tend to have credible content so that users can be more confident of the information they contain. Physicians can also help solve the problem of the cyberchondria by directing their patients to their own preferred sites. This will reduce patient anxiety and frustration, so physicians can use their consultation time more productively.

UNIT 16

# Problem–Solution 4: *It* Constructions; Transition Words to Indicate Steps of a Solution

## Leading a Healthy Life

## 1 Grammar in the Real World

You will read an essay about changes that people can make in their lives in order to have a healthier lifestyle. In this problem–solution essay, the writer describes the process of implementing the solutions.

**A** Before You Read **What are some things a person can do in order to live a healthy life? Why is it sometimes difficult in our modern world to do what is necessary to live a healthy life? Read the essay. What solutions to this problem does the writer suggest?**

**B** Comprehension Check **Answer the questions.**

1 According to the essay, what is the main reason that people are prevented from leading a healthy life?

2 What are some of the beliefs that people have when it comes to healthy eating and exercising?

3 Do you think the writer would think that you have a healthy lifestyle? Why or why not?

**C** Notice **Follow the instructions below to help you notice how the writer uses *it* constructions:**

1 Reread the sentence with the word *it* on lines 7–9 in the first paragraph and the sentence with the word *it* on lines 20–22. One *it* refers to a previously mentioned noun, but the other one doesn't. Which one doesn't refer to a previously mentioned noun?

2 Reread the sentence on lines 31–34 with the word *it*. The writer uses the passive. Does the use of the passive and *it* make the sentence more subjective or objective?

3 Reread the sentence on lines 56–57 that begins with "On the contrary, … " Notice how the writer uses the word *it* to introduce his proposal. What adjective does the writer use after *it* to make the proposal stronger?

# Leading a HEALTHY Life

In the last few decades, the average person's life has become increasingly unhealthy. The rules of modern society seem to have forced many into a stressful lifestyle. As individuals strive to meet the demands of their lives, they often overlook the multiple sources of stress and unhealthiness in their lives. Even though the task is challenging, it is not impossible to make some changes that can lead to a healthier lifestyle.

Many factors can contribute to creating tension in everyday life. For most people, a busy work schedule usually prevents them from dedicating time to other stress-relieving activities. Lack of exercise and not enough sleep are only two of the consequences of such a lifestyle. Also, as time is consumed by work-related responsibilities, individuals tend to have less time to eat well. Many people end up eating fast food as a strategy to save time, which adds to unhealthy practices.

Contrary to what many people may think, living a healthy life does not have to be difficult; nor does it have to be time-consuming. In terms of eating habits, a few changes can go a long way. First, individuals need to be committed to the challenge. Next, in order to have a healthier diet, they should buy low-calorie and low-fat foods that are easy to cook, such as broccoli, cauliflower, carrots, chicken, and fish. Then they can cook more quantities of food over the weekend and freeze the leftovers in small containers so that the food can be consumed throughout the week. It has been argued that freezing the food destroys some of the nutrients. This may be true. However, this solution is certainly better than the fast-food option.

Just as with eating habits, it is a common belief that exercising takes away many hours of an average person's week. However, first, it is important to find an activity that is enjoyable, such as playing a sport or hiking. Even simple activities, like taking the stairs, raking leaves, or sweeping the floor, contribute to keeping someone active. Next, after finding an enjoyable activity, people need to commit to it. This means that people need to exercise regularly and make it part of their routine, just like brushing their teeth or combing their hair. Many people will agree that their level of stress tends to decrease once exercising becomes part of their daily lives.

Maintaining a healthy lifestyle does not have to be challenging but can be accomplished with a series of small steps. Setting a few reachable goals can make a huge difference. Drastic diets, fasting,[1] or very demanding exercise routines are not that likely to generate permanent improvements. On the contrary, it is essential to take a holistic approach[2] to good health. Such an approach starts with healthy food and regular exercise. When these items are part of someone's life, lack of time becomes just an excuse for not adopting a healthier lifestyle.

---

[1]**fasting:** intentionally eating no food for a long period of time

[2]**holistic approach:** a way of solving a health problem by looking at the social, psychological, and physical aspects of the problem

# 2 *It* Constructions

## Grammar Presentation

| | |
|---|---|
| *It* constructions are commonly used in academic writing to make the text more impersonal and objective. In problem–solution writing, *it* constructions are often used when a solution to a problem is being proposed and evaluated. | ***It is important to*** *find an exercise that is enjoyable, such as playing a sport or hiking.*<br>***It has been argued that*** *freezing the food destroys some of the nutrients.* |

### 2.1 *It* Constructions

| | |
|---|---|
| **A** *It* constructions are formed in the following ways:<br>*it* + *be* + adjective + *that* clause<br>*it* + *be* + adjective + infinitive<br>*It* is not the subject. To provide a specific subject with infinitives, you can add *for* + noun phrase to the sentence. | ***It is true that*** *people who exercise usually have more energy than people who do not.*<br>***It is difficult to find*** *time to exercise every day.*<br>***It is difficult*** *for many adults* ***to find time*** *to exercise every day.* |
| **B** *Appear* and *seem* are verbs commonly used in *it* constructions. They are followed by a *that clause*:<br>*it* + *appears/seems* + *that* clause<br>*it* + *appears/seems* + *adjective* + *that* clause<br>*Appear* and *seem* are used when the writer is almost certain, but not completely certain of the truth of the statement. | ***It appears*** *that researchers have made the connection between exercise and mental health.*<br>***It seems that*** *people who eat healthier are frequently in a good mood.*<br>***It appears unlikely that*** *the government will issue new guidelines for healthy eating within the year.* |
| **C** You can use *it* constructions with a modal:<br>*may, might, could*<br>These modals soften claims that follow them. | ***It may be true that*** *people who eat healthier are always in a good mood.*<br>***It might seem that*** *people are not losing weight when they start a new diet program.*<br>***It could be*** *that genetics plays the main role in obesity.* |

**Data from the Real World**

| | |
|---|---|
| Adjectives that frequently occur after *It is* to show evaluation are (in order of frequency): *important to, clear that, difficult to, possible that, possible to, necessary to, better to, impossible that, likely that, true that, essential to, common to, doubtful that, easy to, evident that, unlikely that* | ***It is important to eat*** *a healthy diet and exercise every day.* |
| *It seems* is twice as common as *It appears.* Adjectives that frequently occur after *It seems* are: *likely, unlikely, clear, possible, reasonable, obvious, certain, impossible, logical, probable* | ***It seems reasonable that*** *many people would make the connection between nutrition and physical health.* |
| Adjectives that frequently occur after *It appears* are: *possible, unlikely, plausible* | ***It appears possible that*** *health insurance companies will provide more guidance on nutrition issues.* |

## 2.2 *It* Constructions in the Passive

| | |
|---|---|
| You can use *it* constructions in the passive with reporting verbs. This allows the writer to emphasize the idea without stating (or restating) the source. | ***It has generally been accepted*** *that people who exercise frequently have more energy.*<br>***It was found*** *that certain fruits and vegetables can help with weight loss.* |

**Data from the Real World**

| | |
|---|---|
| Verbs that frequently occur in *it* + the passive form of the present perfect are: *shown, suggested, reported, proposed, demonstrated, determined, linked, observed, documented, called, estimated, used, recognized, known, found, argued, applied, approved, associated* | ***It has been shown*** *that drastic diets are less likely to generate permanent health improvements.* |
| Modals that frequently occur with passive *it* constructions are: *can, should, could,* and *must* | ***It can be argued that*** *schools should be more involved in teaching about healthy living.*<br>Note: *Will, would,* and *shall* are very infrequent in passive *it* constructions. |

## 2.3 Using Adjectives in *It* Constructions

| | |
|---|---|
| **A** In problem–solution writing, certain adjectives can be used with *it* constructions to emphasize the importance of a problem and the effectiveness of the solution.<br>These adjectives include:<br>*accepted, certain, clear, evident, important, indisputable, obvious* | ***It is clear*** *that exercising is good for children.*<br>*From the results of the study,* ***it is obvious*** *that children are healthier if they watch only one hour of TV a day.* |
| **B** Use the following adjectives to show the strength of the ideas or claims:<br>To show that something is certain, use *accepted, certain, indisputable,* or *true.* | ***It is true*** *that children are heavier, but the causes are not clear.* |
| To show that something is possible, use *likely* or *possible.* | ***It is likely*** *that genes also play a big role in health.* |
| To show that something is not likely, use *unlikely* or *unusual.* | ***It appears unlikely*** *that cell phone use will decrease.* |
| To show that something is not possible, use *impossible.* | ***It is impossible*** *to address health without including exercise.* |
| Use these adjectives to show the degree of difficulty:<br>*difficult, easy, hard* | ***It is difficult*** *to imagine restaurants eliminating desserts.* |
| Use these adjectives to show the writer's perspective:<br>*clear, curious, evident, important, obvious, strange* | ***It seems curious*** *that fruit and vegetables are not emphasized.*<br>***It is evident*** *that people's lifestyles contribute to their stress.* |

## 2.4 Using *It* Constructions

| | |
|---|---|
| You can use an *it* construction instead of a statement that directly attributes the idea to someone.<br>Use *it* constructions as a more formal way of presenting information. | STATEMENT<br>***Doctors and health officials agree that*** *people should exercise at least three times a week.*<br>*IT* CONSTRUCTION<br>***It is important*** *to exercise at least three times a week.*<br>INFORMAL: ***She argued that*** *exercising is very time consuming.*<br>MORE FORMAL: ***It has been argued*** *that exercising is very time consuming.* |

# Grammar Application

## Exercise 2.1 *It* Constructions

**A** Choose the appropriate adjective to describe the idea in each sentence about health information. Then complete the new sentence with an *it* construction with the adjective. Use *that* or an infinitive. Use *for* and *not* where necessary.

1 People need to find time to prepare a healthy dinner every night.
a difficult (b important) c unusual

*It is important for people to find time to prepare a healthy dinner every night.*

2 Everyone can eat good food by planning meals ahead of time.
a accepted b likely c easy

______________________________

3 Young people don't usually pay attention to their dietary habits.
a possible b impossible c unusual

______________________________

4 There is a good chance that meditation or yoga can reduce stress.
a possible b unlikely c obvious

______________________________

5 Doctors agree that people should focus on their exercise and eating habits.
a clear b unlikely c strange

______________________________

6 There is no doubt that moderate exercise results in fewer diseases such as diabetes.
a unlikely b indisputable c strange

______________________________

7 There is a good chance that working out regularly improves mood.
a may be impossible b could be obvious c might be true

______________________________

8 We can't really say why some people like to exercise and some don't.
a evident b impossible c reasonable

______________________________

9 There is little evidence that regular exercise can cause physical harm.

a unlikely  b impossible  c important

______________________________

10 Everyone knows that good support systems have a positive impact on one's health.

a curious  b likely  c evident

______________________________

**B** Pair Work **Think of four ideas that you have heard that have a positive or negative impact on health. Discuss them with a partner and give your opinion of the ideas. Then share them with another pair. Include statements that state something is certain, possible, not possible, or difficult.**

*From what we have read, it is accepted that vitamins can be beneficial for one's health. I personally don't think that people need vitamins if they eat well. I have also read that it appears unlikely that cell phone use is harmful to one's health. No one's really sure about this, though.*

## Exercise 2.2 Passive *It* Constructions

**A** **Unscramble the sentences that compare medical beliefs today with medical beliefs in the past in the United States.**

1 a your health / accepted / cigarettes / bad for / it is / that / are

*It is accepted that cigarettes are bad for your health.*

b the body / that tobacco / believed / was / it was / good for / in the 60s,

______________________________

c thought / a person's life / and were good for / that cigarettes / might lengthen / years ago, / it was / his or her teeth

______________________________

2 a been recently / that sugar / one's health / it has / is bad for / shown

______________________________

b a good source / argued / of energy for children / it was / that sugar was / years ago,

______________________________

3 a generally been / is bad for children / accepted / it has / that watching / too much television / now,

______________________________

b suggested / that too much / it / from doing physical activities / has been / television keeps children

______________________________

c children's grades / that watching television / could improve / it was / believed / in the 60s,

______________________________

**B** Group Work **As a group, compare medical beliefs of today with medical beliefs in the past. Share your ideas using passive *it* constructions.**

*It was once accepted that eggs were one of the causes of high cholesterol, but I think that it is evident from current research that they are not a primary cause.*

# 3 Common Transition Words to Indicate Steps of a Solution

## Vocabulary Presentation

| | |
|---|---|
| Transition words and phrases are commonly used to guide readers through the steps in a solution or process. | ***First***, *it is important for people to find an activity that is enjoyable, such as playing a sport or hiking.* ***Next***, *they need to commit to doing it.* |

### 3.1 Using Transition Words to Indicate Steps of a Solution

| | |
|---|---|
| **A** Use transition words such as *first* and *to begin* to introduce the first step of a proposed solution. Use a comma after them when they appear at the beginning of the sentence. | ***First,*** *one needs to acknowledge that a problem exists.*<br><br>***To begin***, *put the problem into words.* |
| **B** Use *after that, following that, next, second, third, subsequently*, and *then* to introduce the next steps.<br><br>Use *at the same time* to introduce a step that happens or needs to happen at the same time. | ***Following that***, *ways to address specific aspects of the problem should be developed.*<br><br>***Next***, *key terms should be clearly defined.*<br><br>***At the same time***, *the scope and effects of the problem need to be identified.* |
| **C** Use *finally, in the end, last*, and *lastly* to conclude the steps. | ***Finally***, *the set of strategies should be implemented.* |
| **D** You can also place transition words such as *next* and *then* in the middle of a sentence, before the verb.<br><br>You can also use *next* at the end of a sentence. | *The scope and effects of the problem* ***then*** *need to be identified.*<br><br>*The people associated with the problem need to be contacted* ***next***. |

## 3.1 Using Transition Words to Indicate Steps of a Solution *(continued)*

| | |
|---|---|
| **E** You can also use phrases like *the first step*, *the second step*, *the third step*, and so forth, to indicate steps of a solution. These phrases are usually followed by *be* + infinitive. | ***First***, *one needs to acknowledge that a problem exists.*<br>***The first step is to acknowledge*** *that a problem exists.* |

## 3.2 Using Transition Words in Problem–Solution Writing

| | |
|---|---|
| Use transition words to link the steps of a solution. This makes writing more cohesive. | ***First***, *one needs to acknowledge that a problem exists. The scope and effects of the problem* ***then*** *need to be identified.* ***Next***, *key terms and ideas should be clearly defined.* ***Following that***, *ways to address specific aspects of the problem should be developed.* ***Finally***, *the set of strategies should be implemented.* |

# Vocabulary Application

### Exercise 3.1 Transition Words to Indicate Steps of a Solution

**A** Listen to part of a lecture about how companies can address specific health problems that occur on the job. Complete the steps of the solution, using the transition words you hear to identify the steps.

**Notes:**

*Problem:* For data-entry workers, sitting at a computer for hours every day leads to weight gain, back pain, neck pain, and wrist pain.

*Solution:* Set up a plan to address the specific problems that workers have.

***Steps:***

1 *The first step is to* identify *the health issues*.

2 ______________________ determine ______________________.

3 ______________________ implement ______________________.

4 ______________________ evaluate ______________________.

**B** Pair Work **Work with a partner and discuss one of the problems below. Using A as a model, write the problem, the solution, and possible steps for the solution. Include at least three transition words. When you have finished, report your problem and solutions to the class.**

- Smokers who want to give up smoking
- Students who don't study enough
- People who worry too much

## **Exercise 3.2** More Transition Words to Indicate Steps of a Solution

**Read the steps below about ways to make health a focus in your life. Number the sentences in the correct order.**

_____ Next, keep a journal for a week and write down what you eat every day and how you spend your time.

_____ At the same time, substitute at least one hour of the time that you spent watching TV or doing some other unnecessary activity with one hour of exercise. Do this for 21 days because some experts claim that it takes 21 days to make or break a habit.

__1__ To begin, acknowledge that you need to focus on your health.

_____ Subsequently, look at your journal and circle the unhealthy foods that you ate during the week.

_____ At the same time, circle the things that you did during the week that were unnecessary or could be cut down. For example, did you spend your lunch break surfing online, or did you watch three hours of TV after dinner?

_____ Finally, evaluate how you feel after three weeks of eating better and exercising one hour a day. You should feel great and have more energy.

_____ Also, hopefully you'll have created a new, healthy habit for yourself!

_____ After you examine your journal, substitute each unhealthy food with a healthy food like fruit, vegetables, or lean proteins.

# 4 Avoid Common Mistakes

**1 Remember to use *It is important to* and not *It is import to* or *It is importand to*.**

It is ~~import~~ important to admit that the problem exists.

It is ~~importand~~ important to find an exercise routine that is convenient.

**2 Remember to use *to* or *for* after *impossible*.**

*For many people, it is impossible* ^to *find the time for exercise.*

*It is impossible* ^for *some people to slow down and relax.*

**3 Remember to use *then, not than,* when introducing next steps.**

First, one needs to identify the sources of the stress. ~~Than~~ Then, ways to eliminate them should be considered.

# Editing Task

**Find and correct six more mistakes in the body paragraph from an essay on ways to improve health.**

It is ~~importand~~ *important* to get an adequate amount of sleep in order to maintain a healthy lifestyle. For many people, it is almost impossible get a good night's sleep. Stress and the demands of work have a tremendous effect on one's ability to sleep. Lack of sleep can also result from certain lifestyle habits. However, it is virtually impossible people to function well without adequate sleep. Studies have shown that lack of sleep can lead to a variety of physical and emotional problems. Therefore, it is import to get at least seven to eight hours of sleep at night because getting the recommended amount of sleep means optimal health and energy, more acute mental faculties, and a better memory. It also means getting sick less and being better able to deal with the stresses and strains of everyday life. Although at times it may seem impossible get enough sleep, there are a few simple strategies for improving one's chances. First, one needs to determine the causes of sleeplessness, such as lack of exercise or consuming too much caffeine. Than, one needs to commit to making a few small lifestyle changes. People who have difficulty sleeping should increase their daily exercise, but not exercise too late in the day. They should avoid consuming too much caffeine and eating close to bedtime. It is also importand to have a regular bedtime and to get the same number of hours of sleep each night. These small changes to one's daily routine can lead to a better night's sleep and improved health.

UNIT 17

# Summary–Response: Past Unreal Conditionals; Phrases Used in Summary–Response Writing

## Privacy in the Digital Age

## 1 Grammar in the Real World

You will read an article that discusses the issue of privacy and computers. You will then read an essay that summarizes and responds to the article.

**A** Before You Read **What are some possible dangers of surfing the Internet? What can people do to protect themselves from these dangers? Read the article. Then read the response to the article below it. What do the two writers suggest as ways Internet users can protect themselves?**

**B** Comprehension Check **Answer these questions.**

1 What two suggestions does the writer of "Privacy and Computers" make for being safe on the Internet?

2 What important issues does the summary–response writer believe are missing from the original article?

3 What other privacy concerns do you have concerning the use of your personal information? What do you do to keep your information safe?

**C** Notice **Follow the instructions to notice how the author of "Privacy and Computers" uses unreal conditionals.**

1 Reread the second paragraph of the article. What happened to the people who went on vacation? Underline the unreal conditional on lines 22–24. How does using an unreal conditional help the writer?

2 Reread the third paragraph of the article. What happened to the man who bought merchandise on a website that did not have a security padlock? Underline the unreal conditional on lines 38–40. How does using an unreal conditional help the writer?

3 Reread the last paragraph of the article. Find the sentence with the *if* clause. Compare this sentence with the sentence with the *if* clause in 2. Which one refers to an imagined past result? Which one refers to an imagined present result? What do you notice about the forms of the verbs?

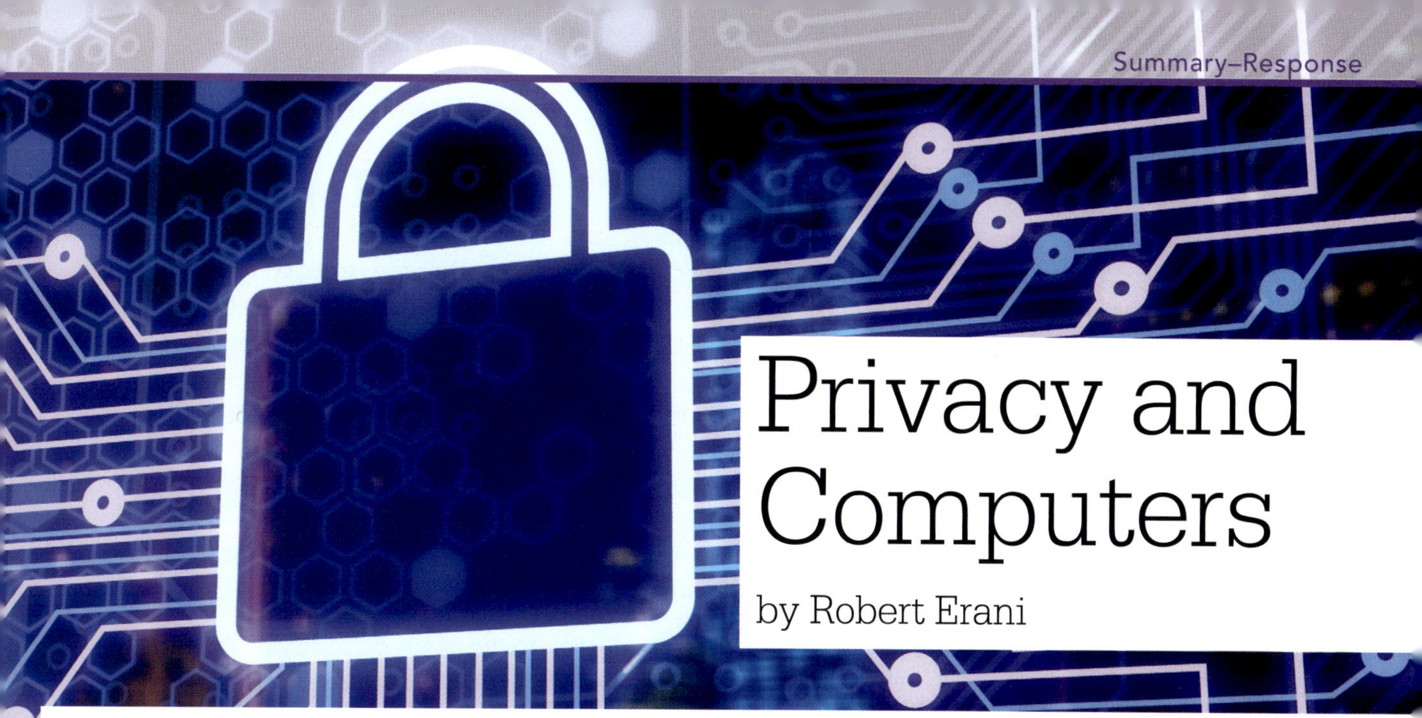

# Privacy and Computers

by Robert Erani

In an era of online social media, people can announce any event to their virtual network of friends, family, and acquaintances within moments. From birthday celebrations to baby pictures, friends get news about each other from texts, tweets, or social networks. In addition, many people use credit cards to purchase products and complete numerous online forms with personal information for a variety of purposes. As a result, personal information is ending up in the hands of other people. There are critics who are concerned by the lack of privacy. Despite such concerns, by following a few common-sense measures, people can use the Internet enjoyably and safely.

In our fast-paced world, social networking sites are, for many people, an important way to keep up with friends and family. The issue now is how open one should be with sharing private information since the information could be stolen by criminals. For example, some people have had their homes broken into because they had posted the details of their vacation online. If they had not posted those details, the thieves would not have known that they had gone away. One way to reduce the risk of this happening is to activate the privacy controls on social networking sites and smartphones. In other words, think about who will see your information and consider how they might use it.

Another important step is to shop only on secure websites so that one's accounts, passwords, and financial records are protected. Some experts recommend that people should treat their online information like they would treat the contents of their wallets. For example, a man bought merchandise on a website that did not have a security padlock, and as a result of this transaction, his bank accounts were emptied. If he had paid attention to the security on the site, he would not have lost his money. However, it appears that people are becoming more aware of the risks of fraud and taking steps to avoid them since the total percentage of incidences of fraud have remained steady. It may be that people who have grown up using the Internet understand its risks as well as its strengths.

The ease of sharing information provides opportunities for crimes and abuses. While it may be impossible to entirely eliminate the risks, if people followed reasonable guidelines to protect important data, they could greatly reduce these risks. The benefits of being able to do such things as bank online, keep medical records updated almost instantly, and share the thrills both big and small of everyday life with friends outweigh these concerns.

## Summary–Response Essay on "Privacy and Computers"

Robert Erani, in the article "Privacy and Computers," explains the issues concerning the sharing of personal information online. According to Erani, one area of concern is that people may sometime share details of their lives online without thinking about the consequences. As the author points out, "The issue now is how open one should be with sharing private information since the information could be stolen by criminals" (para. 2). The author describes a situation in which people were robbed after revealing their vacation plans online. The author further states how important it is for consumers to protect their personal information when they purchase products online. Erani concludes the article by stating that, despite the concerns about privacy, one can still use online services safely by using common sense and privacy controls.

In sum, the author provides a general introduction to the issues of privacy online and offers some advice on how to avoid problems. I agree that insecure websites are a problem, but I disagree with the author's contention that people who have grown up using the Internet are more savvy about using it. Hackers and scammers continue to come up with more sophisticated and convincing schemes. The consumer needs to constantly be wary of them. In addition, the article fails to address the more controversial issues concerning the consequences of posting information regarding health issues, job dissatisfaction, or even political views. This is an oversight because these issues impact individuals every day. It is becoming increasingly common for employers, for instance, to view the online profiles of potential employees as part of their selection process. Despite these shortcomings, the author rightly states that the concern around privacy issues seems to be an acceptable exchange for many people for the benefits of sharing their lives with others.

# 2 Past Unreal Conditionals

## Grammar Presentation

Past unreal conditionals allow the writer to discuss hypothetical situations – untrue or unreal situations in the past – and the consequences of the situations. Effective academic writers use this form to contrast what happened (the "real") with what was possible but did not happen (the "unreal").

*If the author **had discussed** education in his article, the text **would have been** stronger.*

*If this information **had been taught** years ago, we **would not have had** so many problems.*

## 2.1 Past Unreal Conditionals

| | |
|---|---|
| The past unreal conditional is formed as follows:<br><br>*if* clause (past perfect) + main clause (*would/could/might* + *have* + past participle)<br><br>The *if* clause can come first or last in a sentence. Use a comma when it comes first. | *IF* CLAUSE (PAST PERFECT)<br>***If I had read*** *the privacy policy on the company's website*<br>MAIN CLAUSE (*WOULD/COULD/MIGHT* + *HAVE* + PAST PARTICIPLE)<br>*carefully,* ***I would have avoided*** *the problem.*<br>MAIN CLAUSE *IF* CLAUSE<br>***I would have avoided*** *the problem* ***if I had read*** *the website's privacy policy carefully.* |

## 2.2 Using Past Unreal Conditionals

| | |
|---|---|
| **A** The *if* clause gives the untrue condition in the past. The main clause expresses the imaginary past result. | *IF* CLAUSE: PAST UNREAL CONDITION<br>***If*** *she* ***had used*** *separate accounts for work and personal*<br>MAIN CLAUSE: IMAGINARY PAST RESULT<br>*email, she* ***would have avoided*** *trouble.* (The real situation: She used the same email account for personal and work email. She got into trouble.)<br>UNREAL PAST CONDITION<br>***If*** *he* ***hadn't made*** *his passwords difficult,*<br>IMAGINARY PAST RESULT<br>*the thieves* ***would have been able to access*** *his accounts.*<br>(The real situation: His passwords were difficult. The thieves did not access his accounts.) |
| **B** As with other forms and uses of modals, *would have* expresses a more certain (but still imaginary) past result.<br><br>*Could have* and *might have* express less certain results. | *If I had noticed the lack of security on that website, I* ***wouldn't have ordered*** *merchandise from it.*<br><br>*If I had ordered merchandise from that website, I* ***might have had*** *my information stolen.* |
| **C** Use past unreal conditionals to express regrets about past situations or actions. | *If I* ***had insured*** *my laptop, the insurance company* ***would have reimbursed*** *me when it was stolen.* (I regret that I did not have insurance for my laptop.) |
| **D** Past unreal conditionals can also express an imaginary present result. Use *would/could/might* + the base form of the verb in the main clause. | UNREAL PAST CONDITION<br>*If the author* ***had mentioned*** *his sources,*<br>IMAGINARY PRESENT RESULT<br>*the article* ***would be more*** *compelling.* |

## Grammar Application

### **Exercise 2.1** Past Unreal Conditionals

**Read the story about identify theft. Complete the sentences with the appropriate modal and the correct form of the verb in parentheses. Sometimes more than one answer is possible.**

I know that thieves have ways to steal people's identities online, so I'm always careful about the emails I read and the links that I click on. However, I didn't realize that thieves sometimes go through people's garbage to look for personal information. I *'d have been* (1) (be) more careful if I *'d known* (1) (know) that.

Last year, I put a letter that had my Social Security number on it in the garbage. Normally, I shred important documents, but I was in a hurry that day. If I ________ (2) (not be) in a hurry, I definitely ________ (2) (shred) it. A few days later, there was no money in my checking account. I realized that if someone ________ (3) (take) the letter out of the garbage, he or she ________ (3) (have) my Social Security number now. I knew that if someone ________ (4) (find) my Social Security number, they ________ (4) (have) the ability to access my bank accounts, use my credit cards, and get new credit cards in my name.

By the time I realized that my identity had been stolen, the thief had taken all my money and applied for 10 new credit cards. If I ________ (5) (realize) sooner that a thief had found my Social Security number, I ________ (5) (be) able to stop him or her from using it. The identity theft has caused all kinds of problems for me. I can't get a loan to buy a car, and I can't get a new credit card. If someone ________ (6) (not steal) my identity, I ________ (6) (not have) all these problems now.

I shred all my important documents now before I throw them away. Last week, I told my neighbor what had happened to me. She was going to put some important mail in her garbage without shredding it. She immediately shredded the mail. If I ________ (7) (not warn) her, she ________ (7) (have) the same problems that I do now.

## Exercise 2.2 More Past Unreal Conditionals

**A** Combine the pairs of sentences describing an unfortunate event. Use past unreal conditionals. Sometimes more than one answer is possible.

1 I visited my friend Eric for the weekend. I lost all my credit cards and my cell phone.

*If I hadn't visited my friend Eric for the weekend, I wouldn't have lost all my credit cards and my cell phone.*

2 Eric wasn't ready to go swimming on Saturday morning. I went to the beach alone.

3 Eric wasn't with me. I left my wallet and phone on the beach while I went swimming.

4 I went swimming. Someone stole my credit cards and my phone.

5 I forgot the address of Eric's house. I couldn't find the house.

6 I didn't have my cell phone. I couldn't call Eric.

7 My cell phone wasn't password-protected. The thief was able to use my phone.

8 I had personal information on my cell phone. The thief got my bank account numbers.

9 I also forgot to wear sunscreen. I have a terrible sunburn.

**B** Pair Work **With a partner, take turns describing mistakes you have made and ways that you could have avoided making the mistakes.**

*Someone stole my wallet from my purse at a restaurant last weekend. I'd hung my purse on the back of my chair. If I hadn't put it on the back of my chair, no one would have stolen my wallet. If I had put my purse closer to me, I'd have my wallet now.*

# 3 Common Phrases Used in Summary–Response Writing

## Vocabulary Presentation

| | |
|---|---|
| Good academic writers use phrases appropriate to introducing and identifying ideas in summary–response writing. | *The article* ***provides*** *a thorough introduction to the issues of privacy.*<br>*The author* ***fails to address*** *more controversial concerns.* |

### 3.1 Common Phrases in Summary–Response Writing

| | |
|---|---|
| **A** You can use these common subject + verb combinations to introduce the main idea of a summary. They are listed in order of frequency: | |
| *The article + say, state, note, describe, mention, quote, report …* | ***The article describes*** *the problem of privacy and computers.* |
| *The author + claim, explain, call, say, write, argue, cite, establish, start …* | ***The article mentions*** *ways that education can prevent problems with technology.* |
| *The article* is used much more frequently than *the author* in summary–response statements. | ***The author starts the article by saying that*** *technology is part of everyone's lives.* |
| *Note:* Do not use *believe* or *think* in summary–response statements that begin with the words "*The author …*" | ***The author claims*** *that the experts he interviewed for this article were well known.*<br>NOT *The author ~~thinks~~ that the experts he interviewed for this article were well known.* |
| **B** The common subject + verb combinations in (A) are usually used in the present but sometimes also appear in the simple past or present perfect.<br>(See Unit 14 on reporting verbs.) | ***The article quoted*** *many well-known sources.*<br>***The author has argued*** *that individuals are responsible for protecting their own privacy.* |

### 3.1 Common Phrases in Summary–Response Writing *(continued)*

| | |
|---|---|
| **C** Use these phrases to identify ideas by the author of the original text: | |
| *discuss* | ***The article discusses*** *identity theft in detail.* |
| *go on to say* | ***The article goes on to say*** *that the problem is being addressed.* |
| *further state/explain* | ***The author further states*** *that regulations may be necessary in the future.* |
| *also state* | ***The author also states*** *that consumers need to become proactive on this issue.* |
| *according to the author* | ***According to the author****, the government has an important role in this debate.* |
| **D** Use these phrases to conclude the summary–response: | |
| *In conclusion,* | ***In conclusion****, the author predicts that Internet privacy will become one of the most important issues of the next decade.* |
| *In sum,* | |
| *The author concludes* | |
| *Summing up,* | ***Summing up****, the author calls for people to be cautious when giving their personal information online.* |
| **E** Use these phrases in the response part of summary–response writing to indicate what the author omitted or did not consider: | |
| *fail to address/mention* | *The author* ***fails to address*** *the idea that users are also to blame for identity theft.* |
| *not address/mention* | *The author* ***does/did not mention*** *that we are all responsible for protecting privacy.* |
| *Note:* Phrases that use the first person, such as *In my opinion*, are rare in academic writing. They are more common in informal texts like magazines. | ~~***I think that*** *the author*~~*…* |
| | ~~***In my opinion***~~*, the author could have …* |

# Vocabulary Application

## Exercise 3.1 Summarizing Information

Read the summary of an article about privacy on the Internet. Circle the correct words or phrases to complete the summary.

John M. Eger, Chair of Communications and Public Policy at San Diego State University, addresses / claims the issue of privacy in the Internet age in
(1)

his article "Growing Concerns Over Internet." He starts the article/further states (2) by explaining the historical context of the right to privacy in the United States and cites/describes (3) how in 1928, a Supreme Court decision was made to protect the right to privacy. However, he concludes that/notes that (4) our online lives are today being monitored in ways that most people do not even realize. He then claims/goes on to explain (5) how websites use cookies to follow an Internet user's every move. The author acknowledges that/thinks that (6) some sharing of information may provide us with advertisements for things that may be beneficial to us, but then he argues that/sums up that (7) data collectors might collect and share health and financial information, and even connect our names to our data. In addition, according to the article,/the article quotes (8) there are currently no laws that adequately protect our right to privacy. Then, while the author goes on to show/concludes (9) by saying that we need to do something about this problem, he does not mention at all/further states (10) what we can do to protect ourselves.

## **Exercise 3.2** More Summarizing Information

Read the sentences below. Then listen to two people talk about an article on Internet passwords. Make notes as you listen. Listen again and complete the sentences.

1 *The author starts the article by saying that a website* was recently hacked.

2 ______________________ when they create their passwords.

3 ______________________ can break one password a second.

4 ______________________ shouldn't use the same password for multiple accounts.

5 ______________________ says, "I always use the same password for everything because otherwise I can't remember them."

6 ______________________ is abc123.

7 ______________________ is 123456.

8 ______________________ can do to create strong passwords.

# 4 Avoid Common Mistakes ⚠

**1 Remember to use the past participle form of the verb after the modal in past unreal conditionals.**

*If the company had installed secure systems, it would have ~~avoid~~ avoided data theft.*

**2 Remember to use academic, precise words rather than multi-word verbs or idioms such as:**

| | | | | | |
|---|---|---|---|---|---|
| find out | → | discover/learn | start off/out | → | start/begin |
| put up with | → | tolerate | look into | → | investigate |

*Social media users enjoy ~~finding out~~ discovering what products and services their friends recommend.*

*Older users will not ~~put up with~~ tolerate further invasions of privacy.*

*The article starts ~~off~~ with a presentation of both sides of the issue.*

*The author ~~looks into~~ investigates recent developments in Internet security.*

## Editing Task

**Find and correct five more mistakes in the summary paragraph from a summary–response essay on privacy issues and social networking.**

In his article "Privacy and Security Issues in Social Networking" (2008), Brendan Collins ~~looks into~~ investigates the security and privacy problems associated with social networks. He starts off by making the distinction between security issues and privacy issues, highlighting that social networking sites (SNSs) provide ideal opportunities for both types of violations. An example of a security violation that Collins cites is the case of a hacker who shut down a SNS just for fun. Fortunately the attack was harmless. If the attack had been malicious, the personal data of millions of users would have be stolen. According to Collins, SNSs provide ideal opportunities for break-ins because they have so much information, and because so many people have access. As an example, he gives the case of Adrienne Felt, a PhD student at U.C. Berkeley, who found out that there was a security flaw in a major SNS. The program that allowed people to share photos and send invitations also exposed their information to theft. If Felt had not looked into the SNS, many users could have had their information stolen. Collins recommends ways to limit the possibility of violations. Because SNSs are so big, it is impossible to monitor them. Therefore users should take precautions information that is shared. Collins concludes that there probably will never be a solution to these issues and that we will have to put up with threats to our privacy and security.

UNIT 18

# Persuasion 1: Nonidentifying Relative Clauses; Phrases That Limit Overgeneralization

## Violence in the Media

## 1 Grammar in the Real World

You will read an essay about violence on television. In the essay, the writer argues that violence on TV should be regulated by the government. The essay is an example of one type of persuasive writing.

**A** Before You Read **Do you think there is too much violence shown on TV? Who do you think should be responsible for controlling the amount of violence that children watch on TV: parents, the government, or both? Read the essay. What is the writer's main argument?**

**B** Comprehension Check **Answer the questions.**

1 What evidence is given in the essay that violence on TV may negatively affect children's behavior?

2 Why might it be difficult in the United States for the government to regulate TV violence?

3 Do you agree with the writer that violence on TV should be regulated? Why or why not?

**C** Notice **Answer the questions below to notice how the writer uses relative clauses to explain and support his ideas.**

1 Compare the two sentences concerning children on lines 12–15 and 59–60. In which sentence does the writer refer to *all* children? In which sentence does the writer identify a particular group of children?

2 Read the two sentences on lines 44–51, starting with "TV rating and blocking systems . . ." Look at the relative clauses in these sentences. Are these relative clauses essential to understanding the sentences? What information do these clauses provide the reader?

# TV Violence: WHO IS RESPONSIBLE?

**SHOULD VIOLENCE ON TV BE REGULATED?** This question has long been debated. Opponents defend the right to freedom of speech. Proponents believe that some restriction is essential to protect young people from too much exposure to violence. Over a decade ago, in a controversial report, the Federal Communications Commission (FCC), which is the government agency that regulates radio, TV, and Internet communications, advised the government to regulate violence on television to protect children. Since then, many reports have suggested that children who watch violent TV shows and play violent video games are likely to exhibit more aggressive and violent behavior. They may also become "immune" to violence and begin to identify with the characters shown. The American Academy of Family Physicians states that the average American child will have witnessed 200,000 acts of violence on screen by the age of 20. It is clear that the government should take immediate action and control violence on TV through regulations.

Regulation by the government should protect the public, especially children, from overexposure to violence. In the past, courts have protected violent speech and depictions[1] of violence under the First Amendment.[2] Nonetheless, the government regulates TV and film indecency.[3]

According to the FCC, the Supreme Court allows these restrictions so that children are not so easily exposed to indecency. The parallel with violence in the media is obvious. Limiting media violence is much like limiting indecency in the media.

Government regulation will also help parents monitor their children's exposure to violence. FCC Chairman Kevin Martin explained that while parents should always be the decision makers on how to best protect their children from violence, they alone cannot be responsible. The main problem is that television violence seems to have a strong presence in most children's lives. TV rating and program-blocking systems, which are both tools to help parents control viewing, are "not effective," according to the FCC, since networks may not consistently monitor TV shows for violent content. In fact, the Parents Television Council, which monitors TV shows for violent content, states that networks are not doing a good job of rating TV shows. As a result, children have access to inappropriate content. Research conducted in 2017 by the Parents Television Council shows that gun violence has increased on primetime television shows that are marketed as suitable for children's viewing.

Congress has resisted addressing this issue. However, not addressing it could put children, who have young minds that are easily impressionable,[4] at risk. It could also put society at risk for aggressive acts committed by people influenced by violent media. Therefore, the government must act now to regulate media; otherwise, society will have a difficult road ahead trying to control the negative effects of violent media on our children.

[1]**depiction:** an image

[2]**First Amendment:** an amendment in the United States Constitution that allows for freedom of speech in most situations

[3]**indecency:** behavior that upsets popular moral standards, usually as they relate to sexual behavior and nudity

[4]**impressionable:** readily or easily influenced

# 2 Nonidentifying Relative Clauses

## Grammar Presentation

| | |
|---|---|
| Nonidentifying relative clauses provide additional information about a noun phrase. Writers often use nonidentifying relative clauses to describe or identify the proper noun or organization they are citing. The relative clause can add credibility to the expert or organization. | *The Federal Communications Commission (FCC),* ***which regulates radio, TV, and Internet communications,*** *has condemned violence in children's programming.*<br><br>*Parents,* ***who one could argue have the most influence on young children,*** *must limit their children's exposure to violence.* |

### 2.1 Nonidentifying Relative Clauses

| | |
|---|---|
| **A** Nonidentifying relative clauses add more details about a noun or noun phrase. They begin with a relative pronoun: *who, which, whose,* or *whom.* Use a comma before and after these clauses. | *The National Institute of Mental Health,*<br>NONIDENTIFYING RELATIVE CLAUSE<br>***which is a government agency,*** *conducts research on the effects of violence on children.* |
| **B** The information in a nonidentifying relative clause can be omitted and the sentence will still make sense. | *Brad J. Bushman and Craig A. Anderson,* ***who are on the faculty of Iowa State University,*** *have written extensively on violence in the media.*<br><br>*Brad J. Bushman and Craig A. Anderson have written extensively on violence in the media.* |
| **C** Nonidentifying relative clauses are more common in writing than in speaking. | *L. Rowell Huesmann, PhD,* ***whose research on the effects of media violence on children is well-regarded,*** *argues that there is a correlation between watching violent shows and aggressive behavior.* |
| **D** Do not use *that* or omit the relative pronoun in a nonidentifying relative clause. | *The American Academy of Pediatrics,* ***which is a prominent group of medical professionals,*** *has several suggestions about television violence.*<br><br>NOT *The American Academy of Pediatrics, ~~that~~ is a prominent group of medical professionals, has several suggestions about television violence.*<br><br>NOT *The American Academy of Pediatrics, ~~is a prominent group of medical professionals~~, has several suggestions about television violence.* |

## 2.1 Nonidentifying Relative Clauses *(continued)*

| | |
|---|---|
| **E** You can use nonidentifying relative clauses after proper nouns, such as the name of a person or an organization. This adds credibility to the source. | *Susan P. Leviton,* ***who is the president of the Advocates for Children and Youth****, is on the faculty of the University of Maryland School of Law.*<br>*The National Violence Survey,* ***which has examined violence on TV for many years****, released its report today.* |
| A shorter way to indicate an expert's credentials is to use an appositive. (See Unit 12 for more information on appositives.) | *Adam D. Thierer,* ***a senior fellow at the Progress & Freedom Foundation****, believes that parents should decide whether their children play violent video games.* |

# Grammar Application

## Exercise 2.1 Nonidentifying Relative Clauses

**A** Underline the names of the experts in the sentences. Next, write new sentences by adding the additional information about the expert using nonidentifying relative clauses.

1 Jason Edwards reports that the effect of violent content on adolescents depends on how it is portrayed.

*Additional information:* Jason Edwards is an assistant professor of communication at Bradford College.

Jason Edwards, who is an assistant professor of communication at Bradford College, reports that the effect of violent content on adolescents depends on how it is portrayed.

2 A child who watches two hours of TV a day is exposed to approximately 10,000 acts of violence a year, based on research by the Philips Family Foundation.

*Additional information:* The Philips Family Foundation is a nonprofit organization that focuses on health-care issues.

3 Parents should discuss the content of TV advertising with their children, according to Joanna Moore.

*Additional information:* Joanna Moore is the mother of five teenagers.

4 According to Pablo Silva, the best way for children to be active is to turn off the TV set.

*Additional information:* Pablo Silva studies the effects of TV on children's development.

---

5 In 2006, the American Academy of Child & Adolescent Psychiatry determined that children with excessive exposure to violence on television may "become 'immune' or numb to the horror of violence" (p. 1).

*Additional information:* The American Academy of Child & Adolescent Psychiatry provides resources about children's mental health.

---

6 Gerard Jones believes that effective use of media violence can help children vent their anger.

*Additional information:* Gerard Jones is a well-known comic book writer and the author of the article "Violent Media Is Good for Kids."

---

**B** Pair Work **Find the sentences in A in which the relative clauses can be turned into appositives. Say each sentence with the appositive. Then give your opinion of the information.**

*Jason Edwards, an assistant professor of communication at Bradford College, reports that the effect of violent content on adolescents depends on how it is portrayed.*
*I think I agree. When violence is portrayed as something heroic or admired, then I think it is harmful because children always want to imitate their heroes.*

## **Exercise 2.2** More Nonidentifying Relative Clauses

**A** **Listen to a talk show on the effects of media violence on children. Take notes about the speakers on their credentials or information about their background and their opinion on the issue. Finally, write statements about each person. Use nonidentifying relative clauses.**

1 Dr. Marc Richards

*Marc Richards, who is a school psychologist, believes that exposure to violence in the media encourages young children to react violently when they're upset.*

2 Kevin McDonald

---

3 Dr. Marcia Chan

4 Catherine Wong

5 Dr. Eric Lopez

6 Barbara Cramer

7 Noah Friedman

**B** Group Work **Take turns choosing a speaker in A, summarizing the speaker's opinion, and sharing your opinion of the speaker's ideas. Include the credentials of the speaker. After you give your opinion, ask your group members to respond with their opinions.**

A *Marc Richards, who is a school psychologist, says that exposure to violence in the media causes children to react violently when they get upset. I'm not sure I agree with him. It's true that young children are impressionable, so they may think that the violent behavior on video games, for example, is appropriate, but I think family and friends are more influential.*

B *I think I agree with Dr. Richards more. When children see violent images over and over, I think it might make them more likely to use violence when they get angry.*

# 3 Phrases That Limit Overgeneralization

## Vocabulary Presentation

Writers of persuasive essays need to provide facts to support their arguments and points. However, it is important to be careful about the language used to express these ideas. Some phrases can help limit overgeneralizations and make claims more accurate and therefore more credible. Limiting claims is also called "hedging."

*This statement* ***is likely to*** *cause arguments.*

*Television violence* ***seems to*** *be everywhere.*

***In most cases****, parents try to control what their children watch on television.*

### 3.1 Words and Phrases That Limit Overgeneralization

| | |
|---|---|
| **A** Use *seem/appear/tend/be likely* + infinitive to indicate something that is possible but not certain, or to indicate something may not be true all the time. *Seem* is the most common verb in this construction. | *Experts who study violence* ***seem to/appear to*** *disagree with one another's conclusions.* (We do not know all the experts who study violence, but from what we have read, they do not agree with one another.)<br><br>*Children who watch many hours of TV every day* ***are likely to/tend to*** *be exposed to violent programs.* (We do not know that all children will be exposed to violent programs, but we suspect that it is true most of the time.) |
| **B** Use *it* constructions like *It seems that* and *It appears that* when you believe that something is a trend, but do not have enough evidence to support it strongly. | ***It seems that*** *parents are becoming more cautious about what programs their children should watch on TV.* |
| **C** Use these phrases to express limits on your general claims: *in most cases, mainly, typically.* | ***In most cases****, children can tell the difference between cartoon violence and real violence.*<br><br>*Children will* ***typically*** *show higher levels of aggression after watching violence on TV.* |
| **D** *According to* is the most common way to identify a specific source. | ***According to*** *the report, the television industry is not policing itself to the satisfaction of parents.* |

# Vocabulary Application

## **Exercise 3.1** Words and Phrases That Limit Overgeneralization

**A** Rewrite each sentence about the possible positive effects of media violence. Use the word or phrase that best fits the description of the limitation in parentheses: *according to, appears, in most cases, likely, seems, tend, typically*. Use each word or phrase once. In some cases, you may need to change some of the wording of the sentence.

1 Many parents and teachers believe children should not be exposed to any kind of violence in the media. (This is a trend, but there is not enough evidence to support this.)

*It appears that many parents and teachers believe children should not be exposed to any kind of violence in the media.*

2 Children are taught to deny their feelings of violence. (This is true of some children, but not all children.)

______________________________

3 Adults attempt to repress any violent reactions they have. (This seems to be true of many, but not all adults.)

______________________________

4 Media violence allows people to fantasize about releasing their aggression in a safe, nonthreatening environment. (Some experts believe this claim.)

______________________________

5 Violent video games provide players with an outlet for feelings of anger and frustration. (This is possible, but there isn't enough research to back this up.)

______________________________

6 Constant denial of violent feelings, rather than exposure to media violence, makes people react to problems with aggression. (It is very possible, but it is not certain that this is true.)

______________________________

7 Video games portray heroes as violent. (It is possible, but not true all the time.)

______________________________

**B** Pair Work **Work with a partner. Take turns making overgeneralizations about the topics below. Your partner will ask you to limit your generalization.**

- The effects of violent video games on teenagers
- Reasons that children like to play violent video games
- The effects of violence in cartoons and movies on children

A *Violent video games always make children act violently.*

B *I think you're overgeneralizing. In some cases, some violent video games may make some children act violently, but you can't say that is true for all violent video games and all children unless you have research to back up your claims.*

# 4 Avoid Common Mistakes ⚠

**1 Remember to include the relative pronoun in nonidentifying relative clauses.**

*"Violent Video Games: Myths, Facts, and Unanswered Questions," ^which was published by the American Psychological Association, establishes the connection between violence in games and violent behavior.*

**2 Remember not to use *that* as a relative pronoun in nonidentifying relative clauses.**

*The National Institute of Mental Health, ~~that~~ which published the article, is an excellent source of recent studies on the effects of violence in the media.*

**3 Remember to use the singular form of the verb *seem* with *it*.**

*It ~~seem~~ seems that not enough parents take responsibility for monitoring their children.*

# Editing Task

**Find and correct eight more mistakes in the body paragraph from an essay on violence in the media.**

Government's Role in Violence in the Media

There is a major reason that the government should not be involved in solving the problem of violence in the media. Government control of the media is unconstitutional. It ~~seem~~ *seems* that some people feel that the Federal Communications Commission (FCC), is the government agency that regulates media such as TV and the Internet, is the best tool for protecting children. However, many experts disagree. For example, the American Civil Liberties Union (ACLU), that focuses on constitutional rights, believes that government control of the media is a form of censorship. The First Amendment to the U.S. Constitution, guarantees freedom of speech, gives us the right to media that are not controlled by the government. A free and open media is the foundation of democracy in the United States. However, it is important to protect children from violence. According to the ACLU, protecting children is the responsibility of parents, although it seem that many parents are unwilling to take on this responsibility. Caroline Fredrickson, is a director of the ACLU's Washington Legislative Office, points out in her article, "Why Government Should Not Police TV Violence and Indecency," was published in *The Christian Science Monitor*, that parents "already have many tools to protect their children, including blocking programs and channels, changing the channel, or simply turning off the television." She adds that the Parents Television Council, that is a nonprofit media monitoring organization, provides information on their website about television programs that are appropriate for children. It seem that if parents take responsibility for monitoring their children's television viewing, then we will be able to have free and open media and protect children at the same time.

UNIT 19

# Persuasion 2: Noun Clauses with *Wh-* Words and *If/Whether*; Phrases for Argumentation

## Living in an Age of Information Overload

## 1 Grammar in the Real World

You will read an essay that discusses the easy availability of information online. The essay is an example of a type of persuasive writing in which the writer chooses to present opposing views.

**A** Before You Read **How do you find most of your information: in printed sources or online sources? Read the essay. What concerns does the writer have about relying on the Internet for information?**

**B** Comprehension Check **Answer the questions.**

1 What are the two main points in favor of new technology mentioned by the writer?

2 Why does the writer believe that ease of access to information may not be such a good thing?

3 The writer offers readers a choice in the concluding paragraph. What point do you think the writer is making by offering a choice?

**C** Notice **Find the answers to the following questions in the essay to notice how the writer uses grammar in her arguments:**

1 Read the sentence on lines 51–52 beginning with "People who embrace . . ." to notice how the writer uses a clause with a *wh-* word to help present the different sides of the argument. What are the two sides of the argument?

2 Find the sentence in the first paragraph in which the writer states the opponent's view and then responds. What phrase does the writer use to introduce the opponent's view before refuting it?

# So Much Information, So Little Time

WE LIVE IN AN AMAZING TIME, with access to almost unlimited information, entertainment, and opinions. Digital technology offers us new information whenever we are "plugged in." Just the other day, I watched a baseball game on TV, texted a friend, and kept track of the details of my other friends' lives online. I also kept an eye on all the other sports scores as they were happening. I did all this while also having a conversation with my brother. While it is true that digital technology has many benefits, they come at a cost, producing citizens who have fewer critical-thinking skills and weaker social skills.

According to the proponents[1] of technology, easy access to information is one way that people benefit from new technology. When doing research, you do not have to walk to a library, search for books, and read words on paper. Obviously, finding what we need from the Internet is faster, and online searches provide a broader range of sources. Often, however, when people are faced with search-engine results in the thousands or more, their critical-thinking skills may be overwhelmed by the sheer volume of material to read. One study in the UK showed that students skimmed over most information they found. According to this study, they rarely read more than a page or two when completing academic research.

Proponents also point out that technology has increased social connections. People can stay in touch with friends more easily now, sending them birthday greetings, sharing complaints, and keeping each other informed, all online. Naturally, email and social networking websites have facilitated[2] communication. Ironically,[3] though, the tools designed for increased online interaction may actually lead to people being less social. Students rarely need to engage in face-to-face interactions these days either with their professors or their fellow students. Lonely librarians remember when students used to ask them questions in person. Now they more often respond to students' text queries via website help centers. At the end of the day, workers come home exhausted by so much online interaction. Having made themselves accessible online 24 hours a day, they end up sacrificing family time at home as they prepare for the next round of virtual interaction.

Clearly, increased access to information results in added benefits, but it is also true that there is a cost. People who embrace new technology should reflect on what they lose as well as what they gain. There is a choice between touching and smelling a flower grown in my garden and sharing it with one or two friends in the neighborhood, and instead photographing the flower, putting that image online, and reading the responses of my worldwide set of "friends." Perhaps the touch of the real flower should rule.

[1]**proponent:** supporter
[2]**facilitate:** make easier
[3]**ironically:** in a way that is different from what was expected

# 2 Noun Clauses with *Wh-* Words and *If/Whether*

## Grammar Presentation

| | |
|---|---|
| Noun clauses with *wh-* words and *if/whether* are useful in persuasive academic writing, especially to present different viewpoints and then critique those viewpoints. | *Experts disagree on* ***what the benefits and drawbacks of Internet use are for students.***<br>*Nobody really knows* ***if children today have more difficulty with concentration.*** |

### 2.1 Noun Clauses with *Wh-* Words

| | |
|---|---|
| **A** *Wh-* noun clauses start with a *wh-* word (*who, what, where, when, why*, and *how*) and function as nouns. They can act as subjects, objects, or objects of prepositions. In academic writing, they are more frequent as objects and objects of prepositions. | WH- NOUN CLAUSE<br>*Readers have to decide which* ***expert they trust.***<br>*Readers are concerned about who* ***seems the most credible****.* |
| *Wh-* noun clauses use statement word order (subj + verb). Do not put an auxiliary or modal before the subject. | *Students have to learn how* ***they can evaluate sources.***<br>NOT *Students have to learn how ~~can they~~ evaluate sources.* |
| **B** Noun clauses with *wh-* words often come after the following verbs:<br>Thoughts and opinions: *agree, consider, disagree, know, remember*<br>Learning and perception: *see, understand, wonder* | *We need to consider* ***who our main market is.***<br>*I don't remember* ***where I read that****.* |

### 2.2 Noun Clauses with *If/Whether*

| | |
|---|---|
| **A** *If/whether* noun clauses function as nouns. They start with *if* or *whether* and show an alternative choice or a *yes/no* choice. As in *wh-* clauses, these clauses are in statement word order.<br>*Whether* is more commonly used when alternatives are presented or implied. | *Students need to check* ***whether their online sources are current or out-of-date****.* (Alternative choice: Are they current or are they out-of-date? The answer is one or the other.)<br>*I don't know* ***if that website has accurate information****.*<br>(*Yes/no choice:* Does that website have accurate information? The answer is *yes* or *no*.) |

## 2.2 Noun Clauses with *If/ Whether* *(continued)*

| | |
|---|---|
| **B** The verbs *know*, *see*, and *wonder* are commonly used with *if/whether* noun clauses. | *Let's* ***see*** *if we can find an answer on this website.*<br>*Some students* ***wonder*** *whether they should do research online or in the library.*<br>*I don't* ***know*** *if there are computers available to do the research online.* |

# Grammar Application

## **Exercise 2.1** Noun Clauses with *Wh-* Words and *If/ Whether*

Combine each pair of sentences about the effects of information overload on workers and the workplace. Use a noun clause with a *wh-* word, *if*, or *whether*. Sometimes more than one answer is possible.

1 How does information overload affect the workplace? Researchers are studying this.

*Researchers are studying how information overload affects the workplace.*

2 Does information overload make an employee more or less efficient? Researchers are trying to determine this.

______________________________

3 What do employees do when they are overwhelmed by too much information? Employers want to know this.

______________________________

4 Do employees ignore important facts or absorb more when they are overloaded with information? Employers wonder this.

______________________________

5 Do overloaded employees waste time? Corporations want to find this out.

______________________________

6 How does information overload affect employees' decision-making skills? Studies may determine this.

______________________________

7 When do employees feel overwhelmed by information? Researchers wonder this.

______________________________

8 Does information overload increase or decrease productivity? Researchers want to learn this.

______________________________

## Exercise 2.2 More Noun Clauses with *Wh-* Words and *If/Whether*

**A** **Listen to a lecture about information overload. Number the questions in the order that the speaker mentions them as noun clauses with *wh-* words and *if/whether*.**

____ 1 What is the daily volume of new web content?

____ 2 What can we do about information overload?

____ 3 Do you really need to send out emails to people who don't need them?

____ 4 Does each recipient of information really need the information that he or she receives?

__*1*__ 5 How does information overload impact us?

____ 6 Do you have to look at that video that your friend sent you?

____ 7 What are some of the causes of information overload?

____ 8 What can you do to avoid being overwhelmed by information?

____ 9 Can you spend a portion of your day disconnected from technology?

**B** Pair Work **Complete the summary below of the lecture in A with a partner. Use the answers in A written as noun clauses with *wh-* words and *if/whether*. Then share your paragraph with another pair.**

First, the lecturer says that he wonders *how this information overload impacts us* (1) and ______ (2). Then he says he is going to examine ______ (3). Next, he tells us that people tend to distribute information without considering ______ (4). The lecturer also wonders ______ (5). Then he moves on to consider ______ (6). His first suggestion is that people should see ______ (7) to focus on one source of information at a time. Third, he asks people to consider ______ (8). Finally, he tells people to ask themselves ______ (9).

# 3 Phrases for Argumentation

## Vocabulary Presentation

Writers use particular words to present an opposing view, to acknowledge that an opposing view has some merit, and to refute, or disprove, the opposing view.

***It has been argued that** the Internet has caused groups to form more quickly than in the past.*

***Clearly**, the Internet offers access to a wealth of information.*

***However**, some students need more guidance than others in using online resources.*

### 3.1 Phrases That Present an Opposing View

| | |
|---|---|
| **A** Use the following phrases to present opposing documented views: | |
| *It has been argued that . . .* | ***It has been argued that** young people handle information in a much different way.* |
| *It is argued that . . .* | |
| *It has been claimed that . . .* | ***It has been claimed** that it is important for adolescents to spend time away from electronic devices.* |
| *Some researchers disagree that . . .* | |
| *Argue* and *claim* are the most common. | |
| **B** Use these phrases to present potentially opposing views when you do not have sources for your claim. Modals make the claim less strong. | |
| *It might/could/may be argued that . . .* | ***It could be argued that** video games allow children to develop critical-thinking skills.* |
| *It might/could/may be claimed that . . .* | ***It might be claimed that** cell phone use can be addictive.* |
| *Might* and *could* are more common than *may*. | |
| (See Unit 16 for more practice with *it* constructions.) | |

### 3.2 Logical Connectors That Show a Point of View

Use these adverbs as logical connectors to acknowledge a specific point of view or an opposing argument:
*clearly, naturally, obviously, of course*

***Clearly**, increased access to information results in a benefit.*

***Obviously**, few want to return to the old system of information gathering.*

*Internet research is different, **of course**, and it requires specific strategies to get proper results.*

## 3.3 Phrases That Introduce a Refutation

Use these phrases to introduce a refutation or to dispute an argument:

*However, . . .*
*It is not true that . . .*
*That may be so, but . . .*
*(Unfortunately,) this is (simply) not true.*
*While it is true that . . .*

*This is (simply) not true* is the most common of these phrases.

OPPOSING VIEW
*Some claim that violence on TV leads to violence at school.* REFUTATION ***However, this is simply not true.***

OPPOSING VIEW
***While it is true that*** *well-designed video games can help children think creatively,* REFUTATION ***they do not replace physical interaction with others.***

# Vocabulary Application

## Exercise 3.1 Phrases for Argumentation

**Complete the paragraph below about some drawbacks of easy access to information. Circle the correct word or phrase.**

While it is true that / However, it has been argued that (1) easy access to information allows people to learn almost anything they want at any time, there are some downsides to this accessibility. Some people believe that individuals are more productive when they multitask. Naturally / Unfortunately (2), this is simply not true, according to recent studies. Attempting to do several things at once is less efficient than doing one thing at a time. People should attempt to focus on one source of information at a time and one piece of information at a time. Clearly, / It has been claimed that (3) people want to receive a lot of information, though. Otherwise, they wouldn't access so many different sources of information at once.

Also, while it is true that / it has been claimed that (4) social networks allow people to stay updated on their friends' activities, they also create a big distraction. The vast amount of information that we have to sift through cuts into time we could actually be spending with friends. It is not true that / Obviously (5), individuals have to decide on their own priorities, but spending time with friends face-to-face might be more valuable than communicating with them online. A person would probably benefit greatly from trading time spent learning unimportant information for some time spent with friends. It could be argued that / Of course (6), people will not remember the 20 status updates and 5 emails they read after work, but they will very likely enjoy and remember a dinner with a friend.

## **Exercise 3.2** More Phrases for Argumentation

On a separate piece of paper, write a short paragraph for the thesis statement in item 2. Use the example in item 1 as a model. Include the opposing view, an agreement, and a refutation. Use the phrases for argumentation to connect the ideas.

**A** **Thesis Statement:** The college should provide more on-campus child care for students.

**Opposing view:** The college should not provide more on-campus child care.

**Agreement with the opposing view:** There are enough day-care facilities in the community to serve the students who need them.

**Refutation:** The majority of day-care centers do not have evening hours, and most students attend school at night.

**Supporting information:** Many students miss school because they do not have anyone to care for their children while they are at school.

**Body Paragraph:** *Some college personnel may argue that the college should not provide more on-campus child care. Clearly, they believe that there are enough day-care centers in the community to serve the students who need them. However, the majority of day-care centers do not have evening hours, and most students attend school at night. Therefore, many students miss school because they do not have anyone to care for their children while they are at school.*

**B** **Thesis Statement:** Students should turn off their electronic devices during class.

**Opposing view:** Students should be allowed to have their devices on during class.

**Agreement with the opposing view:** Students may need to be in contact with family members or their jobs.

**Refutation:** Electronic devices can be a distraction in the classroom.

**Supporting information:** Students can become easily distracted by their devices and miss important information.

## Exercise 3.3 More Phrases for Argumentation

**Pair Work** Work with a partner and choose a topic from the list below or a topic approved by your teacher. Choose opposing sides and, individually, write sentences to argue for your side. Use vocabulary that addresses opposing views. Then role-play a debate about the topic.

- Are parents who allow their children to spend all day using electronic devices negligent?
- Should people turn their cell phones off when they're out with friends?
- Is it acceptable to surf the Internet and check text messages during class?

A *It has been claimed that too much television is not good for young children. However, children can learn a lot from watching television. They can learn about cultures and families that are different from their own. And they can learn practical information like reading and numbers by watching educational shows.*

B *That may be so, but it is also true that children can learn even more by interacting with humans rather than with an "electronic babysitter."*

# 4 Avoid Common Mistakes

**1 Remember to use *if*, and not *whether*, to express a condition.**

*E-books will be popular ~~whether~~ if they are less expensive than print books.*

**2 Remember that *or not* can immediately follow *whether*, but it can only appear at the end of a sentence with *if*.**

*Experts can't decide ~~if~~ whether or not students retain enough information with online reading.*

*Experts can't decide if ~~or not~~ students retain enough information with online reading or not.*

**3 Remember to spell *whether* correctly.**

*The instructors decide ~~weather~~ whether students bring laptops or smartphones to class.*

*They have not decided ~~wether~~ whether laptops are helpful or a distraction.*

# Editing Task

**Find and correct six more mistakes in the body paragraph from an essay on information overload.**

Information Overload

Opponents of online technology often point to the negative effects of the information age. They claim that ~~weather~~ *whether* individuals use the Internet for research or for social networking, they suffer from information overload. They believe that easy access to information has a negative effect on users' critical-thinking skills. They also cite the fact that online readers understand and retain less than print readers. The fact is, however, that experts have not yet determined if or not there is a difference between reading online and reading print material. There haven't been enough studies to determine if or not there truly are negative effects of information overload. Furthermore, it is important for proponents of this argument to identify wether they are referring to the effects of technology on older people or younger people. For example, their arguments may not be valid whether they consider how digital natives respond to technology. Digital natives are people who were born since the 1990s. They were born into a digital world, and they have been using technology since childhood. According, to the author, Don Tapscott, digital natives process information differently than digital immigrants (people who were born before the 1990s and learned how to use the Internet later in life than digital natives did). Tapscott cites a study designed to show whether digital natives retained more information from a traditional newscast or an interactive webcast. The study showed that digital natives remembered more from the interactive news source. Tapscott also points out that intelligence and aptitude test scores are rising, which further indicates that digital natives' thinking styles have not suffered. Some wonder wether digital natives should adapt to traditional ways of processing information. However, if or not we like it, the information age is here to stay. Therefore, digital immigrants are going to have to adapt to digital ways of interacting with technology.

UNIT 20

# Persuasion 3: Expressing Future Actions; Common Words and Phrases in Persuasive Writing

## Social Media

## 1 Grammar in the Real World

You will read an essay about the impact that social media may be having on college students' academic performance. In this persuasive essay, the writer argues for banning social media sites from college campuses.

**A** Before You Read **What social media sites are popular among you and your friends? What are some possible negative aspects of social media? Read the essay. Does the writer think of social media as having a positive or negative impact on students? Why?**

**B** Comprehension Check **Answer the questions.**

1 What positive things does the writer say about social media?

2 Why does the author want to limit or ban social media on campuses?

3 Do you agree or disagree with the writer's point of view? Why?

**C** Notice **Complete the tasks below to notice the grammar that the writer uses to talk about possible future events and opposing views.**

1 Compare the use of the word *should* on lines 11 and 54. How are the meanings of *should* different?

2 Read the sentence on lines 50–53 beginning with "Based on these concerns . . . " Look at the verb phrase. Does the verb phrase refer to present or future time? What words in the phrase help you to determine this?

3 Look at the use of *would* on lines 38 and 53. Does the meaning of *would* refer to present time or a likely result in the future?

# Social Media on College Campuses

SOCIAL MEDIA HAS REVOLUTIONIZED the way we communicate with friends, colleagues, classmates, and even family members. It is now possible to interact and maintain a relationship with someone without ever meeting in person. There are many positive aspects of these new types of interactions. However, the excessive use of such websites has created a distraction[1] for some users. Some college students spend hours a day "networking" instead of focusing on their studies. To help these students be more successful, colleges and universities should block access to social media in most areas of their campuses.

Social media has been growing in popularity at an astonishing rate. According to the Pew Research Center's Internet & American Life Project, it is estimated that at least 85 percent of college students in the United States use some type of online social media on a daily basis. In fact, according to many instructors, college students are growing dependent on such networks. While there is no doubt that social media has created valuable new ways to communicate and share information, they have also become a distraction for college students who spend time online instead of preparing for their future careers.

Some proponents claim that the social media phenomenon[2] can be positive. Students can join online groups in which everyone shares the same interest, and they can learn how to communicate effectively in this digital age. It has been further argued that, when online, students will discuss current events and issues that they are less likely to discuss in "real life" interactions. In an ideal world, this could indeed be a beneficial way to promote interaction with people from different cultures and backgrounds. Opponents argue that, in reality, some discussions provide a less rigorous platform for ideas because of the lack of monitoring and the informal nature of the format. It is therefore difficult to argue that these postings would add significantly to the students' knowledge base.

Colleges and universities should consider strong policies on the use of social media on campus because students waste valuable study time on it. In fact, some studies report a link between time on social media and grades. For example, an Ohio State University survey indicates that students who regularly use social media study less than five hours per week and have an average GPA between 3.0 and 3.5. In contrast, students who do not use these websites study 11 hours or more per week and have an average GPA between 3.5 and 4.0. In addition, teachers are increasingly concerned about social media use in class. They complain that students are "messaging friends or posting . . . status updates from their laptops instead of paying attention to lectures." Based on these concerns, establishing clear policies for use of these websites on campus is likely to help students focus on their studies. They would spend more time studying, and their grades should improve as a result.

Social media presents a new way to find, organize, and share information and contacts. These visually stimulating, highly interactive websites attract many college students. However, their addictive nature can potentially disrupt[3] student life to the degree that colleges and universities have to take action and ban access to social media in some areas on campuses.

[1]**distraction:** something that takes your attention away from where it should be focused

[2]**phenomenon:** something that is noticed because it is unusual or new

[3]**disrupt:** change the normal direction and create disorder

# 2 Expressing Future Actions

## Grammar Presentation

| | |
|---|---|
| To express plans, predictions, and expectations, writers use *will*, *be going to*, modals, and a variety of words and phrases. | *Students* ***will not*** *be able to access social media sites if colleges ban them.*<br>*Blocking social media on campus* ***would*** *help students focus on their studies.* |

### 2.1 Using *Will, Be Going To,* and Modals to Express Certainty and Make Predictions

| | |
|---|---|
| **A** Use *will* and *be going to* to write about a plan or prediction in the future. *Will* is more common in academic writing than *be going to.* | *The Internet* ***will continue to allow*** *for a greater exchange of ideas.*<br>*Some colleges* ***are going to ban*** *access to social media on campuses.* |
| **B** Use modals *could, might,* and *may* to express possibility in the future. | *The use of social media by recruiters for jobs* ***could increase*** *in the next few years.* |
| **C** Use *should* to express an expectation. | *New technology* ***should make*** *communication more efficient.* |
| **D** Use *would* to express an expectation based on either a stated or unstated condition. | *Banning note-taking on laptops* ***would prevent*** *students from using the Internet during classes.*<br>*If the school implements the ban now, it* ***would see*** *major benefits within the next few months.* |

### 2.2 Using Other Expressions to Express Future Action

| | |
|---|---|
| **A** Use these phrases to write about something that will likely happen in the near future: | |
| *is due to* | *The new version of the phone* ***is due to come*** *out by next year.* |
| *is about to* | *The company* ***is about to introduce*** *a new app.* |

## 2.2 Using Other Expressions to Express Future Action *(continued)*

| | |
|---|---|
| **B** The following phrases can be used to talk about possible future events: | |
| *it is/seems/looks likely that* + clause | ***It seems likely that*** *younger teachers will be more comfortable with educational technology.* |
| something/someone *is/seems/looks likely to* + verb | *Younger teachers* ***are likely to be*** *more comfortable with using technology.* |
| *is/are considering* + verb + *-ing* | *The school* ***is considering prohibiting*** *all unauthorized Internet access on campus.* |
| *anticipate* + verb + *-ing* (suggests that the event is very likely) | *We* ***anticipate focusing*** *only on student performance scores, not other factors.* |
| **C** The following verbs, usually in the present tense, show plans for the future: | |
| *hope to*: not definite but preferable | *The students* ***hope to maintain*** *their high school friendships online.* |
| *intend to*: not definite but preferable | *The university* ***intends to investigate*** *the effects of technology on student performance.* |
| *plan to*: scheduled to happen | *Large technology companies* ***plan to move*** *many applications to phones and other digital devices.* |

# Grammar Application

## Exercise 2.1 Future Possibilities

**A** The managers of a design magazine have noticed an increase in the number of employees who use social media at work. Read the blog post and employee comments about the issue. Circle the correct words and phrases to complete the sentences.

### Friday, May 8

It has been noted that some employees are spending a lot of time on social media during work hours, and productivity has gone down. We really need everyone to be focused right now because we **are about to/are considering** (1) launch our new website, and we **plan to get/anticipate getting** (2) a lot of new business as a result. Because of this, management **is likely to block/is considering blocking** (3) social media websites from the office. However, we'd like to hear what you all think about this. We welcome your comments. We **anticipate having/will have** (4) a meeting next Friday at 2:00 to discuss this issue. All employees are welcome. We **plan to/hope to** (5) see all of you there.

COMMENTS:

Marta G.: Not everyone spends a lot of time on the sites. Most of us check the sites a couple of times a day. Why punish everyone? It **should be/seems likely** (6) that people who waste time **should/will** (7) find other ways to waste time if they can't get on social media.

Erin W.: I like this idea. It's frustrating when my team members don't complete their work because they have spent too much time online. This change **would/is going to** (8) prevent them from spending half the workday online. And my team's productivity **intends to/could** (9) increase.

Tomas K.: I use social media to update my clients on the latest design trends. Some of my clients contact me during the day on this site. If I couldn't use the site at work, I **should/might** (10) lose some of my clients. I **intend/am not likely** (11) to protest this policy if it goes through.

Kevin L.: Friday's a bad day for this meeting. A lot of people **don't plan/are not likely** (12) to attend because they telecommute that day. You should change the day.

**B** Pair Work **With a partner, create a role play between two managers of small businesses who have differing views on the use of social media at work. Answer these questions in your role plays: What are you considering doing? How might the policies affect employees? How will employees react? How do you plan to address employees' reactions? Use modals and phrases that show certainty, prediction, and future action.**

**Student A** You are seriously considering banning the use of social media through the company's computers and implementing strict rules about not accessing them on smartphones during work hours. You strongly believe that these sites cause employees to waste time, do poor quality work, and be irresponsible.

**Student B** You do not believe that social media should be banned at work because you believe that this will create a lot of anger and resentment from employees. You want to work with employees to create a set of policies that everyone can agree with.

A *I'm seriously considering banning the use of social media sites at my workplace because I think they're a major distraction for my employees.*

B *I feel differently. I agree that there might be a need to have policies regarding their use, but I'm not sure that banning is the right solution. There may be other solutions. You're going to get a lot of criticism, you know.*

A *I know I am. I'm planning to hold several meetings about it . . .*

## **Exercise 2.2** Future Possibilities

Listen to two college students, Lisa and Ben, talk about social media. Write *T* if the statement has a meaning similar to the one you hear. Write *F* if the statement has a different meaning. Correct the false statements so that they are true.

*F* 1 Their college ~~has recently blocked~~ *is considering blocking* Internet access to social media sites in some areas on campus.

____ 2 Ben thinks blocking access might help students study more.

____ 3 Lisa is going to demonstrate against it if the school blocks access.

____ 4 Ben will demonstrate against it if the school blocks access.

____ 5 One popular social media site is about to charge people to use their site.

____ 6 Lisa thinks a lot of people might delete their account if the popular social media site charges people.

____ 7 Ben thinks that people will pay to use a popular site.

____ 8 Lisa might use social media if she has to pay.

# 3 Common Words and Phrases in Persuasive Writing

## Vocabulary Presentation

In Unit 19, you learned common vocabulary used in persuasive writing to discuss opposing views. Now you will learn how to use other common vocabulary for persuasive and other kinds of academic writing.

*According to the **proponents** of technology, easy access to information is one way that people benefit from new technology.*

*Some educators **claim** that the networking phenomenon can be positive.*

### 3.1 Common Vocabulary in Persuasive Writing

| | |
|---|---|
| **A** These nouns are common in persuasive writing:<br>When referring to people, you can use:<br>*advocates, opponents, proponents, supporters*<br>When referring to ideas, you can use:<br>*argument, belief, claim, conclusion, evidence, fact, information, problem(s)* | ***Opponents** of social media argue that these communities deter face-to-face interactions.*<br>*The main **argument** used by **proponents** of social media is that it allows contact with people from all over the world.*<br>*Some critics see students' dependence on social media as a **problem**, but there is little **evidence** of this.* |
| **B** These verbs are common in persuasive writing:<br>*acknowledge, admit, advocate, argue, believe, claim, control, estimate, oppose, project, refute, support* | *Some people **believe** that children should not be allowed to text in class.*<br>*A number of parents **support** banning text messaging from schools.* |
| **C** These adjectives are common in persuasive writing:<br>*better, illogical, important, incomplete, little, true, unproved, valid* | *It is **important** to be familiar with the latest technology.*<br>*It is **true** that some people spend too much time in front of the computer.*<br>*The arguments supported by these researchers are **illogical**.* |
| **D** These expressions are common in persuasive writing:<br>*be in favor of* (something)<br>*be against* (something) | *Many instructors **are in favor of** receiving homework online.*<br>*Many teachers **are against** the use of social media in schools.* |

# Vocabulary Application

## Exercise 3.1 Vocabulary in Persuasive Writing

Read the sentences about cyberbullying. Use each word once.

| | | | | |
|---|---|---|---|---|
| argue | ~~claim~~ | in favor of | opponents | proponents |

1 Cyberbullying occurs when people, often teenagers, are teased or humiliated by others on the Internet. Many parents and psychologists claim that it can cause permanent emotional damage to children and teenagers.

2 Some people ____________ that cyberbullying should be categorized as a criminal offense.

3 ____________ of the idea that cyberbullying be classified as a criminal offense are ____________ the approach because they believe it will decrease the amount of cyberbullying among teenagers.

4 ____________ of making cyberbullying a criminal offense do not believe that criminalizing cyberbullying would be effective.

| | | | |
|---|---|---|---|
| acknowledge | against | evidence | a valid point |

5 While some people ____________ that cyberbullying needs to be criminalized, they worry that the law will be ineffective because it is difficult to track the perpetrators.

6 The difficulty of tracking perpetrators is ____________ , but the point may not be convincing in the near future since tracking devices are rapidly improving.

7 Some people who are ____________ the criminalization of cyberbullying say that creating laws making it a crime violates free speech.

8 Some researchers have found that there is ____________ that educational programs in early grades are effective in reducing the incidence of bullying.

**Exercise 3.2** More Vocabulary in Persuasive Writing

Pair Work **Work with a partner and choose one of the topics below. Discuss different views on the topic. Use the vocabulary for persuasive writing in your discussion.**

- Should children under 12 be allowed to use social media?
- Should parents have access to their children's and teenagers' social media accounts?
- Should people be "friends" with their coworkers and managers on social media?

*I believe that children under 12 should be allowed to use social media. I acknowledge that children can get into trouble, but if they use the sites responsibly, they can learn a lot about socializing and computer skills . . .*

# 4 Avoid Common Mistakes

**1** **Don't confuse the noun and verb form of *claim*.**

*The ~~claiming~~ claim that social media is dangerous is illogical.*

**2** **Don't confuse the noun and verb form of *argue*.**

*The main ~~arguing~~ argument against using social media to communicate with people is that it is superficial.*

**3** **Remember to use *according to*, not *according for* or *according with*.**

*According ~~for~~ to a recent study, young people are losing interest in social media.*

*According ~~with~~ to Smith, social media is useful as an educational tool.*

# Editing Task

**Find and correct six more mistakes in the body paragraph from an essay on social media.**

### Social Media

One of the main ~~arguing~~ *arguments* against social media is that people sometimes reveal information on them that often should be kept private. Recently another development has provided more support for this arguing: College admissions committees are now using social media as part of the application process. According for a survey by Kaplan Test Prep, over 80 percent of college admissions officers use social media to communicate with students. The claiming that many colleges make is that they use these sites to attract new students or to stay in contact with former students. However, some colleges admit that they are also using social media as part of the admissions process. The main arguing for using social media is that it helps colleges evaluate candidates at a time when these colleges are experiencing large numbers of applicants. According with many admissions officers, colleges need all the information they can get about applicants in order to make decisions because the admissions process has become very competitive. One college interviewer in a recent survey reported that if she has to choose between two students who are equally qualified in terms of grades and test scores, she looks at their online profiles to make the final decision. In addition, applicants also use social media against each other. According for another admissions officer, his office often receives anonymous messages with links to sites that have negative information on or pictures of other applicants. Many colleges and universities do not have official policies yet on whether to use social media as part of the application process. Until these policies become clearer, prospective college students should keep their social media pages private or remove anything that might make them look less attractive to admissions committees.

# Index

# Art Credits

## Student Book Level 4

The authors and publishers acknowledge the following sources of copyright material and are grateful for the permissions granted. While every effort has been made, it has not always been possible to identify the sources of all the material used, or to trace all copyright holders. If any omissions are brought to our notice, we will be happy to include the appropriate acknowledgements on reprinting and in the next update to the digital edition, as applicable.

## The following images are sourced from Getty Images.

U1: LeoFFreitas/Moment; Gabriel Grams; JayLazarin/iStock Unreleased; U2: Jim Craigmyle/Corbis; Darryl Estrine/UpperCut Images; U3: RapidEye/E+; Martin Barraud/Caiaimage; Zinkevych/iStock; U4: Aaaaimages/Moment; AFP Contributor; MyrKu/iStock; JENS SCHLUETER/DDP; U5: WPA Pool; Brooks Kraft/Corbis Historical; Carsten Koall; Jessica Peterson/Tetra images; Scott Barbour; H. Armstrong Roberts/ClassicStock/Archive Photos; U6: nito100/iStock; Hero Images; U7: Maskot; Hero Images; Hirurg/E+; U8: FatCamera/E+; Juice Images; U9: Anthony Barboza/Archive Photos; Hemant Mehta/IndiaPicture; Rubberball Productions; Astrid Stawiarz; Martin Mills/Hulton Archive; Oliver Gerhard/imageBROKER; U10: Drew Angerer; Francis Dean/Corbis Historical; Tom Stoddart Archive/Hulton Archive; U11: Chris Ryan/Caiaimage; Kevin Dodge/Tetra images; Chris Ryan/Caiaimage; Alexsl/E+; U12: View Stock; Hero Images; Kristina Kohanova/EyeEm; J. Countess; C Flanigan/WireImage; Mint/Hindustan Times; Rawpixel/iStock; U13: Brunorbs/iStock; Fancy/Veer/Corbis; EmirMemedovski/E+; Pinghung Chen / EyeEm; U14: Coldsnowstorm/iStock; Digital Vision/Photodisc; U15: Ariel Skelley/DigitalVision; Andresr/E+; Maskot; Maskot; U16: Natali_Mis/iStock; Adam Hester/Tetra images; Weedezign/iStock; Tein79/iStock; Wavebreakmedia/iStock; U17: Artisteer/iStock; Gajus/iStock; U18: Vladans/iStock; Robert Daly/OJO Images; Miguel Sotomayor/Moment; U19: Busakorn Pongparnit/Moment; AJ_Watt/E+; U20: DragonImages/iStock; Halfdark/fStop; Hill Street Studios/Blend Images; KatarzynaBialasiewicz/iStock.

## Images from other sources

U5: Hine, Lewis Wickes, 1874-1940/Library of Congress; U10: Calamy stock images/Alamy Stock Photo; U11: BDoss928/Shutterstock.

Anafitional

school transcript.